PRAISE FOR
GROW WHEREVER YOU WORK

"There is no straight path to success; we learn and grow from our mistakes. Joanna's book of wise stories and guidance can help all of us get closer to our full potential and dreams."

—Sheryl Sandberg, COO, Facebook, and Founder, LeanIn.Org and OptionB.Org

"Joanna draws upon decades of experience as a leadership advisor, along with real-life stories from high performers, to provide professionals at any stage of their career with an empowering and very practical tool kit on how to grow through challenges and drive toward purpose at work."

—Dominic Barton, Global Managing Partner, McKinsey & Company

"Practical advice from a role model of purpose, passion, and perseverance!"

—Angela Duckworth, *New York Times* bestselling author of *Grit,* and Christopher H. Browne Distinguished Professor of Psychology, University of Pennsylvania

"Joanna Barsh has written a remarkably engaging and wise book about how to deal with the most vexing workplace challenges. *Grow Wherever You Work* offers brilliant and field-tested advice so you can respond with grace and competence to ugly hurdles such as working with the office villain and surviving stretches when everything seems to suck—and for rising to the occasion when it is time to take a big risk. This is the best book of its kind."

—Robert I. Sutton, *New York Times* bestselling author of *The No Asshole Rule* and *The Asshole Survival Guide* and Professor of Management Science and Engineering, Stanford Business School

"Almost every obstacle that you'll face at work has been faced before—and chances are that Joanna Barsh has helped tackle them. In this useful book, she draws on her 35-year-career to coach us to learn from the major challenges of our careers."

—Adam Grant, *New York Times* bestselling author of *Give and Take* and *Originals* and coauthor of *Option B*

"A prominent thought leader on talent and leadership, Joanna helps us turn difficult work challenges into personal and professional growth, spinning gold from inspiring stories, valuable coaching, and the caring mentorship we all want and need. Treasure this book!"

—Eileen Naughton, VP HR, Google

"How do you survive a disappointing performance review? What do you do if your team won't listen? What if work just plain sucks? Top business leader Joanna Barsh has answers to these and other pressing questions that plague us all, as well as the experience to guide you calmly through."

—Jessica Bacal, author of *Mistakes I Made at Work* and Director, Smith College Wurtele Center for Work & Life

PURPOSE PRESSURE
MISTAKE REVIEW
BRING PEOPLE ON BOARD

GROW
WHEREVER
YOU WORK

BULLIES JERKS

Straight Talk to Help with
Your Toughest Challenges

JOANNA BARSH

TAKE A STAND

SUPERHERO ENERGY

McGraw
Hill
Education

NEW YORK CHICAGO SAN FRANCISCO ATHENS
LONDON MADRID MEXICO CITY MILAN
NEW DELHI SINGAPORE SYDNEY TORONTO

MENTOR SPONSOR

LOVE FEAR HOPE DESPAIR

1 2 3 4 5 6 7 8 9   LCR   22 21 20 19 18 17

ISBN: 978-1-260-02646-7
MHID: 1-260-02646-9

eISBN: 978-1-260-02647-4
eMHID: 1-260-02647-7

Design by Lee Fukui and Mauna Eichner

Library of Congress Cataloging-in-Publication Data

Names: Barsh, Joanna, author.
Title: Grow wherever you work : straight talk to help with your toughest
  challenges / Joanna Barsh.
Description: 1 Edition. | New York : McGraw-Hill Education, 2017.
Identifiers: LCCN 2017039530| ISBN 9781260026467 (hardback) | ISBN 1260026469
Subjects: LCSH: Leadership. | BISAC: BUSINESS & ECONOMICS / Leadership.
Classification: LCC HD57.7 .B3677 2017 | DDC 658.4/092—dc23 LC record available at
https://lccn.loc.gov/2017039530

McGraw-Hill Education books are available at special quantity discounts to use as premiums and sales promotions, or for use in corporate training programs. To contact a representative, please visit the Contact Us page at www.mhprofessional.com.

The wise stories inside would not exist without the research participants.
The idea for this book would not exist without my daughters.
The book itself would not exist without my brother.
And my resolve would not exist without David.
We are all connected.
So this book is dedicated to you.

Contents

Acknowledgments

The exact right place to start is with the amazing participants who filled my research with high points, low points, and points of view. Thanks to every company that participated. I am in your debt.

A special shout-out to the story-givers in the book. You know who you are. That took courage, humility, vulnerability, and a fair number of e-mails. By going first, you've encouraged the rest of us. For those whose remarkable stories live on in my files, thank you for that generous contribution. You are the reason I have tremendous hope for our future. Your collective voice is remarkable. Never forget that.

Talent professionals, thank you too. Engaged by the research questions, you jumped in with talent of all shapes and sizes. Your selections shaped this American story: of ambition, hope, challenge, and achievement—a story told by fierce individuals of every background, born in the United States or from almost every corner of the world.

Very special thanks to Anne Thevenet Abitbol from Danone, who imagined closing the gap between generations through open dialogue. Your innovative Octave training was undiluted encouragement.

McKinsey friends and colleagues, thank you too. Karen Tanner blessed this research in its early days; we all miss her. A valiant team volunteered to help mine the data: Lauren Danielle Brown, Srishti Gupta, Kayvan Kian, Olivia Lee, and Smaranda Gosa-Mensing. A giant thank you to Leila Kian, a generous soul who helped even without knowing me. Thank you to Natacha

Catalino, Katy George, Trish Gyorey, and Sara Bernow—readers from Brazil, Sweden, Turkey, and New Jersey! And to the McKinsey diaspora, your support carries me still.

Still more volunteers pitched in so graciously. Nicholas Alers, thank you for offering one man's view through endless drafts. Glynnis O'Connor, you rescued this book from drowning in words. Doug Stern, thanks for being there. And Zach Todd, thanks for being you!

A horde of gifted professionals came on board too. Jim Levine, thank you for reading and reading and reading the pages spilling out of my figurative pen from 2015 on—yikes. You cajoled, questioned, supported, and believed in the mission until we got it right. That brings me to Casey Ebro, my definitive editor. Enthused from the start, you were the book's first fan! You applauded the chorus of diverse voices. Your high standards, adaptability, optimism, and skill made this book better. And thanks to the good people at McGraw-Hill who love books and especially the messages of this one—that a diverse group brings better solutions. That challenges are to be met and not avoided. That growth at work is everyone's right. And it can be fun.

It goes without saying—Gaby and Jetta Garbasz, you're the top. You're the Colosseum! I'm so proud of you for being who you are: tough, smart, caring, funny, energetic, creative, amazing women leaders. I'm honored to be your mother and humbled by your talent. You pushed me to seek answers that would be more helpful and on point for the coming generations of leaders. You held up the mirror with kindness.

Alexander Charles Winter, I'm going to embarrass you, because that's what big sisters do. I brought you big problems, and you sent me into gales of laughter, making them solvable. I feel your expansive heart in every story. You defended all readers, probing to learn what ties us together. Patient, respectful, and loving, you were my no-bullshit gage, vigilant counselor, suggestion box, and early editor, all rolled into one.

There is one more person I'd like to thank, and if I filled up a hundred pages, I would not finish thanking this fellow. You see, I used to be "the cheese," standing alone in that childhood game—believing in myself but doubting, scared. Today, I stand beside David Garbasz, my Relentless Coach, Devil's Advocate, Warrior, and life partner rolled into one. You remind me of all the reasons to keep going. You are the man in the arena. Everyone who meets you is lucky, most of all, me.

Introduction

Who knows when it began, but dirty water was bubbling up from the drain in the boiler room. Sometime around 11 p.m., Gaby and Nick returned home after a grueling day of work. They cautiously descended the stairs to the subbasement. Water was spreading everywhere. Gaby remembered, "I smelled it first. Then I saw the boxes storing important family papers sitting in water. I didn't think. I took off my shoes and waded in. But the boxes were too heavy to move."

She yelled at Nick to help. He refused, stiffly advising Gaby not to touch a thing (too late on that score) and to call the building manager. An exchange of criticisms began, rapidly followed by a few expletive-laden insults. In tears, Gaby dialed her mother. Nick retreated to safety upstairs to call his. Neither mother had much to add.

Panicked, Gaby called the building manager next. He did nothing to relieve her anxiety, replying that no, he wasn't coming over to help and yes, it was most assuredly sewage water. In a tone that communicated *I'm doing you a favor*, he scheduled a plumber for the next day. Now Gaby had to rearrange her day to work from home, *if* her boss would even allow it. She had a sleepless night.

The next morning, she opened her door to Harris, an elderly plumber. A man of few words, he said, "I've done jobs like this for 30 years. This place will be as good as new." Harris then moved the boxes with ease, whistling while he worked. And it was as good as new, for the time being.

The parallel to challenges at work is striking. The expression "volatile, uncertain, complex, and ambiguous" (VUCA) describes extreme military situations, but it has since been adopted as the new normal by the business world. Your job could disappear without warning. Your boss could disappear without warning. People you work with live on the other side of the world—and they want to talk at 9 a.m. *their* time. Expectations are higher; your peers are working harder. And your work challenges are bigger and more intense than ever.

Challenges heighten anxiety and stress. Check. They deplete your energy. Double check. If not addressed, they cause harm in the long term. Triple check. Sound familiar?

Your work is filled with hard challenges that you don't feel ready to handle. They may require difficult conversations, new skills, and tools you don't yet have. Worse, their best friend is fear. Together, challenge and fear can sap your will and render you helpless.

But there's another side to this story.

What if you grew more capable through challenges, working more productively and enjoyably? What if they helped you become more capable? You'd run toward challenges; you'd welcome them. With the right mindset, approaches, and tools, you'd find challenges intriguing and exciting. They'd engage you fully and stimulate your creative thinking.

Reframe. *Challenges are not flashing danger signs, but spectacular opportunities to grow faster and smarter.*

The challenges in this book come from research I've undertaken since 2015. I wanted to tailor my leadership work to midcareer professionals as a follow-up to the Centered Leadership Project, which I founded as a senior partner at McKinsey & Company. Consequently, for this book I interviewed over 200 high performing, high potential rising leaders at Fortune 1000 companies, in addition to startup founders, nonprofit leaders, government executives, artists, actors, academics, journalists, teachers, and other independent thinkers outside of big business. The participants worked at 120 different companies, across industries and functions—and not the usual suspects! Their backgrounds are as varied as their professional lives. Almost 40 percent are people of color. Those born outside the United States or with immigrant parents represent over 40 countries. These remarkable participants shared their personal and professional challenges openly and generously with me. Collectively, they contributed raw experiences from their work and life.

You don't have to love everyone in this book or want to be like them. Chances are, you're going to dislike a few! I didn't include their stories to win your sympathy or compassion but to share important insights that may help somebody—possibly you. By the way, because many of the people in this book have asked for anonymity, I've changed names and circumstances to honor the request. That said, every story is real. Unvarnished.

The collective voice in this book speaks a profound truth: you don't grow *despite* challenges but *because of* them. The stories underscore five themes:

- *Preparation is half the game.* Challenges are made more manageable when you've built the skills and know-how to address them. You don't always have the luxury, but getting ready for challenges will be a critical factor in your success.

- *Asking questions will help you.* Thinking is critical, but it's not what you think. The participants underscore the importance of reflection, soul-searching, and dreaming. Asking questions—big ones and granular ones—is a practice you would do well to hard-wire into your daily life.

- *Talking is a good thing.* Talking to your boss, mentors and sponsors, colleagues, coworkers, friends, and contacts is productive when it helps you address the questions. Interaction generates new energy, which may be exactly what you need.

- *Intentionality is the Do Not Pass Go Until You Do This step.* Lurking beneath your behaviors are mindsets and beliefs that may limit you. With self-awareness, you can choose to stay as you are—or change. As much as you might wish it, change doesn't happen on its own. Consciously shift your mindset and your experience will improve, even if the outcome isn't everything you wanted.

- *Taking small steps frees you to act.* Small steps help you test your way through trial and error, reinforcing your new mindsets and behaviors. Small steps mitigate risk. Take enough of them and they add up.

You'll read about 12 work challenges in 12 chapters. Here's how each unfolds: I introduce the challenge briefly; then share a few more true stories (each followed by my answer to the question "so what?"); and wrap up with recommended tools, practices, and actions. You participate too. You have your own perspective, and you decide what to implement. As one participant said, "I've had enough of school. I don't want to be led by the nose. Let me reach my own conclusions." Right on.

Use the book as you like. You'll experience all of these tough challenges at some point in your career, assuredly more than once. Read from the beginning or start with the most pressing challenge that you face right now.

Think of me as your mentor in a box, or "mentor in a book" more appropriately. I offer more than 30 years of experience helping companies address their strategic, operational, and organizational challenges. I know how to structure problems, analyze the data, reach conclusions, and develop recommendations. I know how to interview and listen intently. That's what underlies the stories, their "so what's," and my counsel. I respect that you may develop your own game plan. Nothing would please me more. This book is for all curious minds open to taking on the toughest work challenges. I hope that's you. I hope you experience work, grow quickly, and above all aspire to greatness. You're reading this book for a reason.

If you're early on in your career, work will be more adventure and less drag when you're open to learning, delighted by challenge, and intentional. Put the tools, practices, approaches, and recommended actions to the test. Learn from the stories of people who faced challenges you haven't yet experienced. But please don't compare. You've got just as much on the ball as the professionals in this book.

If you're midway through your career or further along, there's no time like the present to apply the five themes: preparing, asking, talking, setting your intention, and acting in small steps. Your experiences, skills, and know-how will be godsends, but try to see with fresh eyes too. Remember that if you ask the same questions and do the same things, you'll get the same outcomes. That's not what you want.

Our world suffers a severe leadership deficit on every level. This gap isn't going to close without your help. Choose where to make your mark. Get going.

And I promise, that's the end of the purple prose for me. From here on in, it'll be straight talk, tough love, and "just the facts!"

PURPOSE PRESSURE
MISTAKE REVIEW
BRING PEOPLE ON BOARD
BULLIES JERKS
TAKE A STAND
RISK SELF-DOUBT
SUPERHE ENERGY
MENT PONSOR
LOVE FEAR PE DESPAIR
PURPOSE RESSURE
MISTAKE REVIEW
BRING PEOPLE ON BOARD

1

When Work Holds No Passion

Some people—your mothers or fathers, teachers, maybe your best friend—advised you to get on the right track *and stay on it.* So you worked hard in high school to get into the best college. You pursued the best degree to get the best job. Then you worked hard to advance. When you reached a milestone, you set a new goal. And that's a fine path—just not for everybody.

Alex set out on her own path. She followed her intellectual curiosity and majored in religion, including studies in Trinidad with a bona fide shaman. Unable to find a job after graduation, Alex turned to tutoring. As luck would have it, Alex impressed the child's parents so much that the father decided to give her a chance. He helped her land a brokerage sales job where she worked.

Great news? Something was wrong. A few months in, Alex was dreading work. A year in, the evidence had piled up, but still she didn't act:

> My boyfriend and parents were telling me something was wrong, but I was scared to admit a problem. If I admitted it, I would have to fix it. Brokerage is where the money is, but I didn't like the insecurity. I felt it every day. I didn't know if I would have money for food and rent. I was terrified of failure. After two years, if you haven't paid back the draw, you have to leave.

Cold-calling, I had no idea who I was speaking to. I couldn't see the person's face. I'd just panic and hang up. I was paralyzed. I came in every day and was busy, but I didn't want to do cold calls. It was an epic failure.

Alex lost 60 pounds that year. She threw up every day before work. Mondays were the worst. Still, she wouldn't back out. She was afraid to disappoint the boss who had gone out on a limb to get her the job. Only when the human resources manager challenged her did Alex realize that the work she wanted to do existed—in a different division. It took a few more weeks for Alex to muster the courage to apply for and receive a transfer:

When I told my boss I was leaving, he screamed at me. I ran to the bathroom to cry. He had brought me in and trained me. I owed him. That was the longest year in my life. I slept for a week after that! And went straight into hot water in my new role, but anything was better than cold-calling. Now I feel important and integral to a team. I no longer feel unnecessary and superfluous, and I'm not faking it.

The panic attacks stopped. It was a month before I didn't feel scared at work, it was three months to gain context, and it took six months to settle in. Then color returned to my world.

Today, Alex is working in a different company in the same industry. With renewed curiosity, she is working toward her MBA—exploring what holds her interest.

Our hard work rewards us financially and builds our business skills and experience. But if internal motivation is not there, a rude awakening awaits when we realize what we're missing: passion. We see how far we've traveled for the wrong reasons. It was easier to just keep going. Stepping off the current path felt dangerous, like heading off road at night without lights.

But no one wants to end up on a road to nowhere. Now we're awake and questioning.

This "passion" thing has been glorified and overexposed. If we don't have it, we feel deficient. Each morning, we look in the mirror and think,

Why do I hate my job? We beat ourselves up, feel anxious, and worry that the boss knows. We make excuses. We're overworked, sick as a dog, worried about something outside of work.

Here are the telltale signs that you're missing passion at work: you feel no energy, no positive emotion, and no genuine care for what you're doing. Simply put, you're not interested. That's a red flag, not a personality flaw. Until you discover purpose, passion at work will be elusive. Purpose is what drives you. It offers the deepest sense of fulfillment. Purpose fills work with meaning.*

Finding purpose may be nirvana, but pursuing it is enough to jump-start your energy and interest. The stories in this chapter can point you in the right direction:

- *What questions do you ask to find your purpose?* It wasn't always pleasant or fun, but Nathaniel welcomed adventure to discover the work he truly wanted to do.

- *What can you do if you take a wrong turn?* Realizing she was in the wrong job, Sophie found the help she needed by asking for directions.

- *How do you know when you have it?* Sometimes the pursuit of purpose requires radical openness. That's the challenge Victor faced.

- *What if passion is more about you than work?* Hell-bent on accomplishment, Christine overflowed with passion independent of her work choices.

- *How do you move from vision to action when self-doubt holds you back?* Kavita had always known she was an inventor, but she doubted herself too much to embrace it.

I don't know about you, but I'm tired of superficial talk about passion. Frankly, passion is not a work requirement. If you don't have a calling, chill. If you're interested in learning and growing, that's purposeful and enough.

---

* I'm not one to toot my horn, but if you're eager to learn more about purpose and how you can get some, you might find my earlier book useful. *Centered Leadership* (Crown Business, New York, 2014) will take you through detailed exercises you can do to guide your own exploration.

However, if you're itching to start or renew your search for purpose, do it. You'll generate positive energy through the search itself. Slow down to experience the process. Explore nonprofits, startups, and interests outside of work too. There's no formula and no magic. Purpose exists where it's least expected. Trust in serendipity, trying new things until something renews your energy.

The good news: Passion will find you as you make your way toward purpose.

NOT ALL WHO WANDER ARE LOST

If you're barely satisfied at work, the danger is not what happens if you leave but what happens if you stay for five more years.

Just 12 when his father died of a heart attack, Nathaniel grew up quickly. Back then, he couldn't know that he would follow in his father's career path—guiding young people into work that mattered:

> I took a class in college on sustainability before Gore's book even came out. I became totally obsessed. I shaped my own major by taking classes from many departments. I named it "global human impact studies."
>
> And then I took a job after college with a one-man sustainability consulting firm. That turned out to be a mistake because in six months, it folded up shop. Now I had no momentum. I was at ground zero.

Starting again from scratch was harder than Nathaniel expected. For the next two years, his zigzag path included odd jobs in construction, a master's degree in a Swedish sustainability program, and the Unreasonable Institute program for entrepreneurship:

> I worked like a machine, willing to face uncertainty. I did anything I could during the day, and I wrote grant applications at night. I remember an interview for selling insurance. I was telling the interviewer I was excited about sustainability,

and he said, "What are you doing in my office?" I exclaimed, "I don't know." I got up and left. It was terrible!

My lowest point was something I called "the wilderness." There were nights when I was alone with my notebook, not knowing if I could pay the rent and wondering what I was doing. I felt truly alone, alone in my stubbornness trying to figure it out. I felt crazy. I thought, *How am I going to earn money?* I lost my confidence. I was broke. If worse came to worst, I could ask my mom for money, but the situation forced my brain to become panicky—and that doesn't help you find a solution.

I found inner resources from what had happened with my dad. The worst thing had already happened. I was already not on track, so I could go big. Living month to month helped prepare me. It gave me the grit that started to show later. My greatest strength is the ability to navigate and be comfortable with discomfort!

Over the course of those two years, Nathaniel learned how to be an entrepreneur. He also learned that he loved it:

I knew that I wanted to start a company that helped people find meaningful work. I invited two friends to join as cofounders. We got accepted to an accelerator, and mentors helped shape our vision. Our company was born as a mission-driven recruiting firm. But we were always exploring the possibility of being a software company with the same mission.

In a startup, you have high and low points. It's stressful, and you're in the arena. Nothing is like it. Elon Musk says it's like chewing glass and staring into the abyss. It sounds weird, but that's what it's like.

After four years, I got a call to join a major political campaign, and I accepted. One cofounder split off to pursue the software idea. The other became the CEO of our remaining firm. Looking ahead, I hope to have work that doesn't feel like work.

After the campaign ended, Nathaniel joined a bigger startup whose mission fueled his dream to unlock the possibility in people.

So What?

Stepping off the traditional path can lead you to purpose, but as Nathaniel noted, you're on an adventure in the wilderness. That's not risky early in your career. But what if you're midcareer? Is it too late? There's no time like now. Small steps will pique your curiosity *and* reduce your risk.

Curiosity sparks questions, and big questions spark reflection. Reflection leads you closer to purpose. Nathaniel uses questions like these in his work: "What is it you *want* to do or have more of? Are you willing to take risks to get that? What's stopping you: knowing what you want or summoning the nerve to act?" Uncomfortable questions for sure!

Consider the alternative. If you're barely satisfied at work, the danger is not what happens if you leave but what happens if you *stay* for five more years. If that scenario looks good, you're in the right place. If not, start exploring. If fear kicks in, welcome it. Nathaniel said, "If you're going on a trip into the wilderness, you have to entertain some risk. Some danger is OK." You prepare for contingencies on a camping trip; do the same here.

Develop by stretching to try new things. Raise your hand, not because you're that ambitious jerk who wants to get ahead at any cost but because you're eager to learn and contribute. Even if you decide to stay where you're working—*especially* if you decide to stay—new challenges kindle interest.

Reframe work as adventure. Imagine it through the lens that anything can happen. What small risks did you take today? What did you learn? If your answers are "None" and "Nothing," you've just lost some opportunities.

Not everyone wants high adventure. But adventure that brings you closer to purpose makes life memorable and worth retelling.

WHAT HAPPENS AFTER A WRONG TURN

We do our best to please and gain acceptance. Heading down that path is fine if it helps you explore what you do and don't want.

The middle child, Sophie resolved to do well when she was just five years old, learning to excel in soccer. It was a sport Sophie adored. Her older sister had cerebral palsy; she helped Sophie develop empathy, compassion, and determination. But by college, hairline cracks had appeared in Sophie's relentless strategy for achieving success:

> In college, soccer was like a full-time job that I hated. When I threatened to quit, my coach guilt-tripped me. So I stayed.
>
> My senior year, I was on the field. Someone messed up, but my coach took me out instead. As captain, I sat on the bench, fuming and powerless. I put myself into a deeper hole with a little outbreak. I was triggered by thinking that I was right, but I was unable to convince the coach.
>
> I could have managed better. I didn't put in the effort. I didn't try to change my behavior. I didn't love soccer enough anymore to make concessions.

Those cracks only widened when Sophie graduated. She joined a financial services firm, repeating the pattern of achieving through perseverance, but without interest:

> In college, I didn't find the right people to get inspired. I accepted a job I didn't want.
>
> My parents have always been very black-and-white about a career path. My dad was never into anything but law school; my mom always loved finance and making money. I tried to fit into that mold, and I was miserable. What I was doing was meaningless. It was the same as college soccer. I had no purpose. I slogged it out for a year, but the job didn't get better.
>
> My mom saw me struggling in the field she loved. Maybe she realized she couldn't offer more advice, but she could connect me to a friend who might mentor me. That woman suggested journalism.
>
> At the finance firm, the only thing I had liked doing was writing up research. I had always liked writing. Journalism had been at the back of my mind, too.

So started a six-month journey. Sophie's mentor connected her to three people. Sophie asked them about what they did, what they liked about their work, and what their day-to-day tasks were. Their answers helped her focus on broadcast journalism:

> Once I decided I would love to spend my days doing that, I reached out to an acquaintance who had a friend at one of the networks. That person introduced me to a bunch of people. For months, I had an interview a week. I learned something from each one that prepared me for the next.
>
> Once I found the place where I wanted to intern, I interviewed a dozen more times. It took a lot of imagination for them to agree I could do a good job even though I had zero experience! It wasn't that I believed in myself. It was out of desperation. I wanted the job so badly, and I was so miserable before, that I had no choice. I took risks I would never have taken otherwise.

Ultimately, the company offered Sophie a temporary internship with a modest hourly wage, no benefits, and no promises. Still, the decision was easy for Sophie. A few years in, she knew she had made the right choice:

> My first piece of breaking news was an adrenaline rush! It validated that I will kick ass at this job. It was a Friday, and I had just left DC for New York. A friend of a friend told my friend, who tipped me off. I started making calls. I got a call back from an assistant who confirmed my tip. I was the first to confirm, and it felt great.
>
> Since I've started this job, I've learned so much about myself—I'm smarter than I thought I was. I can do anything that I want to do. I'm 100 percent in control of my fate. And I don't take no for an answer!

A few days later, Sophie found out she had gotten a coveted assignment. As sometimes happens in life, everything came together for Sophie.

So What?

A few wrong turns caused Sophie to switch fields, and when she did, her zest for work went from zero to 80. Beyond that obvious bit of good news, she grew tenfold in self-confidence. Sophie found what she needed by asking for directions, starting with a mentor, and expanding from there. The funny thing is that her interest in journalism wasn't a surprise. Sophie just hadn't been paying attention.

Sophie persevered from the start, but without purpose. The process of learning what did—and did not—energize her uncovered a latent interest. As Sophie fanned that interest, it grew. In turn, that gave her the courage to choose uncertainty over the proven path. But first, Sophie had to free herself of others' expectations. We start out trying to become the right kind of person with the right kind of job. We do our best to please others and belong. Heading down that path is fine *if* it helps you explore what you do and don't want.

Finding purpose doesn't come easily. There are trade-offs. Sophie had to give up something to get something she wanted even more. There's no guarantee that it will work out, but one thing is certain: start searching for your purpose, and life gets a lot more exciting.

ANSWERING THE CALL

*You're bombarded with so many conflicting messages,
so much noise. Let it go by imagining yourself at 70.*

Victor was no stranger to those moments when the universe speaks to you. It was a choice to listen or not, and Victor chose to listen. It happened first in high school during a self-destructive period:

> I ditched so many days off from school in the eleventh and twelfth grades, forging notes from my parents. At the same time, I got great grades. I was raised in a Taiwanese household where I got zero words of praise. If you got an A, the question was, "Why not A+?" I prayed to have the courage to be humbled.

In my senior year, I knew that it was time. I had perfect SAT scores but rejections from every college. I had sinking feelings but could not bear to tell my parents. Then I totaled my car—my most prized possession. I spiraled down fast. At 3 a.m. one morning, I was on the street in front of my house, crying my heart out. I felt so alone and so broken. In that moment, I felt the presence of God around me like a blanket. I realized I had been squandering the gifts I had received.

Since then, I've worked very hard and put my efforts into something more meaningful.

After graduating from college, Victor and his roommate achieved their goal: acceptance to a leading consulting firm. Two successful years later, Victor was interviewing for a private equity job, his next stop on the right path. Then, at the airport, on his way to accept an offer, Victor stopped cold:

All of a sudden, I heard this internal voice. It said, "You're being a coward. You know what you're supposed to do, but you're still just building your résumé."

I had many offers lined up. I turned them down. Then my roommate and I launched our startup with the mission to help businesses and communities thrive. I want to shift culture so that when you walk into a hair salon, you feel you belong.

During his first big round of funding, Victor was following conventional wisdom to raise as much money as he could. He happened to go for coffee with another entrepreneur who told him that getting the wrong investors on board would lead to problems. Victor was warned:

I had made a point of talking about our mission to turn transactions into relationships at every investor meeting. However, some of the investors were just in it for the economics. Some were not great people. We didn't want their money if we couldn't carry out our mission. The scariest thing was not taking those term sheets.

It felt like this baby was my whole life. We had one month of burn rate left and 40 people on our payroll. We funded them with our life savings. It was one of the best decisions I ever made. Right before the money ran out, two supportive investors came through.

I want to serve God and live out his purpose. My goal is to put my life in perspective, remembering why I work. When I don't, I make bad decisions.

I get consumed by work, but I should take my own advice. If you're too busy executing, you won't have the time to think about your life's goals. If you're working 100 hours a week but don't know what you're working toward, you're heading to a crisis!

Even when competitors were scaling quickly and getting great press, Victor held tight to his long-term mission to turn each marketplace into a community. That gave his company the edge.

So What?

Made sweeter by success, Victor's story is less about having a purpose than being brave enough to pursue one. His journey began by embracing radical openness. In turn, that led to greater fulfillment and new energy. If you want that, start by asking what will supply your meaning. Understanding what really drives you will take some soul-searching.*

Articulating your answer is probably one of the hardest things you'll do. You're bombarded with so many conflicting messages, so much noise. Let it go by imagining yourself at 70. What do you want to look back on and remember? Thinking in the long term might lead you to make different decisions today.

Victor opened himself up through religion and philosophy, but there are many doors to deeper reflection. Some find that a repetitive exercise

---

* If meaning is your hot topic, there is no better book than *Man's Search for Meaning* by Viktor E. Frankl (Beacon Press, Boston, 2006). He described three paths to find greater meaning in life: love, creatively engaging work, and nongratuitous suffering. Frankl experienced all three.

stimulates deep thought. Others write regularly in a journal. Or open up with people you trust. If you are brave enough to be vulnerable, they'll try to help. The pursuit of purpose is serious business.

If you need courage to choose this door, this is the precise moment in the show to "call your lifeline."

A MATTER OF PERSPECTIVE

When you exercise choice, you feel more independence and freedom in any job.

Christine inherited vast amounts of internal motivation, resourcefulness, and determination from parents who had left Lebanon and Armenia for America. She also brought tremendous passion to her work. Her story is relevant because of what she discovered. Her passion did not come from a particular sales job in the technology company where she worked but from a daily practice of bringing her full self to bear:

> I make sure I'm present with the right energy to be as successful as I can be for that day—for the long term. That means being open and enthusiastic, making the best decision on what's in front of me, not rushing through, having the bright-eyed and bushy-tailed approach to doing things with love in a genuine way.
>
> Technology has always intimidated me. I don't think I'm smart enough for it, but I made it to the top of my group six years in a row. I don't think about awards; they are the glass things on the shelf or in a desk folder. I don't seek the trophy or compete with others. My focus is different.

In short, Christine is interested in being fully engaged. She focuses on what's most important to her: learning, developing into the best version of herself, and contributing:

> I don't get caught up in the other crap. I don't get caught up in an alternate world of could-haves, should-haves. I don't

get fixated on things that aren't productive: a criticism or judgment. Days can be as long or as short as you make them. If you choose to focus on things that drag you down, that's going to happen.

We live in a very loud and busy world. I learned the hard way to pay attention to the opportunities for greatness that the universe presents. Job or project opportunities can happen fast. I call them "god winks"—they come and go with the wink of an eye. If you're not present, you won't see them.

A passionate being, Christine understood that work wore down her resolve at times. Take unfairness. Like many others, Christine was triggered by it:

Despite my awards, I did not receive a tremendous raise or meaningful promotion over the last six years, although almost all of my male coworkers did. I didn't really have the candid conversation. Part of it was fear, and part of it was getting tongue-tied.

Ultimately, I decided to be bold and advocate for myself with thoughtfulness. When I did, I received a new role and a promotion.

Last year, Christine won the company's top sales award soon after she had her daughter. It was a time to pause and appreciate everything she had.

So What?

Christine proves the case that you can bring passion to work regardless of the job or company. She did it by striving to be present. Such a simple, powerful practice.

Sure, there are days when you don't want to be present: days facing a computer screen, endless traveling, tedious meetings—passion killers for sure. Technology can make it better, but often it makes it worse. Take our tendency to compare ourselves to others on social media. It's a trap! Comparisons kill your self-esteem and steal your meaning.

But most of the time, choosing to be present is a good thing. Mindfulness experts and spiritual leaders tell you, "When you are drinking tea, just drink your tea. Don't drink your worries, your projects, your regrets."* Don't miss the pleasure, beauty, and meaning in this moment by thinking or worrying about the next one.

Even though you cannot control everything at work, you can strive to be at your best. One approach is to set your intention daily. Ask yourself, "What do I want *for* myself today? What do I want *from* myself today?" You'll stray for any number of reasons: crises, urgent requests, daily distractions. When that happens, gently redirect your attention back to your intention without self-judgment or self-blame.

A focus on living each day well is a choice. When you exercise choice, you feel more independence and freedom in any job. That creates positive energy, which leads to more opportunity for growth, which can lead to purpose. Boom. That's why Christine is filled with passion.

Work might bring you passion, but it doesn't have to. *How* you approach work can fuel it. And that has nothing to do with industry, company, function, or role.

SELF-DOUBT GUARDS THE TREASURE

Sometimes, what you really want has been inside you all along.

Kavita sat next to me at a luncheon celebrating a movie about a passionate entrepreneur who invented household products. She was an inventor-entrepreneur, too:

> When I was little, my inventions were things like a rabbit cage cleaner. I was always tinkering. The idea for my startup was my middle school science project, inspired by a stay with my grandmother in India. My parents warned me to be careful about not drinking tap water, but on my first day, I drank

---

* There is a limitless list of books about mindfulness, but if you have yet to locate your favorite one, try my favorite. It's *The Miracle of Mindfulness: An Introduction to the Practice of Meditation* by Thich Nhat Hanh (Beacon Press, Boston, 1999).

some while brushing my teeth. My grandmother gave me a spiced tea remedy. When I didn't get sick, I got curious.

At home, I experimented with spices in jars of dirty pond water. I saw moldy strawberries at the store and the idea hit me. At 17, I was granted a patent for using spices to stop mold. It was designed for people like my grandmother, who were living without access to refrigeration.

Kavita wanted to turn her invention into a nonprofit during college, but advisors offered nothing but caution. So she tabled her idea for designing packaging that would preserve fresh food longer. Kavita doubted herself until a friend who was a physician and consultant convinced her to move forward:

> I had a decade of doubt to deal with before I got the courage to take the first step. When it's your own invention, it feels very personal and vulnerable. My friend encouraged me to apply to a business plan competition, and we were selected. But the expert judges told me that I would not be able to lead the business where it needed to go. With the best of intentions, they felt it was important to convey that I did not have the skills, the experience, or the funding to go forward.
>
> We didn't win. People seemed to think the idea was not worth pursuing. I had a crisis of confidence.

Kavita's lowest point could have been the story's end, but, instead, it freed her to be bold. When she could not imagine it being any worse, Kavita took the leap. She made a packaging prototype with her friend, and they went to the farmers' market:

> The first time we went, it was very clear that there was a serious need. Consumers asked to take it home. A few weeks later, we set up a booth and sold out in three hours. Then people returned to tell us their stories—how they could now afford to eat fresh food that is healthy.
>
> Self-doubt is a struggle. It's not encouraged to share a big idea and big ambition publicly. For me to say that I wanted

to address global food waste, I felt like I was exposing a secret dream. I was looking for someone else to bring my idea
to the world until I realized there was nobody else. It had to
be me. It was almost an act of surrender.

Kavita launched her company, became the CEO, and embraced her
longing to invent. She also married the doctor who helped her make that
first batch.

So What?

Perhaps the invention will succeed, perhaps it won't, but I'm sure that
Kavita will keep inventing. Sometimes, what you really want has been inside you all along. That's not to say that all your ideas (or anyone's) are
good. What *is* good is believing in yourself enough to act. Self-doubt no
longer holds Kavita back.

It may take a supporter to convince you to support yourself. Kavita's
friend played a critical role in encouraging her to take the next step, the
next risk—especially after so many disappointments.

Note that the pursuit of purpose is marked by high points *and* low
points. It's confusing and a mess when you're in the thick of it. You're trying
many paths. Some turn out to be dead ends. Wise people stand in the way,
snacking on your confidence. Early trials fail. This is the stuff that clarifies
and strengthens purpose. Just because you hit a low point doesn't mean you
should quit. Take it step-by-step.

Patience.

Every experience counts toward getting you closer, even if you don't
know it at the time.

PASSION CHALLENGE

Count yourself lucky if you found your calling before school ended. If
that's the case, your strengths, skills, and opportunities have combined
to provide a near-perfect match for work. You're brimming with passion.

Winning on all counts—industry, company, job, tasks—feels almost illegal. If you also like your coworkers, you've hit the jackpot.

Most of us don't find that—certainly not right away. Though recruiters may look for "fire in the belly" or "sparkle in the eyes," nothing is fundamentally wrong with you if you don't have passion at work.

Alex had the opposite: work was making her sick! Sophie persevered on the "right track" without passion too. They both started their search, finding new energy by asking specific, concrete questions about work. Victor and Nathaniel embarked on some pretty deep soul-searching in their pursuits. They asked the big questions. Christine found that passion doesn't depend on work specifics. Intentionality fuels it. Self-doubt bottled up Kavita's energy. Once she let go, the floodgates opened.

Each one of these stories is really about purpose, the driver of passion. Forget passion. Get obsessed with the pursuit of purpose. Happily, the process itself boosts your energy. One cautionary note: It won't happen in a cinematic flash. Don't expect that a "big think" will lead to a sure plan. Your journey will feel uncertain, even uncomfortable. As you explore through trial and error to iterate your purpose, you're learning. You're continuously evolving as is everything around you. Sounds "heavy"? It is.

If purpose is what you want, take the actions that follow.

Investigate Yourself

The first thing you need is data that yields insight—into yourself. The good news is that you already have it. Insights are trapped in your untapped memories. Free them through a bit of digging:

- *Reconnect with what gives you energy.* Give yourself some open-ended time. If you like, start with a mindfulness practice.* Sit comfortably on your chair, with your back straight and limbs untangled, feet on the floor. Close your eyes and breathe in slowly. Breathe out even more

---

* If you prefer a business person's approach to mindfulness practice, you might enjoy this book by Chade-Meng Tan, *Search Inside Yourself: The Unexpected Path to Achieving Success, Happiness (and World Peace)* (Harper One, New York, 2012), or one by Jon Kabat-Zinn, *Mindfulness for Beginners: Reclaiming the Present Moment—and Your Life* (Sounds True, Boulder, CO, 2016).

deeply. Do that three times. Now breathe normally, feeling each part of you loosen, starting with the top of your head and slowly working down to your toes. This takes a few minutes. When you're ready, bring your attention to a few memories.

○ *Think about the experiences or activities that energized you at each stage of your life*. Return to when you were young and work forward from there. Choose a few high points—when you were fully engaged, energized, and drawn to the activity. Put yourself in the moment to feel where the positive energy comes from. Let thoughts and images flow.

○ *Find the patterns*. Looking across your high points, consider what you value about yourself. When you combine what gives you energy and what you value, you'll find your strengths. Understand why you took the path you did (without judgment). Appreciate your honest answers. Anything goes except for "I don't know."

● *Explore your work experiences*. This exercise is best done with pen and paper. By using the lens of your work experiences, you'll discover what you like and don't like about work. If you've done the same job for 10 years, break it down into specific segments. If you've been at your present job for only 1 or 2 years, add part-time jobs from the past. Look at everything, even gigs that felt like a waste of time.

○ *Find the specific tasks, people, and work environments that energize you*. Make three lists if that helps, carefully working through each segment of work. Also note the work challenges that fire you up.

○ *Find what drains your energy at work*. Look for evidence in the specific tasks, people, and work environments you've experienced. Note the work challenges that have bored you or grated on you, although you did them anyway.

○ *Now make some estimates*. What percent of the time has been energizing for you at work? Under 30 percent is a red flag. Decide on your goal. You may be able to go from 30 to 60 percent in your current situation, armed with these insights.

Ask Good Questions

Now you're ready for questions. Go ahead, roll your eyes, but hey, it's important. The practice of asking questions and thinking about them will help you in your search. It's a skill you had and lost as life took over.

Ask two kinds of questions: abstract and granular. The first kind feels like big-picture questions, and the second feels more concrete. If one isn't working, try the other. Your answers may not come easily. Reflection is uncomfortable, but it yields insight that sparks ideas. Here's how:

- *Think long term to get out of your current rut.* Choose abstract questions that intrigue you. Give these a whirl: "What really matters to me?" "What makes me happy?" "Who is my best self?" "What would I most regret not doing before I retire?" And the mother of all questions, "What is the unique contribution that I—and only I—am meant to make?" Ask, and then listen to your answers. If they don't materialize, don't give up. Ask others to describe you at your best. Or take a break and try these exercises.

  - *Imagine yourself in your current job for three more years.* If that feels energizing, spend a bit of time understanding why so that you can do more of what energizes you. If it feels draining, get curious as to what you can do to change that. Identify your degrees of freedom and options.

  - *Now imagine yourself 10 years from now.* Assume that you're healthy and happy in life and successful at work. In other words, take flight. What are you doing? What energizes you? What has become possible for you? Try to release all constraints. If you knew you could not fail, what would you do?

- *Get real about your dream job.* If you're a realist, conceptual thinking may drive you nuts. If so, try these questions: "What do I want to be doing every day?" "What activities do I like to do at work?" "What gets me excited to come to work?" "When am I most focused and present at work?" Find people to tell you about their work as a way to inspire you.

○ *Cast several lines.* You may have several possible interests, so start a chain of interviews for each one. The secret of this process is six degrees of separation. Start by talking to a person you know whose work interests you. Ask that person to refer you to two relevant people. As you continue to interview, ultimately you'll meet the right people, six connections away.

○ *Keep track.* You're about to meet a lot of people! You'll want to maintain this extraordinary network. It is value worth preserving. Let everyone know where you have settled. People like closure.

○ *Make your trade-offs.* Few people find absolute paradise at work. There are always pros and cons, even in a job made for you. So as you find out what you like and don't like about work, clarify your trade-offs. You might hate to travel, but you might still choose an exciting assignment that requires it because you want that opportunity even more.

Declare Your Vision (for Now)

Not the vision thing! Yep. Vision forces clarity. Even if you're just starting out, declare who you are and your purpose. Don't get hung up on perfection. Your vision will evolve as you take steps toward it, because you're growing. Do this:

● *Let your right brain lead.* It's hard to shut down your left brain, but that's the drill. Pick up a journal, clay, drawing materials—anything that allows the images and words to come. Stop thinking or thinking about thinking. Nobody's watching. Just play. Unabashedly. You're searching for what inspires you to get out of bed most mornings.

● *Make a statement.* Once you have a start, declare it. Say it. Write it.

● *Stop and feel.* Reading back your statement, pause and listen to yourself. What do you feel physically? What emotions are you experiencing? If your answer is "Nothing," it's back to the drawing board for you. Go about your business, confident that something's cooking.

● *Punch it up.* Use friends and colleagues as sounding boards to embolden you. Be warned that some may encourage you to do what they would do. Their well-intentioned advice may not be what you need. Accordingly, ask them what inspires them about your vision. Ask them how you might make that even bolder.

Test Your Way in Small Steps

Some people start their pursuit of purpose only after hitting bottom. Naturally, they feel a certain pressure to take extreme action quickly. If that's you, take your temperature. Start by assessing how bad things really are and whether you can make them better. Buy yourself some time. Through trial and error, each small step is feasible and positive:

- *Remove the thorn first.* Perhaps only one or two aspects of your current role are making you miserable. If that's so, raise your issues with the right people. Time and again, people quit when management would have listened and responded. There is no downside to speaking up if you're truly ready to go.

- *Go do something in a small way.* Figure out small steps you can take to test your vision.

  - *Think creatively.* The company is full of temporary assignments and projects you could do on top of your day job. There may be opportunities like a lateral move or shifting responsibilities. Alternatively, you might find a volunteer role outside of work, or you might find something you can start up on your own.

  - *Learn more.* If a different industry or function attracts you, find ways to test whether it could sustain you. Find relevant meetups to hang out with people who have the jobs that interest you.

  - *Make a change.* The time comes when you know—when the excitement for what's next outweighs the safety of staying where you are. That's when you owe it to yourself to "just do it."

- *Before you leave, stay in your role for a year if you can.* If it was the wrong job almost from the beginning, it makes sense to cut your losses. However, the upsides of learning and gaining experience usually outweigh the misery you're feeling. A year is enough time for you to see the full business cycle and develop some skills—and therefore to make a better judgment.

As you take small steps toward your purpose, something starts to happen. You'll distinguish between opportunities and distractions. You'll feel greater joy at work. Even in dark times, you'll still have hope because you're taking positive steps. The process of investigating, asking, articulating, and testing will pay off.

Instead of rushing to the end, think of your work life as a long-running television series. In the next episode, more will be revealed.

PURPOSE PRESSURE
MISTAKE REVIEW
BRING PEOPLE ON BOARD
BULLIES JERKS
TAKE A STAND
RISK SELF-DOUBT
SUPER   ENERGY
MENTOR S   NSOR
LOVE FEAR   E DESPAIR
PURP   SSURE
MISTAKE REVIEW
BRING PEOPLE ON BOARD

2

When the Pressure Threatens to Overwhelm

The pressure marathon started early. You wanted a good job! After that, you wanted to keep your job, find a better one, and advance. Someone was always a little bit better than you. Does it ever end? Nope. When one competitor exits, a new one appears.

Too much pressure creates unintended and unwanted consequences. On Friday night, you admit to friends that you feel anxious, stressed, unsatisfied, or sad and you don't know why. You chalk it up to fatigue and vow (again) to make good on your gym membership. By Sunday evening, when the cycle starts again, you dream about opening a bakery, moving to Portland, going back to school, or anything but this.

Some people thrive on pressure. Some learn to handle it. Take Sally. Television had her at "Hello." After her college internship, she received a one-year extension. But that year, the company had layoffs, and Sally thought she would be out of a job:

> Two days before my extension was up, I received an offer to be a producer at night. I took it. It was a completely new skill set. I had a very tough boss who was a yeller. We would have meetings every day at 9 a.m. for everything that went wrong—after we hadn't slept all night. It was awful. I put my

head down and picked it up. I struggled to get through every day. I never got to see my boyfriend.

Overnight, there are only three people. You have to learn all the jobs. I was a mess, a wreck. I would cry at the drop of a hat. It was way too early for me to be responsible as a video producer. You learn under the most stressful circumstances. Everyone does.

Eight years in, Sally has been promoted a few times since her trial by fire. It has helped her build muscles for handling the inherent pressures of the work:

When asked if I would do it over again, I don't know what to say. That time was so hard physically and emotionally, but it helped me develop. There are a slew of people who would work overnight. If you've determined this is what you really want to do, take the job.

It's still very stressful, and I want to stay home sometimes. Ten o'clock comes around every night. I'm stressed to get the job done, especially when my work depends on someone's signing off on it. Breaking situations are always intense. But I handle these things every day. I'm good at it now.

Sally learned to manage pressure by setting goals, breaking them down into small bites, forging strong mentorships, and building recovery into her schedule. She also keeps her intention in mind: *This is the job I wanted.*

If you choose a highly paid and/or highly rewarding job with highly important tasks that must be completed with high urgency, pressure is a given. You love it, learn to live with it, or burn out. Before going full speed ahead or quitting, gauge your tolerance through these stories:

- *What if you're the biggest source of the pressure?* Brody landed the job he wanted, but his need to be 100 percent right put it in peril.

- *What happens when the pressure ratchets up unexpectedly?* Emma's world turned upside down when her new boss changed the rules.

- *What if you can't help yourself?* Rajat threw himself into his startup, medical school, and business school—creating a dangerous pressure cooker situation.

- *How can you contain pressure that comes with the job?* Christopher lost his way despite loving the work he had long wanted to do.

- *When is it time to throw in the towel?* Maya found her limit in the back of an ambulance.

You might suppose that pressure is greater in certain industries and jobs. Boy, is that wrong. Every industry and every job has pressure. Often, high performers bring it on themselves. That's not to say that everyone suffers from pressure. Despite physical exhaustion, many love what they do. They thrive on pressure, rest up, and learn to roll with the punches.

Pressure is a part of today's reality. Honestly, I don't think you're going to get away from it. And there are positives to pressure, even when you feel like tapping out. Adrenaline kicks in, propelling you to take action, grow faster, and accomplish more. Actually, it's exciting.

Pressure is neither good nor bad. If it comes from within, this chapter will show you ways to release it. If it's part of the learning curve, your new skills will handle it. If it comes from external forces, you can take better care of yourself through the tough periods. You can build in recovery. And you can quit.

In other words, you have options.

MOVING TO THE DRIVER'S SEAT

Few jobs, if any, make absolute perfection a requirement.
Fear drives us in that direction. And we fall short every time.

Brody had watched his father laboring at the oil refinery, undergoing back surgeries, and then suffering from Parkinson's disease in retirement. He had worked so hard and then life passed him by, so Brody thought. But when the recession hit, Brody triple majored in finance, accounting, and management to land a job. Scooped up by an accounting firm, Brody felt secure, but long, routine days were the norm. Wanting more, he switched to a more challenging job at a finance firm—with pressure:

In the first two months, I was drowning because I was run over by people. I was timid and took a hands-off approach to things. Then my boss moved on, and it took five months to backfill his job. I was afraid to be wrong. I was afraid to speak up and tell the SVPs what I thought. I was really concerned with how I would be perceived.

I would go home and be stressed about work. I was miserable.

Fortunately, Brody had a mentor, and that mentor took him to lunch. He admonished Brody to step up. That night, Brody attended an event at which the speaker reinforced the same message:

He said, "People who have to be sure about everything never do anything." You have to take chances, and you're never going to be right always. The timing of my intervention was crucial. I thought, *This is exactly how I feel.* I would not say anything if I had only 95 percent confidence in what I knew. I had been using my boss as a barrier to answer questions so people wouldn't think I was an idiot. I was so afraid of being wrong that I wasn't listening. At times, my view was 110 percent wrong, and it made no sense. Or I defaulted to what everyone else said.

I came in the next day close to drowning, and I thought, *Stand up and start being effective or go find something else to do.* I stopped sitting in the backseat. I started saying, "Let me take this and be on point." My mindset shifted to, *I'm being paid to give my opinion.*

I still feel like an idiot, but I don't worry about it as much as I did before. That's when I learn the most! You cannot be bold and confident and *not* open to others' opinions. If you're closed, you're incapable of working with others.

Plenty of people are 100 times more successful than I am. I don't feel like I should be the CFO in 10 years. I'm not like this guy who started three months ago. When the senior folks patted him on the back, he asked for a raise!

Remember the job that Brody's boss left open? Brody was promoted to fill it. First he became a leader, and then he became the boss.

So What?

Brody almost drowned in self-inflicted pressure. Switching jobs brought new challenges, moving up a steep learning curve first with a new boss and then no boss. To avoid feeling unworthy, Brody tried to be 100 percent right. He became so focused on his words that he stopped listening. Pressure triggered fear; fear triggered distress. Brody was heading to his worst outcome: failing in the very job he had wanted.

Few, if any, jobs make absolute perfection a requirement. Fear drives us in that direction. And we fall short every time, embedding the pattern.

Brody reframed his mindset to relieve self-inflicted pressure. He forced himself to sit in the driver's seat, as scary as that felt. Consciously, he shifted from feeling judged to viewing discussions as valuable collaboration. Naturally, that led to different behaviors. Now he offered his thoughts earlier in the discussion, not minding being corrected. Monitoring the effect, Brody noticed that he was doing better.

So letting go of perfection enabled Brody to perform at a higher level. Ironic?

Not at all.

OPENING NIGHT WITH A NEW SCRIPT

Emma decided that embracing her challenge head on was better than running away. Her new plan required new skills, and yes, it was scary.

Emma first came to New York to perform on Broadway. She was nine years old, living in a new city. Love of art propelled her to a career in a related field:

> Broadway had given me a feeling of strength, independence, and confidence. When I returned to New York for art school, I realized I wanted a job, stability, money, and a station in

life. I wanted to belong. Making art would be enough intellectually, but it was a lot of being alone and festering in my own thoughts. I wanted to be part of something bigger. After college, I joined a luxury goods firm. The owners gave me a lot of opportunity. They believed in me for who I was. I felt like I had found my home.

I didn't have real experience, but I was nailing it! I tailored the way I ran the department to align with my boss, who was an artist. I knew what he would want aesthetically. I developed product in an organic, unstructured way. The boss gave me an idea, and I worked with an artisan. We made up a concept, and then we saw how to make it a commercial endeavor.

A different boss took charge and my approach had nothing to do with what he wanted! He was very unhappy because we didn't do any of the preliminary work you should do. He told me to think strategically, manage my team, and structure the process. I said, "What do you mean? This is a beautiful piece!" He told me I had really screwed up. He gave me an ultimatum: "You need to prove to me you can do this job. Either you jive with me or . . ."

Emma started to question herself. Self-doubt was a dangerous road to travel. It usually led her to impulsive, bad decisions:

I wondered if I would be able to adapt. The most important thing I have is stability in who I am. I started feeling like I should quit, and that's not healthy. So I flew home to see my father.

He helped me see that I could do it. At least I needed to try. I hadn't even given myself that chance. I thought, *Fuck it, I'm going to do it.* I moved from emotional fear and anxiety to being practical about what I had to do to accomplish the goal. There are a million situations like this. I get so emotional, and then I realize there is a practical way to solve the problem. I shifted from *Can I do it?* to *How will I do it?*

Grounded in strengths and with her plan in hand, Emma went back to work with renewed energy:

> I feel like I turned the steamship around in half an hour! I re-organized my team to be able to do the up-front work on the customer and market. I set clear expectations. At first, I had a small team. I had to add strategy team members. That allowed me to iron out details early so that in the back end, we didn't have as much change and rush costs.
>
> I have good intuition. I'm good at making pretty things and getting it done. I hadn't spent time developing my people, growing my organization, thinking strategically. But I had wanted to do this! It was meant to be.

Unexpected pressure invigorated Emma, triggering the adrenaline to accelerate her professional growth. She grew into the vice president of design.

So What?

Sometimes, you're rolling along merrily when pressure shows up unannounced. In a flash, your world is turned upside down. That's the time to turn to a mentor. That person doesn't need to understand the fine details of your job. Business experience, wisdom, and patience are what you need now. It helps if your mentor cares and knows you well, but objectivity is essential.

Emma decided that embracing her challenge head on was better than running away. Her new plan required new skills, and yes, it was scary. Emma managed fear by first remembering her considerable strengths.

Clearly, a person who sang onstage and lived in a strange city at nine years old would have a high level of tolerance for new experiences. If you don't like your world topsy-turvy, ground yourself in an amazing achievement you're proud of. Consider each step in the plan you're going to implement. Visualize learning and changing in remarkable ways.

And when the curtain rises, remember that trying and failing is far better than not trying at all.

WITHOUT LIMITS

Too much self-inflicted pressure is not a good thing.
Sometimes, harsh criticism is the wakeup call you need.

Rajat's parents moved from India to the United Kingdom and then to the United States to offer their sons a better life. They settled in Ohio, and Rajat's father repeated his medical residency, working long hours. Those early days stirred Rajat's intense drive to achieve:

> The people were friendly and nice, but it was pretty obvious that we were recent immigrants. I remember thinking that I should be doing more and better. In ninth grade, I was always worrying, *Can I be more efficient?*
>
> My self-improvement projects built on each other. Every night before I went to bed, I wrote down what I had remorse over, what I regretted—for instance, if I had had a chance to help someone but didn't.

In college, Rajat cofounded a nonprofit startup with the aspiration to bring leaders together for bipartisan conversation. He co-led it through college, med school, and then business school. Hell-bent on impact, Rajat didn't notice that he was spinning out of control:

> I applied to medical school as an alibi so I could work on the startup. I could have taken a pause, but my parents would have thought of it as tantamount to dropping out. Medical school was intellectually stimulating. I found it powerful to be with people in their hard times. At the same time, the startup gave me incredible exposure to the world's issues and top minds. I'm really competitive, and I had to be the best I could in school. I brought that same intensity to my startup.
>
> My third year of medical school was the hardest, when you work in the hospital all day and study afterward. Some days I had to be in surgery from 5 a.m. to 9 p.m. I would fall asleep standing up in the operating room. Thankfully,

I wasn't doing operations! Fridays, I got home at 5:30 p.m. and made a massive mason jar of coffee that held 10 cups. I did my schoolwork and startup stuff. Saturday night was date night. Every date ended the same: after dinner, I fell asleep five minutes into the movie.

I decided to take a break and attend business school. I had an affinity for risk, creativity, and innovation. We were hitting year 3 in the startup, and I knew I had to bring my A game.

At business school, Rajat's mood worsened. He was frustrated that he hadn't accomplished enough. He lost 20 pounds. His health suffered:

A friend and I went out for drinks. The next day, he called. He said we had spent our entire time complaining about work, and I was changing in negative ways. I felt humbled. I was not sleeping and in pain. I was working to death. I had health problems too awful to discuss. I had never valued self-care. I saw it as not much more than what's required to keep a plant happy—you know, nutrition and water.

In college, every day had felt like the best day of my life. I don't know when that changed, but I was beginning to feel like every day was the worst day of my life. I hit a breaking point when I realized I would rather be poor and happy as a simple doctor than miserable with power, status, connections, and no control over my life. That was rock bottom.

It was time to make a few life changes. Rajat let go of the startup's day-to-day operations and returned to med school, reenergized and purposeful. And healthier.

So What?

Attending medical school *and* business school *and* leading a startup at the same time is a lethal recipe. Rajat didn't question the ill effects of rising pressures that he had imposed. Harsh criticism was the wakeup call he needed.

A mindset of punishing work drove Rajat's behavior. He said, "Ever since I was a kid, I had been envious of monks and the monastic life. I was into the intensity and focus of it, working oneself to death." But when Rajat stopped to reflect, he saw that his drive for achievement was backfiring. The more he worked, the less impact he had.

Self-awareness leads to self-correction. However, this is not a fake-it-until-you-make-it kind of thing. If mindset is what's holding you back, you have to replace it—and genuinely believe the new mindset. If you don't, your unhealthy behaviors won't change. They're simply a function of the entrenched, even deeper mindset that's still steering.*

You'd be wise to pay attention.

DRAWING THE LINE

Establish your boundaries in a dialogue with the people you love. They didn't sign up to be on that tough assignment with you!

Christopher's parents, both professionals, divorced when he was four. He believes that's why they made it a point to always be there. Their safety net helped him grow:

> In high school, I came into my own. I ran for student office, thinking, *Why not try it?* I failed at a lot of things but still kept trying.
>
> As a freshman in college, I was asked to be a senior editor on the newspaper. It was the first time I felt really out of my comfort zone. I had no idea what I was doing. The seniors seemed significantly older. It was a big hurdle to tell them what to do.

Christopher studied engineering, starting out as a product engineer in an innovative industrial company before trying a strategy role. Who better than Christopher to understand how pressure builds up steam:

---

* If you're intrigued by the notion that your intent to achieve a goal is thwarted by unchanging behaviors, check out *Immunity to Change: How to Overcome It and Unlock the Potential in Yourself and Your Organization* by Robert Kegan and Lisa Laskow Lahey (Harvard Business School Publishing, Boston, 2009).

Running a good business is what drives me. You're amped up because you're getting stuff done. The low point is the cost of traveling and working on the road. You think, *Is it worth it?*

I took on a role to help one of our businesses develop the market. I was traveling with my team to align the strategies. I felt great; we were making traction. The numbers were good, and the product looked good. Things we were doing made a difference.

But I have a tendency to always want more. When a project is 80 percent done, I tend to look to the next one. Competition is my number one strength. I want to win.

External pressures built up. Although the assignment was exciting, it was taking its toll on Christopher:

I was on the road so much, sometimes for three weeks at a time. I had to take calls in the middle of the night. That's when I broke up with my girlfriend. Destined to get there, it was a real wakeup call. I realized I had only one priority—work.

I missed something along the way: I lost who I was. I was trying to make it all work and not being true to what makes me happy. I lost perspective on what was important. I didn't set any boundaries. There was no limit. I don't have any regrets because I learned a ton about myself. I'm young enough that I can make stupid mistakes for a while.

If you value the people around you, set boundaries. What's acceptable is in the light of another person. You have to have a conversation. I'd say, "I have this huge project. It's important for me to learn and grow. I won't be here much. Is it OK? Not OK?" You figure it out together openly and honestly.

There is a cost associated with being successful. I struggle with that. I don't know what winning looks like now. I don't know what my priorities should be. Do I get an MBA? Do I chase a dream of money, a better job, a bigger title, and a corner office that I'm not even sure is real?

I'm always planning for a future that is unplannable. I was like that as a kid. What do I actually want? What would make me happy? I don't have an answer. That's the journey of life. Everybody is trying to answer that unanswerable question.

A few years in, Christopher was promoted to product manager. Most recently, he joined a cutting edge bioengineering startup, still pondering.

So What?

When things got harder, at first Christopher pushed harder. When it got more painful, he tolerated more pain. Once Christopher realized that relieving pressure was his responsibility, bingo! He could choose to contain it or live with the consequences.

Travel nightmares are irritating, and looming deadlines fuel compulsive behavior. What do you do? Compromise healthy eating. Work longer hours. Boil over. Instead, estimate the pressure up front and determine what's acceptable. If you're excited for the assignment, good for you.

Establish your boundaries in a dialogue with the people you love. They didn't sign up to be on that tough assignment with you! Boundaries help set their expectations too. Limits also help you restore needed physical and emotional energy.

Set aside the philosophical questions for when you're in stable waters. It's not good to ask them when you've just had a wakeup call—that's the moment when you'll be least likely to find inspiring solutions. Pressure usually comes in waves. Wait for the calm between them.

In the words of a friend, "Strike when the iron is cold."

THE TIPPING POINT

You can have it all, but you never have it all at the same time for long. Things come into equilibrium and feel nearly perfect—momentarily.

Maya grew up in a tight-knit, conservative Indian family. She remembers the first time she got to be on her own. She had always been a rule follower, but in that summer high school math program, she made her own decisions. Still Maya worked hard to please others throughout school, torn between what she wanted to do and what she should do. After college, she started in banking:

> I took the job because it was the hardest to get. I wanted to put myself in situations where I would be uncomfortable. I had spent my senior year in college knowing I didn't want to go. Two years into the job, I crossed the line to miserable.
>
> People were the tipping point. Even in a job that was really tough and not what I wanted, if the people were great, passionate, kind, visionary—that would have made it for me. It wasn't the case, though. There was the issue of fairness too. People got in trouble for things that weren't their fault.
>
> That summer, I broke my leg on a weekend. The first call I made from the ambulance was not to my family but to my boss. I said I could not send the slides that night. Without asking about me, she lost it. So I went to the hospital, went home, and worked on the slides. That's when it hit me: *What am I doing?* I was determined to finish the program, but I was hobbling around on crutches, working 110 hours a week. I had no idea how I would survive.

For support, Maya got involved with the women's network. She launched a successful initiative, work improved, and she received a promotion. That was when Maya decided to leave:

> It was exciting to turn in my BlackBerry and walk out the door. It was a beautiful sunny day. A huge burden had been lifted off my shoulders. I called my mom. Things got muddy then. She freaked out. She yelled and screamed. So I hopped on a plane and went to see my grandparents in India. I had taken that job because it was what my parents wanted and what everybody told me to do. My mother could not understand how I could leave.
>
> I only knew what I didn't want to do. A few months later I moved back home and got an incredible nonprofit job.

I was put on so many transformative projects and had the business skills to be able to contribute. I thought, *I can completely do this!*

At her new job, Maya stayed up all night working, joyfully. And with each subsequent work move since then, she has embraced new challenges—and pressures. When we talked last, Maya was a new mom and spearheading digital transformation for the company, leading her biggest team yet.

So What?

Maya's story explores the question, "When do you cry uncle!" Consider both sides of it. Is the job giving you what you had hoped to learn or do? If so, can you survive the struggle? If your misery is too great, reconsider. You don't want to get stuck in Dante's seventh circle so early in your career. What's your answer? Though Maya's story was about a first job, that same rubric works for every stage of your career.

Before you act, envision what happens next. Walking out the door is thrilling but complex. You feel relief—and some disquiet. Then what? Like Maya, maybe you want it all. You can have it all, but you never have it all at the same time for long. Things come into equilibrium and feel nearly perfect—momentarily. The converse is also true. Pressure boils up and threatens to destroy, but then it dissipates.

Maya's favorite quote sums it up: "The fundamental question of life is not what you want but what you are willing to struggle for."* Reframe struggle as a good thing. It means you are learning and growing.

Remember: What is not obvious today will be clear in time.

TAKING ON YOUR

PRESSURE CHALLENGE

We all work hard to succeed. Our rewards are many: financial independence, recognition, impact, personal growth, enjoyment—all worth

---

* Mark Manson, "The Most Important Question of Your Life," *Mark Manson* website, November 6, 2016, https://markmanson.net/question.

our effort. The higher those rewards, the more pressure we feel. It's part of the package.

What kind of pressure do you have? Jobs contain structural pressures. Sally had a daily show to produce. Christopher's work was on the road and unpredictable. There is the pressure of a steep learning curve. Sally, Brody, and Emma had to learn on the job, and quickly. Third, we bring our own pressure to work: Brody, Christopher, Rajat, and Maya battled limiting mindsets of perfectionism, winning or losing, unrelenting drive, or striving to please.

In most cases, managing pressure is a learnable skill. Learn it and either the pressure will lessen or you'll handle it better. If you're struggling to get the better of work pressure, consider the following recommendations.

Identify What's Driving the Pressure

What's really going on at work? Without self-judgment, unpack the pressure you feel by asking why, why, and why again:

- *Collect the facts.* Find where the pressure is coming from. Make your lists and circle the drivers that really bother you.

  o *External pressures due to industry, company, or job:* How can you tell? Notice whether everybody in the role, the company, and maybe industry experiences the same kind of pressure. Traders yell; journalists fight deadlines; doctors battle to save lives; consultants suffer travel overload. The pressure cooker exists. If it's getting to you, think about whether it's worth it.

  o *Temporary:* Learning new skills is uncomfortable, even painful, but work improves—usually sooner than you expect. If learning is causing the pressure, review your situation regularly. If it's driven by the culture or your team configuration, gaining skills may be insufficient without other changes.

  o *Internal:* Sometimes you create the pressure all by yourself. With a conscious effort to uncover and shift your mindset, that's going to go away.

- *Understand why it bothers you.* For example, maybe you just received a new assignment and you're ready to panic. Why? Afraid that you'll fall short? Keep asking why until you get to the bottom where nothing seems worse: *I'm going to fail* could turn into, *I'm not good enough*, and that could turn into *I am unworthy*. See where I'm going? You're unearthing the fear that accentuates pressure. Accept that you're human. You're not invincible. You're also not a robot! And that's a fact.

Reframe the Pressure

As you get used to the environment, learn more skills, and get comfortable in your role, pressure may lessen. To make the decision whether to stay in the role, take these steps:

- *Review progress against your goals.* Remind yourself why you wanted the job: what you liked about the company, what skills you were eager to learn, what you wanted to achieve. Break down your goals into bite-sized milestones. With those in hand, create your development plan. You don't have to follow it to a T, but a plan helps you see how today's action fits your longer-term goal. Pressure may be tolerable if you're learning what you set out to learn or having the impact you desired.

- *Check whether you can relieve pressure, at least in part.* By talking to colleagues and your boss, you may find creative solutions. Can you shift your tasks or change your schedule in a way that allows relief? What best practices do colleagues live by? If you learn that pressure exists for you in every environment, it's a sign that changing jobs is not going to make things better. Turn inward for solutions.

- *Know when enough is enough.* There are days and weeks when you're ready to throw in the towel, but after the deadline is met or you've mastered a skill or the boss changes, you're glad that you stayed. Before you explode, review your rhythm at work. There should be high points along with the lows. If you don't feel elated ever, that's food for thought.

Manage What You Can Control

Work can be exhausting, so much so that you lose perspective on why you wanted to be there in the first place. Regain your perspective by reaffirming why you're working:

- *Focus on inputs, not outputs.* Turn every pressure-filled challenge into learning and you'll reduce the pressure. You cannot control being a success, but you can give it your best effort, learn a lot, and improve.

- *Set boundaries.* If you start out with no limits, guess what's going to happen?

  - *Do a reality test.* The best way to know if you're working without boundaries is to ask someone close to you. Lost in the forest, all you see are trees that look alike.

  - *Be honest with yourself.* If you want to hit it out of the ballpark more than anything, forget boundaries. But tell the people who presume a relationship with you. Close friends and family have goals too. Take them into account before making decisions.

  - *Engage in a real dialogue.* Pressure also comes from unspoken expectations and resentments. And they're not always about work. Talking things over relieves pressure.

- *Let go of something.* You cannot do it all at once, so figure out what others can do, what really doesn't need to be done (or done right now), and what only you can do.

  - *List your commitments.* Draw a two-by-two matrix with low and high importance versus low and high urgency. Write down all your commitments. Make the most important and urgent ones your top priority.

  - *Negotiate what to let go.* If you have too many top priorities, negotiate with your boss to hand off something. As embarrassed as you may feel, it's better to let others know what's realistic than to let them down later. People hate that kind of surprise.

- *Set up a review ritual.* At the end of each week or month but not before a critical deadline, take 20 minutes to appreciate your experiences. Without judgment. First review what you did well and what you learned. It really helps to write it down so you don't forget. Now turn to what you'd like to do better, with specific and clear language. Watch out for a tendency to blame or judge. If you hear your internal critic scolding, bring your attention back to what you appreciate about yourself. Review your performance regularly and reset as the situation changes.

Take Care of Yourself

When the pressure is unsustainable, you've got to do something about it. Here are tactics to find relief soon and over the longer term:

- *Lean on someone.* The higher the pressure, the more alone you can feel. But you're not working in a vacuum. The people around you can help relieve the pressure—by being a sounding board, a coach, or a helper.

  - *Find someone more experienced.* If you're an individual contributor on the team, go to your boss or mentor or a colleague you trust. They have more tenure and more experience; it's worth knowing what they have to say. Consider this a two-way street. They're probably feeling pressure too.

  - *Tap your network.* Your support network outside of work can help, including everyone from partners to friends to mothers and fathers. Just keep in mind that some people in your network may increase your stress. Find the people who do not have an ax to grind.

- *Start small.* Partners, friends, parents, and colleagues (even strangers) can see that you're sliding, but only you can do something about it. In small steps, redesign parts of your life to make it easier to do. Start with a shift in mindset and take it from there.

  - *Find out why you're not taking enough care now.* Why are you suffering? Sure, work sets up horrible conditions. You're allowing it, and you can decide what to accept.

  - *Replace the mindset that has become the barrier.* You may be pleasing someone else instead of standing up for what you want. Align your needs with your new mindset.

  - *Monitor your behavior.* You're not out of the woods yet. Watch what you actually do versus what you said you would do. You don't need 100 percent compliance, just enough to reinforce your mindset.

Too much pressure dampens enthusiasm for any job. It can disrupt your performance and destroy your job satisfaction. The more you can calm the internal drivers of pressure, the better able you'll be to master external pressures that come with the territory. That's not to say it's your fault—this is a no-fault zone. But it's your responsibility to find out what's going on.

And when the pot boils over, it's up to you to lift the lid.

PURPOSE PRESSURE
MISTAKE REVIEW
BRING PEOPLE ON BOARD
BULLIES JERKS
TAKE A STAND
RISK SELF-DOUBT
SUPER   ENERGY
MENTOR S NSOR
LOVE FEAR   DESPAIR
PURP   SSURE
MISTAKE REVIEW
BRING PEOPLE ON BOARD

3

When Your Mistake
Feels Colossal

I n a job interview, you're asked about a failure, but they don't really mean it. Senior leaders brush off the question too, modestly professing too many to recall—all small, of course! Experts proclaim that failures are a badge of innovation courage to be celebrated. But failure is not like success for one obvious reason: it's painful. The scars last for a long time. Anybody who tells you otherwise is spouting nonsense.

A mistake is a cousin of failure, a pint-sized learning opportunity. Though short-lived, mistakes are painful too. They bring on shame, embarrassment, remorse, anger. Often, they're joined by fears: we're imposters, we're not worthy, we let others down. To squelch fears, we'd do anything to avoid mistakes, which increases their surprise factor. We hate making them.

That's why we love to read about *other people's* mistakes. Lynn, a product manager in a tech company, made a few, each one compounded by the last:

> We were trying to launch a feature by a certain date. I allowed myself to be influenced to take an easier route. My manager also thought that this path would work well, but after starting, a senior executive didn't like the way we were

implementing. He called my manager, who then forgot he had agreed to the decision.

My manager told me, "Maybe we did discuss it, and I didn't listen as closely as I should have. At any rate, client experience should not be compromised. Let's do it the right way." The internal team was upset that we had to start over. I told them I had accepted a compromise that maybe I should not have. I felt as though I'd lost credibility with them. I was hard on myself. I felt bad.

I have not exactly stopped beating myself up. I worry about changes, and I feel guilty when I deliver this type of news. My manager said, "This is software development. People should be prepared for change!"

I've learned to push back. I should trust my gut. If we're compromising too much, I should put the brakes on. I should go back to my manager to slow the delivery. I would love to be perfect. I don't like people being upset with me. I know it's impossible to please everyone, but that's hard for me to believe and accept.

In the end, Lynn launched the product feature on time without compromise. What looked like a mistake turned out not to be one. But Lynn struggled with feelings of guilt and trying to please.

Mistakes are mess-ups with unwanted consequences. Once they happen, we take action to avoid making them again. Then it's time for recovery. Recovery separates the successful people from those who stay mired in the past. The process for recovery is learnable, as you'll see from these stories:

- *How do you bounce back from your broken promise?* In a new role, Bill saw an opportunity to impress that turned out to be a trap; he put his best foot forward and fell in.

- *What happens when your mistakes are inevitable?* Caught like a deer in the headlights when a senior client questioned her, Janelle didn't know what to do.

- *What do you do when the mistake was entirely your fault?* Caitlin's mistake overshadowed what should have been her triumph.

- *How seriously should you take your mistake?* Jorge prided himself on intellectual rigor and professionalism, strengths he needed in order to fix a mistake of consequence.

- *What can your mistake really teach you?* What felt like a disaster led to a positive outcome Paulina could not have predicted.

- *How do you recover from a mistake you cannot fix?* Isabella could do nothing but figure out how to move forward.

All of these stories have satisfactory endings, and no, I didn't stack the deck. Every story is real. Cringe-worthy. And accompanied by a bag of uncomfortable emotions that will last well beyond their expiration date. Sure, they might have been avoided had the person had enough sleep, less stress, more time, greater focus, or seasoned judgment. That's why mistakes get made.

Get ready to root for these imperfect heroines and heroes. Then prepare for your own mistakes—the ones you won't see coming—and grow from the experience.

PROMISING THE IMPOSSIBLE

Why is it so hard to pause and say, "Let me get back to you?"

Bill's father owned a 1965 Chrysler 300. It broke down often, so Bill and his dad spent Saturdays working on the car and hanging out. His father was a nurse, but early on, Bill knew automobiles would be his deal and trust would be his ticket to success:

> I spent most of my life at church. It's where I got my integrity. Honesty is key no matter what. The only way to trust somebody is to believe what they say. It's the same at work or in football. Without integrity, no one wants to hang out with you.
>
> Being one of the first in my family to go to a Fortune 500 automotive company was a big deal for me *and* my family. It took time for my manager to warm up to me. At my

first job in my first year, I stayed at my desk on a computer all day except for bathroom breaks and a 30-minute lunch. It wasn't too bad, but it wasn't good.

At the same time, I was making more money than I ever had. I couldn't walk away just because someone was micro-managing me. I could not go back home. Now, I could be out of the office for a week and no one would mind because there is so much trust. Not being boxed in is freedom for me.

Yet Bill's mistake story was about a breach of trust. Taking on a project midway through, he first met with senior management:

They looked down the table at me. They said, "We can't believe it's so late. The new guy has to deliver it in four days." I said, "I'm going to get it done." A few of them started to laugh. After I left the room, I talked to some people. I found out it was impossible to get it done in four days, but it could be done in four *weeks*.

I asked to meet on day 4. They were not laughing then. I felt embarrassed, but I said, "I'm not going to have it done today, but here are my plans. Here's when I will get it done." They were happy. They wanted to know what I did and didn't know. It was a breath of fresh air. They said, "Good. We expect you to have it done. Come back every other week to review progress."

You better believe that I delivered! That mistake will never happen twice. I learned from my dad. He never committed to anything he could not do. He said, "I will do my best to make it happen. That's all I can promise." If you don't know, don't make something up. Don't just say something because you feel you have to. I learned to make sure my yes is really yes.

Delivering led to more success and more responsibility. Assigned to be the liaison between China and U.S. manufacturing and engineering, Bill turned to trust building again:

People don't only want to know what you *know*. They want to know that you *care*. They believe you're going to make them do it your way. Ask what they think. Take the time to listen. That was a shocker for the local workers.

They have a big deal dinner with all types of food. Even though we put in 15 hours a day, I felt that I had to go and eat things I didn't want to eat. I wanted to show that I would be part of their culture. The next time we had an issue, they thought, *Bill said it, so we should hear him out.*

Delivering every time, Bill advanced steadily, earning financial independence and more trust too.

So What?

We all break promises without considering the consequences. Whether it's due to excitement about a project, a desire to please, or feeling cornered, it's easier to say yes in the moment. And then, poof! Broken promises erode trust quickly, as Bill learned.

Bouncing back is hard, but it's doable. Bill shows the way. Get the facts and revise your plan. Fess up and offer your new solution. Meet expectations without another hiccup. Of course, it's better not to make commitments we cannot keep in the first place.

Why is it so hard to pause and say, "Let me get back to you"? You first have to believe in yourself. Faith reinforced Bill's self-esteem and confidence. That and having an older brother twice his size! Growing up with his brother as his protector, Bill didn't get pushed around. That's exactly what you need. The next time someone urgently requests something, imagine you have a big brother standing beside you. Even if you feel pressured to overcommit, your big brother won't allow it.

Let him do the talking.

CAUGHT IN THE HEADLIGHTS

Until we gain experience, we all make mistakes of judgment.

Growing up in Trinidad, Janelle and her parents worked in the shop first opened by their Chinese grandparents. So three generations toiled and made sacrifices for Janelle and her brothers. Their persistence inspired Janelle to value financial security, expertise, and perfection. She joined a financial institution to satisfy all three. Everything went well until Janelle faced live fire:

> Our clients were CFOs and treasurers—very senior and much older. My boss was not able to make this meeting. The CFO client asked questions I didn't know the answer to. I felt extremely *not* confident! I thought, *Shoot! I should know this!*
>
> I made something up on the fly. In the moment, I thought that was the best course of action, which was wrong. I thought it would go under the rug and not come up again, but obviously it did. A more senior colleague approached me later and said, "I don't think this answer is right." That was a slap on the wrist.
>
> I should have said to the client, "I don't know, but I will get back to you."

Janelle found the right answer and buried it in a follow-up e-mail to the client. The deal went through, but she continued to wrestle with her mistake:

> I don't think the client stressed about my wrong answer, but I will never forget. It makes me second-guess myself every time I say something. There were so many things going on. Every time I see the guy who corrected me, I think about it! I was extremely embarrassed.
>
> A lot of people say incorrect things and move on. I'm the kind of person who likes to be credible and trusted. I have to be right. So much of this business is just perception. If you say something wrong with confidence, 9 out of 10 people will believe you. I grew up being self-critical. I'm more self-conscious. But taking things too personally holds you back.

The wrong answer has been long forgotten. Janelle put her experience—surviving live fire—to excellent use from that time on.

So What?

Janelle's boss did no wrong by throwing her into the meeting on her own. It was a way to help her grow. Fielding a difficult question from a client is no fun. This is one of those mistakes that everybody makes—once. Until we gain experience, we all make mistakes of judgment.

Stand in the other person's shoes to see a better way. The receiver would rather wait a little longer for confidence in the right answer than question whether the quick answer was wrong. Saying "I don't know" builds trust. Confident people don't have a problem saying it. Even experts don't have all the answers; they do know how to get the answer faster.

You can prepare for live fire. Practice your mantra: "I don't know the answer. I'll get back to you [pick a reasonable deadline]." Practice calming yourself down ahead of time. When the questioner or the question is tough, take time to absorb the question and form your response. Get used to not knowing the answer. If fear is lurking nearby, recognize that you're imperfect *and so is everyone else.* And if you do make a mistake, think, *Did anything terrible happen? I'm here and safe.*

This game is won by being at bat more of the time. Step up to the plate quickly and often. To do that, learn to let go of perfection. It saps energy. Seeing only black-or-white with no shades of gray breeds risk aversion. Who says you have to be the best at work or the best at (karaoke, weight lifting, parenting, or whatever)? Who says you have to have all the answers? You did. If you're not the best, that doesn't mean you're the worst. If you say something wrong, you're *not* failing. You're pretty good and maybe even better than that.

Operating well under fire is part of the job. With practice, the adrenaline rush may become a pleasure.

THE SUN WILL COME OUT TOMORROW

Mistakes fixed quickly do less damage.

Caitlin grew up in a suburb where no one else was Indian, and it seemed like they were all better off. Then, several surgeries put her in a wheelchair during high school. Perhaps those challenges reinforced her soaring ambition and creativity—and impatience. Caitlin's teachers encouraged her not to settle, but instead, to do whatever she wanted:

> I realized I had to form myself in a new way, change my entire life. I taught myself guitar, took up writing for the school newspaper, and learned how to talk to people. I developed a self-deprecating sense of humor. I'm definitely not one of the smartest from my school. But I wanted the chance to be awesome!
>
> For example, as captain of our high school math team, I would read our public announcements on Monday mornings just like a varsity athlete captain did. In college, I made a feature-length Bollywood movie even though I couldn't sing or dance. My parents told me, "Just say yes to everything. Whatever people ask you to do."

After college, Caitlin joined a Wall Street trading firm. At first, she thought the screaming traders hated her. But after a while, Caitlin learned to respond calmly and rationally to them. Gaining confidence, she invented a new approach to doing a trade, and her boss approved the implementation. Minutes later, Caitlin messed up:

> I bought instead of sold! It felt like a nightmare. I felt completely sick. How could I have done this? Everyone makes mistakes, but my mistake overshadowed the cool thing I could have done. We ended up losing significant money.
>
> My boss was upset. Every few minutes he asked me for the numbers, which stressed me out more because I was selling as the market moved. It took a few hours. I thought I should start looking for another job.
>
> After I completed the sell, he asked for the final loss. I said I was so sorry, and I explained what I would do to be more careful. I promised not to do it again. He started calming down. By the end of the day, he said, "OK, these things happen."
>
> I had a couple of really good friends at the office. We went out for drinks, and I vented. They assured me that my

mistake was stupid, but it happens. Even now I cringe because of the stupidity of it.

The next morning, my boss said, "You cannot do this again. It makes me look bad." That was the worst sentence in the entire conversation. I felt bad, but trading requires attention. I left the problem in the dust and acted normal.

Since then, I've made my way back, replacing that mistake with better performance. Whenever I do something slightly off, I freak out and double-check. Paranoid is another way of putting it.

Over time, Caitlin bounced back. She noticed that other people made dumb errors too, and did not get fired. She collaborated with a colleague to implement her idea successfully. Her last words? "It was awesome!"

So What?

Alarm bells and flashing lights can be paralyzing, especially when you're struggling with cognitive dissonance. Two opposing thoughts collide: *I'm a good worker* and *I made a terrible mistake*. But mistakes fixed quickly do less damage. Summon your inner relentless coach to respond. There will be time for crying later on. Own the mistake immediately, genuinely apologize and be contrite, and swing into action to repair the damage.

It may take a while for your boss to calm down. It may take longer for you to stop cringing. The sting of mistakes lingers for a reason. It makes us vigilant and careful to avoid making the same one again.

RECOVERING FROM A WHOPPER

The good thing about mistakes is that when they're done, they are done. It's what you do afterward that counts.

Born to proud Caribbean professionals, Jorge does not remember an easy childhood growing up in Florida. He saw himself as the outcast, less valuable than others. That said, the fortitude and resilience he developed helped him rebound at work years later:

> My parents got divorced when I was 11. It was dramatic. Not an experience for kids to see. It made me more sensitive to people and their feelings. I don't try to confront people. Instead, I try to resolve conflict.
>
> Over time as I thought about it more, I used logic, and it made more sense to me. I can be rational to a fault. It made me realize that I like to be intellectually stimulated.

Jorge stayed on the "right track": college, financial analyst, business school, and investment firm associate—always successful. So his mistake came as a surprise:

> We were trying to standardize a set of accounts as much as we could. I was taking a ton of time to make sure all their details were correct. But a few months after the clients had signed their new agreements, I realized I had made a really big mistake. The firm lost a lot of money.
>
> I had missed one area, partly due to inexperience. It was something we always harped on to get right, but I didn't check it. I asked a colleague what to do, and he told me to let it go, do nothing. I felt I needed to tell now rather than later. Normally, I would have talked to my boss, but he was traveling. So I called my boss's boss. I thought I was going to get fired!
>
> My boss was upset when he returned, but he resolved it and told me to stop worrying. He said others had made bigger mistakes that had cost a lot of money. I should have believed him, but the firm wrote a big check to make up for the mistake. The most senior head of our team took responsibility on behalf of the firm. I needed his OK.

Anxiously, Jorge waited for his probation. He prepared for a call that never came:

I was trying to be diligent. I don't think it was possible to work harder. I estimated to see if I could pay for my mistake. That gave me some comfort. Then I prepared a sheet with the lessons I learned and rehearsed them with my wife. I took it with me everywhere in case they wanted to meet.

The important lesson was that whenever you have a complex process to make heterogeneous things uniform, you need a point person. You have to at least create a way to pull it together into one macro snapshot. Though I missed something, the person who owned the macro view would have found it.

At year end, the mistake did not show up in Jorge's review. It was time to move forward.

So What?

There are two kinds of people: those who make mistakes and admit them and those who just don't admit them. Definitely the first kind, Jorge treated his mistake as serious. His strong values guided him to quick action. Waiting would have compounded the mistake. His boss might have found out and asked, "Why did you wait to tell me?"

The good thing about mistakes is that when they're done, they are done. It's what you do *afterward* that counts: helping to fix the problem, repairing the damage, and avoiding another one like it. Jorge figured out the root cause and came up with a solution, and he was ready to discuss it if asked. He learned a great deal from that mistake, which was forgiven and forgotten.

The hardest part is letting go of strong emotions like shame, embarrassment, and remorse. It's hard work to move on, especially without the closure that comes from punishment. Jorge gained some comfort from carrying his lessons around. And a fast-paced job is a blessing: tomorrow brings more work and new issues to focus on.

So watch out. If you ruminate, your mistake will take on a life of its own. Powerful emotions will cloud the objective reality. The worst outcome of making a mistake would be to miss its silver lining—the lessons it holds.

THE DAY IT HIT THE FAN

Unless you're hell-bent on self-destruction,
ironically, mistakes accelerate your learning.

Paulina started her life in Poland, moving to Canada at eight and then to the United States for college. Who could have predicted that Paulina would earn a PhD in molecular medicine and get a coveted venture capital job after?

> I will forever remember moving to Canada from Poland. I went to class not understanding a single word of English. I hadn't seen my father in so long I called him "Mr. Dad." I cried myself to sleep. All I wanted was to go back to my little village. Over time, I realized that if I could do all of this, there would be nothing in this world that I could not accomplish.
>
> I knew I was in college to get a 4.0. I studied after everyone went to bed. I was so happy and serene. I realized I could handle four majors if I wanted, go to med school, get a PhD, anything! It sounds cocky, but I felt empowered to do what I wanted.

Confident Paulina did not factor in mistakes getting in the way of a meteoric career. At the time, she was working on a deal with a brilliant entrepreneur who was a close friend of the venture capital CEO:

> My boss told me to figure it out on my own—the science, the medical application, and whether there was a business. We were going back and forth on whether to proceed.
>
> At one point, I miscommunicated that our firm would be in for tens of millions of dollars. The entrepreneur had thought the investment was across the finish line, but it wasn't. He was really mad and said, "How are we even having this conversation?" I hung up thinking, *How do I fix this? No one is ever going to do business with me again. I'm not meant to do this. I can't do it!*

The entrepreneur called the CEO next, pissed that we'd been at it for four months and were still not investing. The shit hit the fan. The CEO called me. I laid out what I thought had happened. I said, "I think I fucked up."

That's when the plot of this story and Paulina's fortunes zigged when she thought they would zag:

The CEO said, "I just want to let you know that there is nothing wrong with this moment." I thought, *What in the world does he mean?* He said, "I'm going to figure out whether we want this deal or not and socialize it with the team. We owe an answer." He felt there was nothing more to be done. We just had to decide.

I felt disappointed but thought, *I have done three years of great work here, and this is my one mess-up. I can learn from it; it isn't so bad. The worst case is I will get fired. I have a wonderful family. My life will go on.*

My boss knew this was a learning moment. You have to get in it deep enough that you can mess it up. Otherwise, you cannot get to the next stage of your career.

Everyone at the firm found out what had happened when they met to decide on the deal. Then the CEO handed the reins back to Paulina. She repaired her relationship and joined the venture's board. Paulina's career continued on a rocket-ship trajectory.

So What?

Feeling invincible, Paulina had single-mindedly created her opportunities in life. Making a mistake was human but mortifying. It felt disastrous in the moment, and it almost was. When the entrepreneur exploded, Paulina was not equipped to handle the difficult conversation. Luckily, the CEO turned it into a teachable moment. This story doesn't focus on his heroism, but he intervened at the right time to make the experience productive.

Paulina's mistake taught her to face tough subjects without trying to please. She learned that directness builds trust and that getting help is not a weakness. Unless you're hell-bent on self-destruction, ironically, mistakes accelerate your learning.

STILL STANDING

In the moment of shock, you stop thinking. You need oxygen to think. The past has already happened, so breathe deeply.

Isabella's background is as colorful as her career. She lived in the Middle East until third grade. When her father returned to his home in Southeast Asia, she came to the United States with her mother and sister. For Isabella, life and struggle go together:

> We had a lot of things, but when we came here, money ran out. Our mom was college educated, but she had to take any job she could. I didn't understand. I felt the rug pulled out from under us. That made our family stronger.
> Life gets messy. I must always be on my feet if circumstances change.

Isabella had a passion for television, despite the all-night work and harsh environment. She enjoyed it enough to laugh at the high points along with the low ones. We celebrated her biggest achievement before discussing her biggest mistake:

> I was the only one chosen from my show to cover a very important event. It was huge! I had no idea what I was doing. I always worried about messing up. The senior leader told me I did a great job. I've always felt good about my achievements, but you don't believe in yourself as much as other people believe in you.
> The morning after the president was elected, I was responsible for the cold open, which is the first piece of video that airs on the show. It was a very big deal, just my editor and me doing it. That was my entire focus that week.

We were done early, about midnight the night before, but we were exhausted from pulling late hours. My editor lay down on a couch to nap. Before our 5 a.m. airtime, I had a hard time getting him up. The machine was a little slow too. Then it happened. You hear the anchor's voice. You hear the new president speaking. All you see is black.

It was the first and last time I had black air. We didn't get the footage out on time. I got yelled at: "Why didn't you get help?" In that moment, everyone was screaming. I would have been yelling at myself too, but my jaw locked, and I couldn't open my mouth. I was so upset. I thought I was going to get fired! I thought it was the end of the world. They told me to take the day off after seeing the dentist.

Later, Isabella's boss debriefed her on what she should have done differently. They fixed the tape for the West Coast release. Much, much later, Isabella saw her mistake in a new light:

Though it's a reflection on the network, I realized that it's fine. At the end of the day, it's just television. You have to move on to the next story. It's not life and death! These things happen. It makes you aware.

It took me a while, but every night, I had one or two new stories. If the feedback from the next five stories is great, then the shitty feedback from one story is dulled.

So What?

When the walls come crashing down, what do you do? Isabella's family challenges had prepared her to handle it. She knew that the first thing she had to do was breathe. Sometimes, it's all that you can do.

When you're threatened with clear and present danger, your amygdala rushes into action. Your amygdala doesn't distinguish between physical danger and the emotional kind. It kicks into gear before you know it. In the moment of shock, you stop thinking. You need oxygen to think. The past has already happened, so breathe deeply.*

If you're wondering what to do next, put more points on the board. Each new success diminishes your mistake a little more. Recent successes can transform your career trajectory.

Then there is emotional recovery. Your mistake may feel like a loss (as in, lose your job or lose your health). Many struggle with residual feelings long after the mistake has been forgotten by others. Take that seriously. Just when you need to move on, remorse and guilt hold you back.

Be kind to yourself on the road to recovery.

MISTAKE CHALLENGE

We *all* make mistakes, regrettable mistakes that hurt. What separates successful mistake makers from those whose careers nosedive is this: strong recovery. Mistakes don't get better with age; in fact, unclaimed mistakes may lead to questions about your competence. Cover-ups complicate matters. Assume others will unearth your buried mistakes. That undermines trust and calls your integrity into account. Mistakes are your responsibility; you're accountable. Given our globally connected environment, the consequences might be bigger than you think, so take note.

Work is full of ways to make mistakes. I shared a range to assure you that mistake making is universal. Lynn second-guessed herself. Bill overpromised. Janelle misspoke due to lack of judgment. Caitlin implemented poorly. Jorge didn't catch an oversight. Trying to be nice, Paulina avoided

---

* Daniel Goleman coined the term "amygdala hijack" in his book *Emotional Intelligence: Why It Can Matter More Than IQ* (Bantam Books, New York, 1995). Diane Musho Hamilton, a conflict mediator and author, offers tips on how to respond instead of react in the moment of an amygdala hijack. Her advice includes focusing on curiosity in the moment to stay present; letting go of the story running through our minds; feeling our physical presence acutely; and breathing slowly and in rhythm. Read more in her short and helpful article "Calming Your Brain During Conflict," *Harvard Business Review*, December 22, 2015.

a necessary but difficult conversation. Isabella dropped the ball. They all deserve praise for their generosity to share.*

Even though these are early and midcareer mistakes, you can learn from them if you're much further along. The moral is not to avoid every mistake in the first place. Rather, success results from regaining your balance when you're thrown off it. Our capacity to make mistakes is infinite, but we can learn to mitigate their impact.

Confirm Your Mistake and Acknowledge It

Fatigue, time pressure, and angry bosses are all red flags that a mistake is about to happen. It's easy to miss the ringing alarm bells and flashing red lights when you're in shock. So do this:

- *Size it up.* Know what you did, confirm that there really was a mistake (not a near miss or peccadillo), and estimate the damage. If you cannot quantify the loss, determine the nature of the damage—for example, (potential) client upset or quality issue. If you're telling yourself that your mistake was tiny, then before you make a decision, find a colleague to validate whether the mistake requires action.

- *Fess up.* It's human to sweep mistakes under the rug for fear of retribution. However, if you're already feeling stressed, chances are that your mistake was material and should be communicated. That doesn't mean putting on a hair shirt to punish yourself.

  - *Alert your boss.* The business world is not black-and-white, so it's likely that your boss is in a better position to judge the extent of your mistake and the best fix. If your boss is not around, get help from someone more experienced than you.

---

* If you're keen to read more stories of mistakes, including some doozies I've made, you can in *Mistakes I Made at Work: 25 Influential Women Reflect on What They Got by Getting It Wrong* by Jessica Bacal (Penguin Group, New York, 2014). No matter that only women share their mistakes—men can learn from these too. Although it does make you wonder whether a group of 25 influential men would have been as forthcoming.

○ *Apologize.* Apologize right away, calmly and rationally.* This is the unpleasant part, but if you can, stay focused on what can be done to fix the mistake. Once you've apologized, it's your responsibility to move the process along.

Design Your Plan for Change

Planning will help you avoid making the same mistake twice. If you're in the thick of a crisis, figure this part out later. Once the mistake has been fixed or someone else is fixing it, you have time to regroup:

● *Find the root causes.* Once you've found the weakest link, figure out how to eliminate it through process redesign. Here are a few simple fixes.

  ○ *Stop making promises on the spot.* Before you make the next one, check that you can, indeed, deliver on the commitment.

  ○ *Rely on others' judgment.* Check with other people before releasing important information.

  ○ *Build in pauses.* Before you rush to execute, pause for a minute to think rationally. Do a sanity check.

  ○ *Increase your checks and balances.* In a spreadsheet mistake, for example, add in a third-party check. If you're working alone, add in a short break and then do a clean-sheet review. If you can, double-check your work in the morning after a good night's sleep.

---

* Making a genuine apology is not as simple as it sounds. Katie Heany breaks it down into four parts: (1) Choose your words with care. For example, say "I'm sorry for" and never "I regret if." (2) Show genuine remorse for what you've said or done. (3) Show responsibility and ownership by using the active voice because the passive voice suggests that it simply happened. (4) Briefly explain how you'll make sure it never happens again, because many apologizers are recidivists whose apologies do not seem genuine. There's more helpful advice in her article "The Apology Critics Who Want to Teach You How to Say You're Sorry," NYmag.com, June 8, 2017. The article refers to another one by Susan McCarthy in *Salon:* "How to Say You're Sorry: A Refresher Course," Salon.com, August 23, 2001. McCarthy gleefully recommends offering an apology without inserting the word *if,* which both qualifies the apology and absolves you of any responsibility. Frog lovers beware as the article explores the example of apologizing for a frog's death in a multitude of humorous ways to make the point crystal clear.

- *Match your vigilance to the risk.* The bigger the inherent risk, the more careful you should be. Think about the implications before acting. Not all mistakes are good. Some matter a lot. But if the cost of a mistake is negligible, that's a different story.

- *Identify a behavioral change.* If your solution is simply to work harder, head back to the drawing board. Working harder is no guarantee. In fact, you're almost certain to repeat your mistake! You have to change a behavior, such as keeping your eyes on the road and not staring at the tree you don't want to hit.

Start Your Comeback Now

Recovery starts as soon as you've committed the mistake. Sounds weird, but you'll be judged based on what you did during and after the crisis as much as or more than on what you did to cause it:

- *Be present and on the case.* You may or may not have a role in what happens next. Sometimes, the boss fixes your mistake. Sometimes, it's up to you and your team. There will be times when what's done is done. In all cases:

  - *Avoid the deer-in-the-headlights response.* It's natural but unhelpful in a crisis situation. If you're paralyzed in a mistake meltdown, change your physical state to affect your emotional state. For example, wash your face or drink some water. Give yourself that quick break of a minute or two to reengage your thinking brain.

  - *Set aside your feelings, and focus on the task.* Your instinct may be to apologize every chance you get. Park it. There is no place for emotions when you're under the gun. Your genuine wish to apologize was already honored when you fessed up. Repeating your apologies can boomerang.

  - *Stay on it until the mistake is resolved.* Don't behave as if it's business as usual unless your boss indicates you should. Assume urgency, and do what it takes, which may entail late hours or extra tasks. The situation may not improve for a while, so stick with it. Whatever it takes, be there—on the job and present.

○ *Get out of the way if needed.* If others have taken over, please don't create extra work or heighten the emotional tension. If someone takes the mistake out of your hands, assume your job is to get back to work.

• *Get help to recover.* Others can help you repair and learn from your mistake. You'll get a double benefit: their insight will make you stronger, *and* you'll get them on your side.

○ *Reach out to friends and colleagues.* If your boss responded with anger, turn to people who care about you personally. Friends and colleagues have their own mistakes to admit, and in a weird way, that's going to make you feel better. By the way, this is not the ideal time to talk to people who don't know you at all. If you're brand new, find the person you know best.

○ *Connect with those who are affected.* You may need to reach out to clients or internal customers affected by the mistake too. It's good to apologize once and solicit their input to improve your process. If you're not sure whether to reach out, ask your boss. He or she will know if that's going to help or compound the issue.

○ *Structure your conversations.* Make sure your conversations are constructive by keeping a positive goal in mind. For example, ask others how they closed the chapter on their own mistakes. Avoid apologizing for the fourth time.

• *Make recovery your business.* Think of your own repair next. Tap into everything you can do—physically, mentally, emotionally, and spiritually—to move on.

○ *Use physical activity to get relief.* A brisk walk or an immediate workout has therapeutic effects. Your brain needs a rest, and if you provide one, it will thank you.

○ *Get some hugs.* You need three to five times more positives to effectively counter one negative thought. You're a high integrity person trying to do a good job. (Four to go.)

○ *Relieve some stress.* Turn to an activity that helps you relax, such as listening to calming music, practicing meditation, getting a massage, watching sports with friends, or rereading a favorite book.

○ *Get to work.* Some jobs move so fast that this is natural. If not, consciously shift from obsessing about what's done to losing yourself in new work.

○ *Continue to focus on recovery.* Most people assume they're done, but the need for recovery is ongoing. Continue your recovery activities until you have the physical, mental, and emotional stamina to move past the mistake.

● *Put points on the board.* Delivering new successes helps you diminish the mistake's impact on your overall performance. It has the added benefit that you can come back to the situation with the objectivity of distance. As you focus on results:

○ *Make sure to appreciate yourself.* Keep that journal, and every week, review your accomplishments—for example, your quick response time, your wisdom in alerting others, what you learned, or a silver lining. Note what you've learned and also what you'd like to improve or learn going forward. Months later, you'll find your journal more useful than a CliffsNotes for your job.

○ *Notice your changed behaviors.* If you're stuck, remind yourself that you've got an improved approach. Reframe the work at hand as an opportunity to demonstrate that you've improved.

○ *Take a longer-term perspective.* Imagine looking back at your mistake in 3—or 20—years. Most mistakes shrink with the passage of time. One day, your mistake might be a story you're delighted to share with junior people who deeply admire you.

In the end, there are no pills to erase the memory of your mistake. I empathize if you're still mortified, but when your seniors review your performance, they won't be looking at your mistake. They'll be looking at what you did next.

If that's not enough to get you moving, consider this: while you're punishing yourself, other mistake makers are overtaking you. Make sure you're not using your mistake to sink your progress. That's 10 times worse than making the mistake in the first place.

PURPOSE PRESSURE
MISTAKE REVIEW
BRING PEOPLE ON BOARD
BULLIES JERKS
TAKE A STAND
RISK SELF-DOUBT
SUPERHE   ENERGY
MENTO   ONSOR
LOVE F   DESPAIR
PURPO   ESSURE
MISTAKE REVIEW
BRING PEOPLE ON BOARD

4

When Your Review Whacks You

A close relative of mistakes is the disappointing, lousy, gut punch performance review. Getting one is not a rare occurrence. Almost everybody experiences it. Few lead to separation. If you get started early, you can avoid one, but that's not our focus here. Receiving it is.

Receivers experience a wave of negative emotions: disbelief, anger, denial, resentment, sadness, hurt. We react like a pendulum, swinging between extremes: "That jerk!" "I'm the dummy here." "I hate my job!" "I can't do anything right!" "They threw me under the bus!" "Who's going to hire a loser like me?" "That @#$%!!"

Most people expect a decent review. They worked hard, accomplished a goal, and thought things were going reasonably well. Surprise! Shock makes the news hard to hear, let alone understand and process. What receivers usually don't realize is that givers of feedback are triggered too. They show it by curtly handing you the news or woodenly reading from notes. That makes the conversation even more difficult.

There is another way to experience a lousy review.

Jeff's warm welcome had me at "Hello." He described his Midwestern parents as former hippies with the mentality of loving others. His dad always made it home for birthdays, taking the red-eye to be there. But growing up, Jeff drove himself to achieve goal after goal. Then in his junior year, he shattered his leg in a soccer accident. Lying in the hospital for three weeks, Jeff began to open up to relationships. He began to see beyond milestones. He understood his parents' mentality.

That's why Jeff is the right person to share how it feels on the other side of the table. Years ago, he was in charge of college graduate hiring and training:

> We started with 50 candidates for an analyst position. We narrowed the list down to 10. We all met and liked the final candidate, but my boss and my boss's boss thought she wasn't right for the job. But she was dynamic and smart, with a good education. I hired her, and it didn't work out. I had always gotten strong marks. This was a real shot in the face. I felt I had failed her and myself.
>
> We had met for her three-month review. It's hard to put this into words—seeing her getting emotional, crying. It's tough to hear the other's view when it's opposite to yours. She felt that she had not gotten time with me, that I was intimidating. I'd never heard that. She also made a comment about not feeling part of the team. That shocked me, but it was how she felt. I wish that I could have made her more successful early on. I saw things happening, but I had taken no action.
>
> I told her to tell me what she needed to do better. I was just trying to be a person. I thanked her for her feedback, and I said I would take reflection time. The meeting ended abruptly. I went home in a bad mental spot.

That night, Jeff got on a treadmill at the gym, spending two hours thinking. A self-proclaimed people pleaser who wanted things to work out, he had to come to terms with being management, like it or not. Jeff realized that all bosses could be intimidating, and he resolved to do better. The next day, they met again:

> I told her I did not see the progress or the hunger, and I wanted to learn what she was seeing and feeling. I went through her points and asked her to think about whether it was a job she liked. If so, we would work on it together.

There are two sides to every story. You can't just react. You have to think through your feedback. Over the next two months, things got better. She felt a lot more comfortable and continued to work hard. Eventually, we both realized it wasn't the right fit. She found another job, which was a better fit. We've stayed in touch.

By accepting ownership, Jeff treated his analyst as he'd like to be treated. He appreciated that it was a *performance* review, not a *person* review. Jeff's story underscores that whichever chair you sit in, the human being in the other chair is being judged too.

The sting doesn't disappear overnight, but a disappointing review offers real benefits: accelerated learning and development. When the pain recedes, you'll be left with the gift of new insight and know-how, as these stories show:

- *What if your poor review is a complete surprise?* Will's faux pas revealed a development need he didn't even know he had.

- *What if you don't want to act on your review?* Ife had achieved excellence but found her review disappointing nonetheless.

- *What if the review feels totally unfair?* In 12 months, Julia had three bosses, and the third one rated her average for the year.

- *How can you turn a disastrous review into a gold mine?* Aria's review sent her down an emotional spiral until she asked for help.

- *What does a good review look like?* Everybody should be so lucky as to have a manager like Sara.

Most people focus on the issue of fairness, missing nuggets of gold hiding in plain sight. If your review leads to action, you're the winner. You found gold.

Focus first on recovery and then development, with help from your reviewer and colleagues. Of course you have other options. But if you leave without making good use of this disruption, you'll have wasted the opportunity.

IT'S NOT FUNNY

Other than in a crisis, there is no time when
apologies are not welcome.

Will had been an entrepreneur ever since he resold the treats his parents brought to summer camp. In high school, he launched a web design business, and became an EMT. Will had planned to become a doctor. Loving business, after college, he joined a large industrial company with an aspiration to grow as a leader:

> Prior to becoming an EMT, I wouldn't have considered myself a leader. But when you're a crew chief in charge of three others and the patient, you don't know what you're walking into. If you're not confident, people take advantage. You need people skills to empathize.
>
> I adapt the way I speak and try to understand the feelings people have when I'm speaking to them. I can sense when people don't feel right, and I try to change that. That helps me in my career now.

Bringing empathy to his work was something Will had to learn. It all started with a bit of harmless joking (so he thought) at the leadership boot camp:

> When my friend asked what the supervisor looked like, I said, "She's really big." I had picked a random trait and said the opposite. It was a prank. When she walked in, my friend asked the supervisor who she was. He had no idea. There was an awkward moment when she wondered why people were laughing.
>
> I realized it was a bad move when she looked around, puzzled. She asked once and then she asked twice. I thought, *This is not going to go well.* I decided to tell the truth in order to protect my peers. I explained why people were laughing, and she said, "I don't get it." It turns out that she was sensitive about her weight. Clearly, I had made a big mistake.

The class moved on, but the incident wasn't over as evidenced by Will's year-end review. Surprised, he met with the review team to learn more:

> My assignment leader had rated me reflecting my positive performance, but when my rating went to that supervisor for review, it was bumped down two grades. My rating was decreased for "soft skills" because I had called her fat behind her back. I had forgotten all about it. The premise of the joke was complimentary. We were in a hotel, all recent grads, and joking around. It was a place where social activities like beer pong were mixed with work. I would never joke in an ambulance. I never meant harm.
>
> That's when it hit me. I had not apologized because I had not realized the extent of her hurt. I thought an apology wouldn't help in the moment. I remember acknowledging the misstep as we were talking about something else, but I don't think I ever said, "I'm sorry." I felt horrible that I had hurt someone. I was embarrassed, too. Now I'm glad they rated me poorly.

Will took his poor review to heart. He apologized and worked hard to repair that relationship. Back on track, Will advanced to vice president of innovation development.

So What?

Will was so proud of his empathy skills that his review created cognitive dissonance. He struggled with the feedback that he lacked soft skills. That unpleasant surprise turned into a fabulous lesson! Will had assumed that others knew the thoughts, feelings, and intentions he had not expressed. He realized that the other person had unshared thoughts, feelings, and intentions too. Standing in her shoes taught Will that things are not what they seem to be.

Will's second lesson was not apologizing right then. Other than in a crisis, there is no time when apologies are not welcome. And just like other types of mistakes, an apology gets harder to make the longer you wait. Will got caught up in overthinking how to seem sincere. He turned a molehill into a mountain through inaction.

Ultimately, Will accepted the development need he didn't know he had—a terrific outcome of his poor review.

I'M OK, AND YOU'RE OK TOO

There is plenty of space between
good enough and absolute perfection.

Ife's journey began in Nigeria. Her next stops were New York and Silicon Valley. With an older sister setting a high bar for diplomacy, playing by the rules, and following a traditional path, Ife took a different direction. Successful in her own right, Ife led her team to a notable app release. She received a great review. And she quit after working "one year, 11 months, and 20 days:"

> Launching something pivotal to the company was important to me. It was our product team's biggest project, talked about at the all-staff meeting. I was pushing for it to be amazing up until the day it launched, pulling things out and putting things in because I didn't feel it was good enough. Others didn't see those flaws as deal breakers. I saw them as mediocrity. When you're working with people who don't strive for perfection, you feel you're making compromises.
>
> I got a much higher rating than before and was gratified. Then I didn't get promoted, and I felt I was not valued by the company. I knew I needed to leave. I was never given a reason. I heard that I didn't have executive presence. Like what does that mean? Maybe they think I'm not nice enough.
>
> The initial phases of my getting feedback are not positive. The second I get feedback, I get super defensive, and I want to explain my perspective. Then I get really quiet. Why didn't I make it perfect? Once I step back, I'm able to replay and see the feedback as a way to improve.

Ife came into that project guns blazing. She didn't like "feedback sand-wiches," couching critical feedback between complimentary language, but her manager asked Ife to adapt to the company's culture:

> At every review, my manager started with the positive, but I don't care about that. I want to hear things I need to work on. I seek out the people who dislike me because they're more honest. I appreciate saying it the way you see it. But that's not how you get ahead.
>
> I didn't know how to do the whole schmoozing thing, playing the game. I'm like Kobe Bryant—I came in, scored the baskets, and didn't make friends. I didn't spend enough time up front getting to know the team. Instead, I gave un-filtered, honest feedback. That's hard to digest from someone you don't know.
>
> I felt compelled to stay a while longer. I hadn't done enough and couldn't leave knowing that. However, at some point, it became clear that I was selling myself and the com-pany short by forcing myself to stay. They wanted me to be someone I wasn't. I needed them to be something they weren't ready to be.

For a long time, her words rang in my ears. All's well that ends well: Ife resettled in a late-stage tech startup whose culture welcomed direct and in-ventive producers.

So What?

Sometimes, you choose not to act on a review that's more about cultural fit. Ife exercised her choice and left. Nonetheless, she missed an opportunity to question her own beliefs, using her review to grow.

Ife's passion for excellence energized the team. However, her judgment was tough on everybody, and reviews were her yardstick. She said, "If I reach for the stars, I will fall to the moon. But anytime I accomplish some-thing, the bar just moves, and I'm discontented until I get there again." I admired her spirit; I worried about her pursuit of perfection. It made good things taste bad, including a good review.

An unrelenting focus on perfection means you forget to appreciate others and yourself. There is plenty of space between good enough and absolute perfection. Park somewhere in between without giving up the push that comes from striving for excellence.

By shifting to learning as a measure of success, we appreciate others more and accomplish more too.

THE GIFT OF UNFAIRNESS

We don't build our careers; the people we know do.

Julia's story begins in Brazil and continues in south Florida. Her father's drive inspired her, as did his zeal for travel. Julia's mother inspired her too, as a connector and nurturer. In turn, Julia developed her own strengths:

> I am who I am because of the people who helped me get this far. I have insatiable curiosity and passion to absorb everything. Knowledge is addicting: the more you learn, the more you realize the world is big. There's so much out there that you don't know about. My mother says I'm like a drunken cockroach when it comes to learning.
>
> Getting married and divorced in six months was a transformational moment for me—and a rebirth. You learn your strength when you fail. I was surprised by my resilience. You buckle down and grow out of the dirt much stronger.

Julia's love of learning and her resilience were tested at work when the financial institution reorganized. She had three bosses in one year and a disappointing performance review:

> I had been working for the third boss for about two months. I didn't formally report to him; there was an open role between us. He gave me a rating in a written performance review, not what I was looking for—average. That killed my ego. I scheduled a meeting to discuss it, but there wasn't much to discuss. I ended up crying, feeling like the justifications were ill based.

In that moment, I realized it was my fault. The impression of the work I was doing was not the work I was doing. He gave me the advice that I had to showcase myself and report up the next time. He didn't change the rating.

Julia met with her two former bosses. One thought she should tell human resources; the other invited her to his team. Neither solution seemed right. Julia's strengths kicked in. She returned to work, determined:

> I will be successful if I have continued to grow. I consider myself successful right now. So it's about growth. I learned then that the politics of an organization matter. I have some weaknesses. I didn't defend myself at all. I didn't speak up. I didn't sell myself. If you don't take care of yourself, if you don't have thick skin, nothing happens. I had to toughen up, fight for and defend myself.
>
> The next day, I came in to work, extremely professional, but I had decided to leave. Three bosses was a hell of a year. I waited for the financial crisis to end. It gave me more learning than I could get from a book. Then I got my MBA and a new job.

Julia joined another global financial services company, where she was recently promoted to senior vice president of operations.

So What?

Julia is no angel. As she reeled from the shock of a review that felt unfair, her first reaction was to stew. She had so many good reasons. The team was not functioning well. The position above her was a revolving door. She had no immediate boss. The reviewer had limited exposure. Only when curiosity got the better of her did Julia shift from blaming to learning.

In particular, gaining other perspectives helped her open up. You need your network when times are tough. That's when relationships matter most. Until then, nurture your network constantly. Julia said, "Don't network as if it were a fad or you were a machine. We don't build our careers; the people we know do."

There's one more thing that Julia learned—the value of a great boss. Reorganizations disrupt relationships; your boss may disappear. There are a lot of great bosses out there. You deserve one. So before you switch companies, try to switch roles.

THE BRUTAL FACTS

*It's easy to become your own worst critic,
doubting yourself at every turn. Instead, conjure up a voice
that speaks to your superb chance to develop.*

Aria is a woman of the world, a British and U.S. citizen from an Indian family. Intellectual curiosity, strong ideals, and high achievement have always fueled her purpose:

> I started becoming interested in economics as a way to help women. I talked to my aunt, who was an investment banker. She laughed and said little in finance is socially redeeming. I rebelled, switching from medicine to finance.
>
> I loved using economics as a tool for social justice. In the summer after freshman year, I went with two classmates to a rural Argentinian microfinance bank for women. We designed a detailed survey to determine social impact. The survey was really well thought out, but it turned out to be a total disaster in reality!
>
> A lot of the women were illiterate. We didn't speak Spanish well. We had underestimated the poverty. We were insensitive and naïve. I ended up traveling on foot to interview women in their homes. Theory can disintegrate in practice. The most you can do is humanize it.

Wiser and more determined, Aria joined an investment firm as a data analyst. Not challenged enough, Aria asked for a move. A year in, she transferred to research. After two months on a steep and rocky learning curve, Aria received her performance review. She doubted whether that had been a good decision:

I had wanted to learn the skills. I was nervous because I thought I didn't have the qualifications. My boss was honest. He said, "You really have a lot to learn here. You're not up to speed. You show your stress, and that's not going to help you." I took that whole review as a personal failure. I wasn't automatically a star. I assumed I wasn't going anywhere and would not progress.

The next day I woke up in tears. I thought, *I don't think I should be here. I don't have a right to be at my job!* I was a total failure. It was even more painful because the move had been my decision. I thought, *This means I'm no good.*

It was as if everyone around me were speaking a different language. I would go to meetings with my boss and come out with notes that made no sense at all. I didn't even know what questions to ask. I thought that because I was a high achiever, the transition would be easier. Now I had to figure out how to get better when I didn't know what "better" looked like!

My best friend at the firm was in the same group. She had been there for a year and was tasked with training me. It was embarrassing to admit that I needed help. I put a lot of undue pressure on myself because she was doing so well.

Fortunately, Aria turned to three people for help. First, her mother showed her the review's valuable insight. Next, her friend turned out to be terrific day-to-day support. And third, her boss became a wonderful coach. The more projects Aria completed successfully, the more confidence she gained. In time, she proudly advanced.

So What?

A horrible review can trigger an extraordinary learning moment. When things don't automatically line up, you have an opportunity to stop and reflect. Take Aria's case. From thinking she was at the top, Aria spiraled down to feeling worthless. She viewed herself in extremes (*I'm the best! I'm the worst!*). That caused her to lose sight of her strengths, along with a few minor details like being brand new in the role.

It's easy to become your own worst critic, doubting yourself at every turn. Instead, conjure up a kinder voice that speaks to your superb chance to develop.

Aria's coaching didn't happen by accident. She had to swallow her pride, ask for help, and accept it. Her coaches had to make time. Once she was open to learning and receiving feedback, Aria made steady progress. She didn't change overnight. It takes time to accept yourself realistically—neither star nor fraud.

Aria's capacity to develop will be essential for a leader whose goal is to make a meaningful difference to women's empowerment someday—including her own.

WITH A LITTLE HELP FROM MY FRIENDS

Most people want fast feedback when their performance falls short. Waiting till year-end for the shock-and-awe effect is cruel.

Sara, I can honestly say, is a star whose life did not set her up for success. Bravely overcoming adversity, Sara brought great humanity to her e-commerce job:

> I grew up in an alcoholic household. My senior year in high school, I had my daughter, and I changed to a school for pregnant and parenting teens. I had to give up being captain of the volleyball team. I moved out of my parents' home at 19, working to pay bills while attending college at night. My daughter and I lived on food stamps. I've also been in recovery for many years.
>
> We all have our own struggles. Mine instilled gratitude in me. I get to come to work today! It also shaped the way I manage people. Humans are messy. When things go amuck, that's a part of life. It's not about me anymore. I profoundly impact five people's lives—and their families. I need to understand what I can do to help them.

Sara's compassion and insight featured when it came time to review someone on a team she had inherited:

He rated himself a 4, and I rated him a 2. It was very hard to look at him. He looked so deflated. I used examples of what he could do to get to a 3 or 4 rating. He thanked me. Perhaps it was his personality not to fight back or get defensive.

It was hard for him to admit he was not in the right role, but he still wanted to stay in the company. He knew he was having difficulty keeping up with the technology. I was clear about my standards and expectations. I spent time bringing him back to why it's important to do things the way we do on the team. It's not arbitrary.

After this difficult conversation, it became easier to offer my help. I tried to build trust. I asked what brought him energy and what drained him. With 10 years of experience in operations, he had a network. He understood enough about technology. He had integrity and a positive outlook.

Sara helped her team member find a new role one level up, a better fit with his strengths. But her second experience with giving a poor review was tougher. An early hire she made under pressure turned out to be a poor fit:

He came from a very structured field where there was time and space for problem solving. I didn't ask the right questions. I should have found out if he had an obsession with the way things work, if he was comfortable with ambiguity. I missed those big red flags. I should have waited. I cannot teach curiosity and obsession. He had zero self-awareness that this role was not right for him. I knew another role would be better, but he thought he could hang on.

I became impatient with his continued inefficiency. Look, this is a tough environment! Having him on a performance improvement plan was incredibly difficult. I knew he was miserable. Another part of me thought, *I have to run a business. I cannot have the rest of my employees burning out.* He accused me of harassment. I worked with my manager and collected documentation.

The day Sara handed in the papers to let her first hire go, he resigned.

So What?

Giving poor feedback is as challenging as receiving it. How you prepare matters, especially what you do on day 1. In addition to setting expectations and clarifying your standards, share why meeting these standards is important. And be realistic about expectations. Your excessive pressure dampens your team's performance.

Let people know regularly how they're doing. Most people want fast feedback when their performance falls short. Waiting till year-end for the shock-and-awe effect is cruel. Appreciate that a poor review affects the person's livelihood; take care to show respect.

As Sara learned, you can be authentic *and* adapt your management style to help the other person grow: "When I walk into a conversation, I've already thought about what I'm trying to leave with. If I really want the other person to perform well, how I speak to him or her changes."

Experts call this a difficult conversation for a reason. If you're the giver, remember that review is not about you—but you're instrumental to the outcome. If you're the receiver, keep in mind that when you develop and advance, the giver deserves some praise too.

TAKING ON YOUR

REVIEW CHALLENGE

Receiving a disappointing review sucks. If you work for yourself, it comes in the form of a customer who walks away. If you work for a small firm, it comes when colleagues trash your idea. And if you work for a larger company, it comes in the form of the dreaded review. Aaaagh.

Newsflash: Almost everybody receives at least one disappointing performance review. You haven't been singled out for martyrdom. Now for the upside. A poor review is really an extraordinary opportunity disguised as a smackdown. In three years' time, you'll thank the person who set you on this course. Let's take that again—in slow motion.

Few people enjoy criticism. Sometimes the feedback is public, and that hurts even more. It unleashes unpleasant emotions. It usually affects compensation, and nobody likes that. So what's to like?

The truth.

If you can shift from an emotional stance of blame and protection to learning, you can grow from the nuggets of truth offered. Will stumbled right out of the gate, and he learned a valuable lesson. With curiosity and openness, Ife sought the truth, but she chose not to adapt to a culture she didn't value. Julia's review may have seemed unfair, but she reaped benefits from it nonetheless. Aria stepped off her downward spiral to seek development she needed and wanted. Despite being caring and attentive managers, Jeff and Sara had to learn how to deliver a helpful review and subsequent coaching.

If you are a receiver—or a giver—of the review, you can improve your experience too.

Gain Perspective on Your Review

Reviews can feel unfair or unduly harsh. That's the shock-and-awe part. With openness, you may find that the review is neither unfair nor extreme. You don't have to accept everything. In particular, use the associated difficult conversation to glean from it all that you can:*

- *Look for the well-intended message.* Without judging yourself, find the review's message. Trust me, there's at least a grain of helpful truth in your review. You're not a horrible person. You're not the worst performer ever. You just have some growing to do.

- *Face the review fresh.* After your first reading or discussion, turn to another activity. Physical activity can change your emotional state. Do something that will take your mind off the injustice, insult, or condemnation until you cool down. When you're ready, take a second look. If you're still struggling, pretend that you're reading someone else's review.

- *Move from blame to curiosity.* It's easier to absorb a poor review when you're curious about how to improve. "What can I learn from this?" is a better question than "What did I do wrong?" Assume that everything in the review is true and that the reviewer cares deeply about you.

---

* Another one of my favorite books is *Difficult Conversations: How to Discuss What Matters Most* by Douglas Stone, Bruce Patton, and Sheila Heen (Penguin Books, New York, 2010). There are all kinds of difficult conversations, many tougher than giving or receiving feedback. Try this book if you're a conflict avoider at work—or at home!

Your boss wants you to thrive. So get curious about what more you can learn.

- *Put things in perspective.* The review is also a reflection of the company culture versus how you show up. It might feel like a life-and-death battle, but you're not dying. It's just a job, and you get to decide what to do about it. You might decide to adapt or move on if the cultural fit isn't right.

Make Your Plan and Align with Others

No matter how objective you are, you're constrained by having only one perspective. This is not to say that you should shout out from the rooftop! Find the people you respect and ask for thoughts, not sympathy:

- *Hold a second conversation with your manager.* Even if you had a positive review and a great first discussion, it's worth a second one. Don't wait too long. A few days is fine; more time leaves room for you to stew and for your manager to delay. The second discussion enables you to ask follow-up questions and dig into learning.

    ○ *Make a connection.* Show that you care about what the person is saying in the moment. That doesn't mean you have to agree. Keep the lines of communication open; you'll receive more insight that way.

    ○ *Stay calm or withdraw.* If you're being reactive, you're no longer learning. Take a break to recenter. That's another way of saying, be a logical, rational, thinking person.

    ○ *Thank your manager even if you feel angry.* Standing in your manager's shoes, appreciate how hard it is to give feedback. Forgive poor delivery and accept positive intention. If you strengthen the connection, you'll enlist your manager to coach you. That makes you a better manager in turn.

- *Collect multiple perspectives.* If you have a mentor or sponsor, schedule a discussion. Remain open, regardless of what you hear. You're asking a more experienced person to read your review, offer advice, and recommend next steps for you. Even if your mentor's view is wildly different from yours, take notes. If you can, find three different perspectives. This process gives you time and distance to understand your review, learn more about yourself, and regain your footing.

- *Decide on your next steps.* It's up to you to make your development plan. Make sure to close the loop with your boss and the individuals you've reached out to. Align on what success looks like and how to measure your progress.

Get Going on Your Development

You know what to do: forge relationships, work in a more effective way, build and demonstrate new skills, and solicit ongoing feedback. Take these steps along the way:

- *Find a peer coach.* Enlist someone with more experience who will work with you. Why would anyone agree to do that? It's personally gratifying and professionally rewarded. Show reciprocity in at least two ways:

  o *Thank your coach regularly.* Shower your coach with appreciation through e-mails and in person when you meet. Your coach deserves the praise, and it makes you both feel good.

  o *Let the boss know.* Make sure your boss and boss's boss know what a great job your coach is doing. Giving credit to someone else only makes you look better (it demonstrates confidence).

- *Sign up witnesses.* Ask your boss or team to alert you when they observe you mastering the skills or approaches flagged in your review. It's human nature to categorize people and never change. To disrupt that pattern, ask them to look for positive evidence that you're changing. As their brains do that work, their opinion of you will change!

- *Keep a performance file.* As you develop, it's important to take notes so that you can remember at review time. If your organization has eliminated formal reviews, it's even more important to note how you're developing and achieving the organization's goals.

○ *Collect the compliments.* Save the notes and e-mails that people send to thank you or praise you. It will make you feel better on a down day.

○ *Focus their attention.* And when you've done something amazing, be sure to send (and save) an e-mail to your boss describing that amazing thing in terms of the company's interests.

○ *Prepare your review ahead of time.* Be sure to assemble a fact-based summary of your year to help your evaluator note each milestone, your impact, and witnesses. Be even in tone.

Become a Good Feedback Giver

If you're getting ready to give feedback, make it your intention to help the other person perform at a higher level. Keep sympathy for your family and friends. It may feel better because you're commiserating together, but that's like jumping into the hole to help the other person instead of throwing the person a rope to climb out. Once you're in the hole too, no one gets out. Instead, practice these skills:

• *Listen without judgment.* The other person may see a different side of the story. Acknowledge what you're hearing and how that person feels. Stay away from judgment words like "good" and "bad." Watch that you don't slip into giving advice. Save that for coaching the person in later sessions.

• *Ask genuine questions.* Design questions that solicit better understanding of what the other person is thinking, how he or she feels, and what he or she wants. They're usually open-ended. Watch out for questions that put the other person on the defensive. Avoid questions that start with "why."

• *Create space.* When a conversation is uncomfortable, it's natural to fill awkward silences. Instead, give the other person a chance to reflect and feel. Practice patience; use the time to feel empathy.

• *Treat each person with respect.* Regardless of the performance issue at hand, the person sitting opposite you deserves your respect. You're alike in many ways. And if you were in his or her shoes, that's what you would want.

The company's intent is to get great work out of you. Once you're done being angry, focus on the how. At a minimum, you'll learn that people don't always see you the way you see yourself. It's up to you to show them.

You want to do well in your career. So what's next? Once again, it's your choice.

5

When People Don't Come On Board

Perhaps you're leading a team of people old enough to be your parents. It's possible that you've never met them because they work somewhere far away. They don't report to you, but you're responsible for a work product that requires their inputs. And they have their own goals, different from yours. What the #%&* are you going to do?

Management 101 says that to achieve early impact, you should prepare objectives, a plan, metrics for success, and your communications. The more complex and global the assignment is, the more planning, measuring, and presenting you do. But what happens?

Progress stalls.

Michael experienced something like that. Just promoted to manage the industrial plant's finance function, he was younger and less experienced than the people he managed. Closing the books was his team's biggest job. They were always rushed and late. With an internal audit pending, Michael was worried:

> Early on, I tried to get a ton of stuff done. I didn't ask people for help. I thought if I asked my staff a lot of questions, I would be proving that one of them deserved the role more

than I did. That turned out to be the dumbest thing! You can't just google how to do your job.

I thought, *I'm going to be audited on something I don't even know if my staff does.* This wasn't like cramming all night for a test. I had to cooperate with my staff on a whole different level. At my next staff meeting, I printed out the list of controls and asked who did each one. Then I met with each person to learn his or her core, daily tasks. Then over the next month, I spent a day shadowing each team member. It sounds so silly!

Michael worked with his team on process improvements they found together. What used to take the team until 9:30 p.m. was done without error by 4:30 p.m.:

No one was checking my work. I was the top person for finance accounting for this facility. I felt I had to have everything perfect. A mistake would have been unacceptable.

I was 27 years old. My staff had an average age of 55 and over 20 years' experience. That got into my head; I thought they would begrudge me my role or be hesitant to follow. Well, it turned out not to be the case. A guy who had worked there for longer than I was alive came up and thanked me. And I had been so scared to take on this team!

Michael's story shows in a nutshell how important it is to bring others on board. A well-performing team always outperforms the individual. The people in this chapter have struggled with similar challenges:

- *What if they don't like you?* Casey was on the fast track until a new assignment played right into her blind spot.

- *How do you deliver on mission impossible?* Leading a global project to deliver her radical vision, Emily's approach wasn't working.

- *How do you mobilize people when you don't have common ground?* Kelly had to increase productivity in the plant after the employees had just lost their overtime benefits.

- *How do you create cohesion among opposing voices?* After months of working together, Tatiana's peer task force was stuck in the eleventh hour without alignment.

- *Why the heck aren't people coming on board?* With his father in critical condition, Greg left his dream job to take on a serious issue in desperate need of leadership.

Once in charge, you know you're not going to get it done by yourself. That's obvious. It's also obvious that people need to feel respected, valued, and heard. If you're leading 50 or 100 people globally with limited authority, that's a tall order.

The stories that follow will help you harness the power of the community. It's a must-have when you've just been assigned to turn straw into gold by morning.

A FISH OUT OF WATER

Sometimes you have to go slow to grow faster.

Casey grew up in a one-company town. Her hardworking parents and neighbors felt secure until that company went under. Naturally drawn to a long-standing, more adaptive industrial institution, Casey wanted to make it on her own two feet. She was competitive, she worked hard, and she was succeeding:

> I worked for an individual known to be a difficult character. He took me under his wing. He was direct and driving, but he also called out "Atta girl!" at the end of the day. Later on, I asked what he recognized in me at 25 years old. He said, "You were resilient. You bounced back no matter how hard I was on you. You were coachable and could learn. I knew you would take whatever training I was able to give, and you would get better."
>
> A key value for me is being told that I did a good job. It's not about the reward, but personal validation. Without it, I question whether I'm truly successful. I think it goes back to

the way I was raised. I wanted to make my parents proud. If I did anything to disappoint them, it would crush me.

In 2010, Casey's boss championed her for the inaugural class of the superstar leadership program. She got in and achieved its highest award. From there, Casey rotated into a sales role in a good, stable division where colleagues had years of service. Things felt very different:

> I was a fish out of water. I didn't fit! People were like, "Shut up and go back to your desk. You make us look bad." Our program sponsor called me and said, "I'm getting feedback that it's not going so well." I told her, "I can't be in a coma." She replied, "This is a really profitable business. Get with the program!"
>
> So I had some good conversations. I was told, "The people around you are intimidated, and you make them feel like they're not contributing. They don't like you. You can continue like that, or you can develop some emotional intelligence and adjust." I felt like crying. I want people to like me. Belonging has always been something I have struggled with. My worst fear is to walk into a room and not know anybody. I could crawl under my desk. My behavior was driving animosity. It hurt my feelings, and it was hard to hear. I care, but I have a tough time connecting. I tend to focus on what needs to happen versus how or why it happens.
>
> Coming off of two intense roles, my urgency made me aggressive. I tried to slow down. I did more face-to-face interaction instead of e-mail. I started asking questions, and I listened more. I tried to take an equal number of actions that helped other people, working more to support them to close their stuff rather than just hammering them when they didn't deliver. It was way out of my comfort zone to go have coffee rather than shoot off a voice mail.
>
> I told people that I owned this and was working on it. I tried to be really transparent. One of the guys who would make fun of me ended up being a great advocate. He appreciated that I admitted I was wrong.

Slowing down, Casey didn't feel like anything was happening, but it was. Her performance improved, and she advanced once again.

So What?

Propelled by a strong work ethic, and an underdog self-image, Casey was on the fast track. When that formula stopped working, she was at a loss. In her new situation, Casey could achieve success only by building relationships. Not everyone shared her definition of success or drive. She had to take time to listen in order to adapt.

Casey believed that the person who gets the most stuff done wins. Boy, was she mistaken. Relationships and community matter just as much. Only when she faced her fear of connecting could Casey engage in the uncomfortable, and essential, work of forging relationships.

Sometimes you have to go slow to grow faster.

WINNING OVER THE SKEPTICS

Having a bold vision was the easy part of mission impossible.

When Emily found a job in 2008, she considered herself lucky. Still with the same automotive company today, she is thriving. That's because getting around obstacles is her strength:

> In high school, my friend stole my form and signed me up for a harder math class. At the same time, my boyfriend said I would not be able to take a harder science class. That made me mad, so I took both classes. I started to enjoy them and realized they were useful.
>
> The arc of my career working in technology is in part fueled by someone saying I could not do something.

A few years back, Emily was assigned to lead a global project on groundbreaking electronic technology with new industry standards. This was a much, much bigger challenge than Emily had ever faced:

My leadership on the value proposition was unpopular for a multitude of reasons. I recognized the right solution for the consumer. Our battery took 24 hours to recharge versus 5 minutes to fill up with gas. I spent a lot of time trying to get our charging time down to 2 to 3 hours—but my vision was 20 minutes. I pushed forward and got support from other areas of the vehicle team to pull my own leaders along. My mentor helped me get allies. But then he left.

I had made clear decisions that allowed the team to focus. I just knew it was the right thing to be competitive. But my new manager was weaker; he was not comfortable because those decisions were unpopular. We were almost two years in without true buy-in. Competitors were launching their technologies.

Word came down that the vehicle development timeline was being shortened. I could not create a production-ready patch in the revised time frame. My new charging technology was pulled, but the other teams needed it even more than before.

Emily had gained three key supporters early on, but she needed six. It was a stalemate:

My current boss's boss had said, "Absolutely not." But I don't take no for a first or second answer. I was working in Europe to get the drawings done, and I happened to go with a friend to a Christmas party. The head of engineering for one of our brands was there. We were introduced, and he blurted out that I must be the most important person in the company. My jaw dropped! Realizing that someone saw the project as important helped me see that it was. My U.S. group had not been excited about what I was working on.

After that, I got buy-in from every engineering group. They couldn't afford to wait 24 hours for their test cars to recharge. That was our turning point.

Empowered, Emily worked with the policy group to drive standards with suppliers globally, with marketing to support consumer acceptance, and with manufacturing in Asia. She led regional integration teams and the core technology team. Overcoming obstacles kept Emily busy 24/7:

> I had to move from visionary to communicator. I had updated and shared my presentation, explained it, or reexplained it once a week for three years. If you've said it 30 times, that's not enough. If you can't win over your grandma, you probably haven't explained it well enough.
>
> It's about sharing at the right time when somebody is ready to hear. You cannot be five steps ahead. I listened to every concern. I had to show empathy and speak in terms that the receiver used. Each party had a stake. I had to not take it personally.
>
> Every time we had a vehicle built with a software release and it worked a little bit better, I loved it.

Even more satisfying, Emily and her pioneers paved the way for subsequent teams to follow a smoother process.

So What?

Having a bold vision was the easy part of mission impossible. Making it happen added all the value, but it was a lot harder. For that, Emily needed to mobilize support here, there, and everywhere.

Most people assume that to be great at communications, you must be a persuasive speaker. That's half true. Emily presented her pitch dozens if not hundreds of times, but she would not have succeeded only by presenting. She had to learn to listen deeply. By listening to others' issues and concerns, she knew what obstacles to work on and address. That brought the influencers on board, who in turn brought others along.

This insight feels counterintuitive. Most people launch a project by talking. Who knew that listening would be far more effective than telling?

IN HIS SHOES

It took deeper listening skills to recognize what the team really wanted.
It's rarely about what people say, but what they feel.

Kelly had a trust advantage: her openness helped her adapt. Case in point, she grew up with no interest in having kids—until meeting her future husband's large and close-knit family. Today Kelly is a mother of four. Being open enough to adapt drove her success in the body shop manufacturing plant. Kelly was only 25 at the time:

> It was a complete unknown, a recipe for disaster. I was nervous. There were 60 United Auto Workers (UAW) employees, and the *lowest*-seniority guy on my team had 30 years in the plant. After 2008, we went from unlimited overtime to zero. The employees had relied on that money to pay for homes. I was thinking about how people were going to take it and how this was going to reflect on my performance.
>
> We also had a very tough target: 80 jobs an hour. First, they tried to not make rate in order to get the overtime back. I was worried about anger and sabotage. I had to find a way to motivate them.

Kelly used emotion—fighting negative with positive—to find common ground and win over the team:

> I thought, *Really? No, they can't just hate me! These people are going to like me!* I pictured them as grandparents, parents, friends, and neighbors. That made them human. I told them about my children and showed them photos. It's hard to watch someone you know struggle. I let them know I cared about them and their work experience so that they would care about me.
>
> I was friendly, and over time, they became friendly. Even when they were mean and disrespectful, I was nice to them every day. I had an older brother, and that helped because he's on the rougher side.

I looked at what else motivated them. The guys worked close together and talked a lot. I walked the line and listened. One guy would give me clues, like his kids' sports scores. I found that they just wanted to have fun every day—not doing the same thing. We identified appropriate job switches. I included them in focus groups on how to improve the workstation. I realized that they were motivated by attention.

No one liked to be the slowest, so they all worked at the same pace. I started to post their times on the wall—all three shifts—and they began to compete. Some people wanted to win and worked faster. Most just didn't want to be last, so everyone's time sped up. In days, they went 10 jobs an hour faster. They liked the competition.

Some stations were slower, like the door line. I was working hard for months and not getting there. My internal goal was to narrow the gap—80 sounded impossible. I told everyone we could get there, but I didn't believe it. I never let on. The first time one of my door lines made the goal for an entire day, it was amazing. We had cake and celebrated as a whole team! I was pretty surprised. After that, the guys kept their momentum. The overtime issue was no longer the focus, and we moved on.

Six years later, Kelly joined another auto company in a new role, open and ready for a new experience.

So What?

I could feel Kelly's excitement over a crackling phone line. There seemed to be no common ground when she started, but once Kelly viewed her workforce differently, there was plenty. She got there by standing in their shoes. It took deeper listening skills to understand what the team really wanted. It's rarely about what people say, but what they feel. That takes openness, empathy, and the capacity to notice.

I challenged Kelly on wanting to be liked. Kelly agreed on its importance to her, but she didn't let that interfere with her managerial responsibility. Clear on standards, she showed a couple of workers the door for breaking shop rules. Clearly, you can understand what someone chooses not to express without having to be a friend.

Empathy made Kelly a brilliant manager, enabling her to adapt the work for the good of both company and employees.

LISTENING LIKE YOU MEAN IT

It's not about lining up supporters to
win the debate. Lead by noticing.

Her Cuban-Dominican father was a truck driver, but Tatiana didn't know him. Growing up with her mother and brother in Florida, she had high aspirations:

> Before I was even a thought, my mother's experience of com-
> ing to the United States shaped me. It made us different.
>
> In third grade, I had a teacher who was great but strict. I
> told her I was bored. She said, "Boredom is a state of mind. If
> you are bored, that means you are boring!" I cried! But from
> then on, I kept busy and pushed myself to do new things. I
> started writing to convey what I learned and felt about the
> world around me.
>
> I am the first in my family to go to college. I won a full
> scholarship to graduate school. That was acknowledgment
> of my work so far and that this is the right path for me. That
> journalism program was one of the best things I've done,
> even if I'm not a journalist today.

It was journalism training that helped Tatiana make her mark in the consumer goods company's leadership program. Challenging? Very:

> Growing up, I had been shy, not liking attention. I struggled
> with confidence. Here I was in a group of the company's fu-
> ture leaders. I had to step far out of my comfort zone. I could
> not doubt that I was a mistake and didn't belong. I felt both
> excitement and fear. You always question, *Should I be here?*
> *A lot of smart people could have this opportunity. Why me?* I

don't think you overcome it. You just get more comfortable in your own skin.

For several months, Tatiana and her peers worked together on a business project. Their recommendations to senior management were due, but they weren't ready:

> The project was completely out of scope for what I do. We had seven on our team, from India, Australia, China, Colombia—all different backgrounds. You learn that you're not going to be the strongest at everything. That's the point. You have to figure where you can add the most value.
>
> It was 11 p.m. We were in a conference room. Ideas were coming up. I wanted to understand why old ideas were resurfacing and why people were not agreeing.

Things started to fall apart. Tempers flared. Team members lost confidence in the conclusions. Tatiana listened as each person got his or her point across and then reloaded to defend the point. She waited for a pause. Thirty minutes later, Tatiana intervened:

> We had tough times where we could not agree. I was experienced in that, so I helped lead the group toward resolution. When somebody is stuck or being difficult about moving forward, they just want to be listened to. If you really capture what they're thinking and draw in elements of their idea but also respond with the path you're on and why, you bring them on board. If you're too abrupt, you might create a showdown.
>
> I've realized what it's like to be on the other end, when you don't feel like you're being listened to. It can be really hard to voice your opinion. You're worried that people could think you're an idiot. Of course you're not! When you think of the greater good, you find a way to contribute. That gives you courage to speak up.
>
> You don't have to be the loudest person in the room to make your point. Wait till everybody talks themselves out so they listen to you.

With Tatiana's help, the task force got its act together in time. Of course, senior management was delighted with their recommendations.

So What?

Tatiana fulfilled a leadership role that people often neglect. It's not about lining up supporters to win the debate. Lead by noticing. Listen with objectivity to the opposing voices, reflecting back with empathy. Others will be too busy talking to listen.

In addition to listening actively, use silence as a tool. Most people want to fill the awkward void—with anything. By keeping silent, you give others the opportunity to come out of the corner, to shift from advocacy.

That night, Tatiana noted that everyone was extraordinarily anxious. The only way to create cohesion was to observe and remark. It was a high risk strategy that took guts. And it worked.

It usually does.

SHARING THE BURDEN

Telling people what to do fails to bring them on board.
Even superb salesmanship makes little difference.

Greg talked his way into his dream job as a sports magazine reporter. That dream, however, was short-lived. Greg quit to help his father, whose heart was giving out. The window for a new heart donation was closing:

> We were living in the hospital together. He was very sick. I was trying to be a good son. I talked to all the doctors about how the organ donation system worked. At first, the answers to my questions made no sense. The hospital CEO's son had had liver transplants, so I brought all my answers to talk over with him. We became friends.
>
> I had more access because, with a baby face, I looked 16! I walked in, and everyone let me into their underwear drawer. I got real answers. The more I dove in, the more I saw that it was an "old boys' club," a status quo–protecting industry that never would correct itself.

I remember reading Malcolm Gladwell's *Tipping Point* all night in the hospital. I read a story about a woman who spent a year at church preaching about breast cancer awareness and getting nowhere. Then she switched to training hair salon stylists, which led to a spike in self-exams! I sent that story in an e-mail to every industry CEO. No one replied.

The only perfect part of my dad's entire process was the surgeon who put the new heart into his body. Everything before that wasn't healthcare at all. So I ran around looking for people to help me. I met my cofounder, and we invited the man who wrote the 1968 donation regulation to be our advisor. His wife was the woman from the breast cancer story! When I met her, I was speechless.

Most people feel that the world happens to them, but they are happening to the world. My favorite quote is, "You are not *in* traffic. You *are* traffic."

As sometimes happens, the universe shone on Greg's father. He was heading to the hospital for end-of-life counseling on the last day for a possible donation. His cell phone rang. A 26-year-old heart donor had just died.

Mobilized by that experience, Greg launched Organize with a mission to optimize the donation system. But how could he bring the right people on board?

If you only tout progress, you don't get people to care. If you want them to spend their time on your issue, get them involved in solving your problem. I learned that most people care more about working on really hard problems than seeing the solution.

Every important relationship started this way. The person would come back three days later and say, "You're right. I can't get this fucking problem out of my head. It's driving me nuts! We need to work on this."

That one insight—engage people by inspiring them to work on the problem—enabled Greg to attract Al Roth as an advisor. Roth, a Nobel laureate, had spent decades researching market design in nonmonetary markets, including kidney donor chains. There was no one better to bring on board!

So What?

Telling people what to do fails to bring them on board. Even superb sales-manship makes little difference. Instead, inspiring them to help solve the problem yields better results. Greg's favorite quote from Antoine de Saint-Exupéry explains: "If you want to build a ship, don't drum up people to collect wood and don't assign them tasks and work, but rather teach them to long for the endless immensity of the sea."*

The more complex your assignment, the more urgent your time frame, the bigger your coordination task, the more control you feel you need—especially when lives are at risk. Naturally, you push harder. The more control you exert, the less people feel engaged. Don't confuse commanding with engaging. How many of us look in the mirror and see control freaks? Letting go is difficult, but it's essential to bringing others on board. It's good for your health too.

Ultimately, Greg invented a work policy to help him let go of control. Once a week, he asked everyone on his team to complete the sentence "Wouldn't it be fucking awesome if . . ." It lightened the mood and engaged others.

It also encouraged dreaming, which was often lost in the day's traffic.

—————— TAKING ON YOUR ——————

PEOPLE CHALLENGE, PART I

Who doesn't want to help achieve a positive impact in the mission or business? Sounds great, but it means being dependent on others. Even individual contributors hiding in cubicles at the end of the hallway depend on others for their success. The world of global companies has gotten bigger, badder, and more complex. The projects are sprawling. It's all about the people, people.

But what's a person to do when so many people in the organization don't want to come on board?

Everyone in these stories had to find a solution. Michael crossed an invisible barrier to enlist his team. Casey faced her fear of connection. Emily

---

* Antoine de Saint-Exupéry, *The Little Prince*, (Mariner Books/Houghton Mifflin Harcourt, Orlando, FL, 2000).

shifted from presenting to listening. Kelly stood in the shoes of her workers. Tatiana used close observation. Greg revealed his problem. Everyone learned a powerful lesson that you know too: without others, your impact is limited.

Bringing others on board entails building or rebuilding trust. Most people think that's about reliability. That's part of it. You have to deliver what you promise. If you don't—if you miss the deadline or execute poorly—you erode others' trust in you. However, there's more. You'll inspire more trust if you practice openness, acceptance, and consistency. Here's how.

Identify the People You Need to Engage

It's uncomfortable to connect with people to promote your own success. It's easier to muster your courage in service of a mission. So your first step is to identify the mission and who can help you achieve it:

- *List everyone who affects success.* Identify angels and blockers who can make or break your project. Look all around inside the company and outside too.

- *Identify the key people.* Fewer than 10 people are really instrumental to your mission. Who are they? If you don't know, ask around. You may have taken for granted the people who matter most. Explore your organization's networks. The most influential and respected individuals are usually the best connected—not necessarily the most senior. Put them on your list even if you don't have a relationship yet.

- *Shape strategies to work around blockers.* The people who could slow you down are the most troubling. If you can solve their issues, they may shift to advocacy or let you pass. It's not always possible because politics can muddy the waters. If that's the case, look for others in the organization who can help.

Shift from Managing to Engaging

When you manage, you plan, make checklists, measure things, and tell people what to do. Instead, engage them by asking questions, listening, encouraging, supporting, and inspiring. It's a mindset change from *I don't have time to meet* to *Getting others on board is my most important priority.* To bring others on board, find the best way to connect:

- *Stand in the other person's experience.* Take the time to learn what's important to the other people involved. When you take their issues seriously, you do more than check off one more meeting. You show that you respect them and care.

- *Actively inspire that person to trust you.* You must go first. As the other person begins to trust you, he or she will come on board. Take four actions in tandem.

  - *Be reliable.* Reliability extends to timeliness, quality control, and honoring commitments. Deliver what you promise, plain and simple. Or don't promise!

  - *Be open.* Share what you think and feel so that others know where you're coming from. When you're not transparent, they assume you're holding something back. Telling people that you cannot tell them the whole story is better than withholding. People generally see through masks anyway, so be politely straightforward.

  - *Be accepting.* If people don't agree with you, assume that they have a good reason. If they differ from you, respect that. If you agree in the meeting and then criticize in the hallway, they'll find out. Talk to them directly. Chances are that you can address their issues and bring them on board.

  - *Be consistent.* People are quick to smell fishiness. They want to hear it straight from you when things change. Imagine how you would feel if someone told you one thing and did another, even if that person was trying to please you. So align your words, actions, and beliefs.

Get Others Invested

Keep in mind that building engagement is more than bringing doughnuts to the meeting. How you lead matters. Engage with purpose, a positive mindset, trust, and energy:

- *Form your team.* Teams form by connecting to the mission and to each other. Get curious about their whys (why they want to work on this, why they believe in it). Appreciate their strengths. Postpone your traditional kickoff meeting devoted to the plan, timetable, assignments, and metrics until that's done. Then pull out the spreadsheets, or better yet, involve others in preparing them. Take the time to build a high performance team now. You won't regret it.*

- *Get interested in others.* If you're worried sick about the stretch assignment you've been given, it's normal to obsess about your to-do list. Instead, figure out who needs to be engaged with your mission.

  o *Get curious about what other people think and feel.* As long as you're talking, you're not learning. Safeguard time for listening in one-on-ones and group discussions. Close the loop so that people know you've heard them. Take good notes and summarize impartially. (Hint: People love it when you write down their exact words—they feel as if their contributions have been recognized.)

  o *Be clear on your ask.* People may be willing to help if they understand what you really want. Since you don't want to go to the well too many times, figure that out first. Put it in positive language, answering the why and how. Then listen with respect. What are they thinking and feeling but not saying? Paraphrase what you think you heard to confirm it.

  o *Don't manipulate!* It's normal to say what people want to hear to get their agreement or to please them or to achieve some other end. Be careful that it doesn't bite you from behind. People talk to one another; they forward e-mails. There is no such thing as secrets.

  o *Move on, but loop back.* Uninvolved and undecided voters may come on board much later. It's a good idea to come back to them once you have small wins. Ask for their help again. No one wants to be left behind.

---

* Not sure what a truly high performance team is or how to get one? My former colleagues Scott Keller and Mary Meaney, both wonderful consultants, have summarized that and more in a book to help you improve your chances of building a high performance team and culture. Consider this: there's a lot more than top talent to an all-star team. The secret is entirely in how the team operates. The book is called *Leading Organizations: Ten Timeless Truths* (Bloomsbury, London and New York, 2017).

- *Spark engagement by caring, listening, and helping.* One thing is certain: directing people works some of the time but not all the time. So how do you win over busy people with competing priorities and objectives?

  o *Help the other people.* The people who help you may be simply generous, but there's always something that you can do for them in return. That's reciprocity, an integral part of business. Learn their priorities and objectives before pushing your agenda. Take a side step to help people with their issues in order to get their help in return.

  o *Reach out for one-on-ones.* People can always say they're too busy, but you won't hear their thoughts if you don't ask. In particular, reach out to those who are silent in your meetings or on your calls. You'll want to hear every voice, especially those who are too shy or reticent to speak up in groups. They could have been distracted or bored, but they also might have objections worth hearing now instead of at the eleventh hour.

  o *Ask good questions.* Examples might be these: "What does great look like to you?" "What is in the way of achieving our mission?" A good question opens up thinking. You'll know it by the energy in the room.

  o *Celebrate small wins collectively.* This helps underscore that success is won by team effort. Put others in the spotlight. Spread the love and feel it come back to you.

- *Listen without feeling the need to control.* Being the leader doesn't mean proposing all the ideas or judging everyone else's. Sometimes, you can be more engaging through quiet intervention.

  o *Be present, not dominant.* Your presence signifies the meeting's importance. Be alert and quietly engaged but don't feel the need to run things. Use your face and body language to show your engagement. Monitor how much airtime you use too. There is no rule of thumb, but if you're speaking much more than your fair share, that's telling.

  o *Protect the silence.* If you want better or fresh ideas, endure some silence to get them. Resist the temptation to jump in. Above all, stay off your smart phone! Good things usually follow when others fill the void. Spend that time sensing the group's state of being. Naming what you feel can bring the group together.

o *When you intervene, do it without judgment.* Discussions repeat, heat up, or veer off track. It happens! You may feel frustrated, anxious, irritable, or maybe triggered. Pause. A few deep breaths help, as do physical actions like pushing back your chair. When you're calm, intervene. It can take many forms: observe what's happening, name your emotion, or ask if people feel ready for action. Avoid siding with anyone. Your objective is to eliminate a roadblock and lead the group in a better direction.

Of course, you weren't born yesterday. You know that some people won't join you no matter how nice you are. Their self-interests may never align with your mission. In business, the best idea doesn't always win.

But do all of the things in this chapter and collect every chance for success. When people do come on board, you'll be unstoppable.

6

When You're Working with an Office Villain

t's common knowledge that every office is chock-full of terrible bosses and coworkers: bullies, jerks, tough characters, sharp elbows, crazies, bad guys, sociopaths, pieces of work, and more! There are days when it's you against them. Rose-colored glasses and tolerance can help when your boss is having a terrible day. However, they're not the full solution. Putting your head down will power you through a few days or weeks. But when you're in the ninth circle of hell, tortured by someone who enjoys it, you have to take action. Your life won't get better until you do.

It's not easy to distinguish a real jerk from someone who acts like one. Matthew faced that challenge in his new role at a global retailer. He was excited for the job, but things began darkly:

> My confidence was low. I was still fairly new to the company. Others felt they were entitled to or had earned the right to the management role I was given. When I looked to them to learn or develop, I was closed off. I felt pushed to the side if I had questions or ideas. My boss was focused on himself.
>
> I felt alone. I knew that they didn't understand why I was there or why I was deserving. I didn't want to fail, and I didn't want to quit. So I continued to push forward.

After we became best friends, one manager admitted that he was trying to get me moved out or fired. I became another one's supervisor. She felt I had taken a job meant for her friend. She had a reputation of being tough and not caring.

Matthew wasn't paranoid; they *were* out to get him! Instead of stewing, Matthew rebuilt his confidence, focused on what he could control:

I didn't worry so much about what others said about me. I couldn't control that. I went to my manager for feedback, and I didn't take it personally. I set small goals and achieved them. I built on that to improve.

In time, the woman I supervised became a good work friend. As I understood more, we broke through. She had built a wall—a barrier—taking in everything everyone had said, and that had shaped her personality at work. I helped her overcome her issues to reach her own goals. That was a high point.

We created one of the company's strongest logistics teams in the country. The things I remember are not the numbers but the people I've helped who can grow the business. That gives me goose bumps. That keeps me going still.

Had Matthew judged his team members, he would not have tried to connect, and the team would not have succeeded. He gave others the benefit of the doubt, realizing that not every person who seems like a villain is one.

In the following stories, some of the tough characters had issues of their own: a bad day, management politics, an overflowing plate, job stress. Others were certifiable, inexcusable. Hopefully, this spectrum will help you calibrate your own situation:

- *How do you deal with a belligerent jerk?* Kayla was blindsided when she found herself handling a well-known and verbally abusive individual.

- *When is it better to just walk away?* Some monsters poison everything they touch, as Hannu learned—the hard way.

- *How do you call out meanness?* John felt compelled to stand up to his former boss after she intervened to scuttle his promotion.

- *What if your fear is the bully?* Despite excelling at everything, Tara found happiness elusive.

- *Why would you ever work for a boss with a bad reputation?* Caleb took the assignment knowing that this boss would be very difficult to work for, based on two reports.

The world of work is full of villains. It's also filled with generous people who will coach you, teach you, and support you. Almost everyone is redeemable despite exhibiting demonic behaviors now and then. Few people think of themselves as jerks. You may act like one at times and not even realize it. I know I do.

The responses in these stories are well matched to the situations encountered. Every one belongs in your tool kit, preparing you to take on the next villain you meet at work.

THE JERK WHO THREW A TANTRUM

After the shock, her first thought was to protect herself.
It wasn't personal.

Kayla had wanted to work in publishing ever since college. She found a spot in public relations, but as her experience shows, unsavory characters can be part of the job:

> I took this novelist to a television interview. We were in the green room. A Japanese woman and her assistant were with him, filming B roll for a promotion. He had an Asian female friend with him too. TV stations don't allow other film crews to work in the building, so the show's producer asked them to leave, and they did.
>
> When the author finished hair and makeup, he saw that I was the only one there. He demanded to speak to the producer, who hadn't realized the author's friend was not part of the crew. Actually, no one had to leave; they just couldn't film.

The novelist lost it. He started screaming: "I want to speak to the head of the network! My lawyer is going to speak to you! I want to speak to your lawyer!" He accused everybody of being a racist and believing that all Asians looked alike. He screamed at the producer: "It's impossible to make this up to me!" I thought the producer would burst into tears. The author was shaking with rage. It was a disaster.

I was frozen, afraid to move because the author might turn on me. He had been exceedingly rude and condescending in e-mails, but I didn't know about his rages. It was pretty scary. I was trying to maintain my composure and maintain a relationship with the producer. I wanted us to stay on track for the interview. Then the novelist did the interview as if nothing had happened. That was even scarier. Everyone thinks this man is so charming. People have no idea that he is seething underneath.

Kayla kept it together. Once she took leave of the author, she rushed back to the office to see her boss. She didn't know if she could continue for two more days:

There was no reason to cry or be upset about failure. I had done nothing wrong. I just couldn't believe a person would behave this way and that I had to witness and be subjected to it. I was so uncomfortable.

No one was surprised. My boss put our next actions into motion. My boss's boss sent me an e-mail to apologize. Everyone came together to help. Then I e-mailed the show's producer and apologized, stating it was a misunderstanding, but the author's behavior was unacceptable.

It was obvious that we could not fix the problem. I had to suck it up and do a few more events, seeing the author again. We worked it out so that the editor went on the other interviews—not her normal role.

When Kayla dropped off the author at the airport, she was relieved. He continued to bully her by e-mail, calling her an idiot for getting a date wrong. It took Kayla years to be reconciled to what happened:

You never know what's going to go down. You're not going to like everybody you work with. I had lingering anger and frustration.

I knew I had done a good job and that my mistakes were small. It was such unnecessary drama that I thought, *I don't need this in my life*. I had never seen a person change so dramatically in an instant. It was unexpected. Amazing.

Looking back, Kayla would have liked to have gotten through the experience more calmly, but she knew the novelist's behavior reflected only on himself.

So What?

Verbal abuse is completely unacceptable, but Kayla showed professionalism in handling the situation.

After the shock, her first thought was to protect herself. It wasn't personal. Kayla did the right thing and framed the situation well, not taking responsibility for the author's behavior. Both of those instincts enabled her to unfreeze quickly. When the immediate danger passed, she swung into action. Her first stop was her boss, another good decision. Her boss validated that the conflict was not about her. Together, they decided what to do.

There is always a trade-off. Kayla could stay and reap the career opportunity reward or step aside to avoid further conflict. She chose to stay with the author, a decision mitigated by having a colleague join as a buffer. Third good decision, although Kayla would not have been judged had she decided to hand off the burden.

Hats off to Kayla for her courage! There are plenty of belligerent jerks out there. You have to be prepared to deal with them.

THE MONSTER WHO TURNED GOLD INTO DUST

Sometimes the only thing to do in a
bad situation is to cut your losses and go.

Hannu grew up in a very small town in Finland, an only child. Passionate about physics and mathematics from the start, life was lonely. So he left home for college and a life of mathematics and science with like-minded colleagues:

> I was in Edinburgh learning about string theory, as was Sam. We were fascinated and enjoyed it, but about 10 people in the world cared. Sam wondered how to use mathematics to solve real-world problems. We got our idea for the startup in a conference where companies were recruiting academic mathematicians. Our big turning point was when we took part in a business competition. The judge became our advisor, and then we made her CEO of our consulting startup.

Dream come true? Not quite. Things took a turn a few years later when the CEO brought her husband into the firm:

> We started with trust. Things were going well for a year or so. He was an older Frenchman, charming and friendly, with a background in psychiatry. He was only our advisor and not involved with the work.
>
> But at some point, it became a rule that he attended client meetings. He was very aggressive, and we lost some clients. After that, he started to edit every report. Sam and I tried very hard to understand him, but it was difficult. He had elaborate ideas on AI, with no substance. When we pointed that out, he exploded. He shouted and swore.
>
> He would never apologize; he blamed us. The CEO would speak to us individually about how badly we had behaved, and she would schedule a meeting where we apologized to him. It got worse. We could not write a single e-mail without his approval. Our e-mails went through him, and then his wife, and back to us. He started to get paranoid. He was convinced that Chinese spies had hidden microphones in the office.
>
> The couple had kept our salaries very low, using dividends instead. We had a draconian shareholder agreement

that meant that we would lose our entire stake if we left before five years. We also had a noncompete.

Hannu was in denial with many good reasons for why. But he could not ignore his deteriorating health:

> It was pretty scary. This was our company, our shared dream, and we had built it from scratch. We had hired really good people and developed them. We had good clients and an exciting space project under way.
>
> I generally have quite an optimistic outlook. I believe that most problems are solvable. I thought the CEO and her husband would change through discussion. They might go away. I feared that the CEO's husband had more business experience, and maybe I didn't know how things worked. He said he could try to be less volatile and we could all work on the communication, but nothing really changed. We had the stress of attracting clients, carrying our staff, and travel.
>
> Sam and I began to experience panic attacks. I got them every Sunday night and every time I checked e-mail. I had shortness of breath, pressure in my chest, butterflies, and a cold sweat.

Nine months later, Sam and Hannu faced the facts. They went to see a lawyer and prepared for a showdown:

> The CEO requested a letter from us outlining her husband's contributions. Instead, we prepared a letter with our lawyer. When we finally met, they exploded, calling us snakes, scorpions, and other unflattering names.
>
> During that meeting, we maintained a veneer of complete calm. We had pulled the trigger. We had the satisfaction of standing up to the bully.

Six years in, Hannu and Sam walked away from the company they had founded. Hannu went on to cofound an exciting medical devices startup, and Sam became a successful software contractor.

So What?

When the CEO's husband turned into a monster, Hannu didn't comprehend the severity of his situation. Without prior experience with abuse, he adapted like the experimental frog in water that is heating up one degree at a time. Another way to explain it is Martin Seligman's concept of "learned helplessness."* Passivity enabled Hannu to endure the pain, but it stripped him of free will.

It's important to prepare to protect yourself, but how? Hannu suggested, "Try to imagine the evil twin of the person. What would that look like? How would you react?"

Sometimes the only thing to do in a bad situation is to cut your losses and go. Luckily, work was not Hannu's whole life. His relationships helped him build the resilience he needed to walk away, not a moment too soon.

THE MEAN GIRL WHO INTERFERED

Whether his colleague felt shame or changed her ways was irrelevant. John had proved himself the bigger person, able to forgive.

John's mother raised him on her own as she studied and worked. When she decided to homeschool John, his outlook on life changed forever:

> I was in fifth grade in a public school, looking for validation from friends, when my mother snatched me out of that environment. She was a teacher by nature, always doing math with me, but I also got to explore what I was interested in. I begged for a keyboard.
>
> At Christmas, I got one and started producing music. Music gives you the ability to express things you don't know how to express with words. It relieved my stress; it helped me connect. Music shaped my identity in my community. It has done a lot for what I bring to work.

---

* Martin Seligman, long considered the father of positive psychology, began his research with learned helplessness. You can read more about how these experiments helped shape our understanding of why people give in and how to get out of that rut in the book *Learned Optimism* (Vintage, New York, 2006).

Although not well off in material things, John's mom, grandmother, and uncle loved him deeply. At the end of his first year in college, he won a scholarship to study business and his world opened up:

> My mom cried, obviously. My family has a history of work-ing-class jobs, but she wanted me to have a better life than her. She pushed me to apply. I thought business was great be-cause we need more entrepreneurs in the black community. And I'm a nerd! I loved it.
>
> I joined an African-American fraternity. I was very am-bitious, and this put me in line with a lot of black men who showed me what professional looks like. I realized how much intention I could have.

Still, John started work in a big retailer with self-doubt that grew more powerful when a former colleague intervened to hold him back:

> In my first few months, I was trying to get my bearings at work. I was the inventory planner on a team with an experi-enced merchant. She reminded me of the characters in *Mean Girls*—cliquey, fashion forward, popular. Two months in, I got feedback that I had areas for improvement. Taking that to heart, I improved and was placed on other teams.
>
> A few years later, I started having conversations about moving to a new category to broaden my experience. A meeting was set up, and the new manager was going to take me on. I was pretty excited!
>
> On the morning of Friday, the 13th (it was), I received an e-mail I should not have seen. It involved several manag-ers including my old manager, the new one, and that mean girl. She was dragging my name through the mud. Had she seen my numbers, she would have known I was top tier, but her early impression had lasted. You wonder how people per-ceive you who do not interact with you.

John's response surprised his managers. He behaved with understand-ing, setting aside anger and regulating his response:

When I saw the e-mail, I was shocked and hurt. Then I became angry. Feedback is a gift, but this wasn't. People smile in your face, and then they say mean things behind your back.

I asked my manager how it all went down. She had tears in her eyes; she was embarrassed. But I took it graciously. The incident enabled my leaders to see how I dealt with adversity. That boosted their confidence in me. I met with my prospective manager. He still offered me the lateral promotion. I took the same role in a different category.

I'm now cautious in how I deal with people who see me in a limited way. Even though my manager defended me, I realized I had to be smarter about how I focused. Retention and engagement of blacks and Hispanics are challenges overall. We're working in predominately white institutions. Instances of racism or prejudice are happening all over. It's why companies lose great talent.

I have friends from the best Ivy League colleges, and I'm friends with people who have criminal records. I'm hyperconscious. A lot of friends are struggling with the world around them.

Promoted next to manager of diversity and inclusion, John's new responsibility was companywide leadership development and engagement. Good things are happening.

So What?

Lashing out in response to bias and unacceptable behavior would have been understandable. Instead, John responded with compassion. He shared, "That merchant could have had better training on how to listen and engage in difficult conversations. Middle management may have huge gaps in their leadership. We're going after the 'frozen tundra' who really don't understand how to coach people not like them."

Whether his colleague felt shame or changed her ways was irrelevant. John proved himself the bigger person, able to forgive. His leadership in the situation inspired others. In return, he ultimately received the opportunity to foster inclusion and help others who don't have a voice.

More than he had bargained for.

THE 24/7 CRITIC

Live more in the present. That means letting go
of past decisions and, for the moment, future ones.

Tara had it made. Popular and class president in high school, she went on to a top university. There she got top grades. Offered a job by some choice tech companies, Tara was also accepted by two business schools. It doesn't get any better than that. But in her first year after college, the company Tara joined restructured. No matter. She took the generous severance package and began to weigh her options:

> Weirdly, I didn't panic. Initially, I was excited about the layoff. It was a great opportunity to try something else; I was nervous I would not maximize that opportunity, though. What if my choice was not optimal?
>
> There were all these things I had wanted to get done in that job. I thought I should have accomplished more. With another month I would have gotten so much more done! I started thinking, *Did I have any purpose while I was there?*
>
> I was nervous about finding the next step. I got a startup offer pretty quickly, but I wasn't sure I was 100 percent excited. It was a substantial pay cut. That was unimportant. I felt unsatisfied and nervous about making the wrong decision. Should I go somewhere with a good brand name? I still have misgivings today. I question if I did the right thing. What else should I be doing? Honestly, I know there's no way to know if it's good for my career. But even in college, I still wondered, *Should I have gone to the other college I got into?!*
>
> My way of coping is to go over the decision and see if the benefits I thought I would get are turning out to be true.

The startup job fit Tara's criteria, and after more consideration, she joined:

> I liked knowing everyone. I sat next to the CEO. In my second week, I led a companywide meeting! I led the charge to change our analytics infrastructure. It felt like a big step up.
>
> I was a little nervous because I felt like I wasn't ready to have the analytics responsibility. Maybe I should have gone to a place where people would train and teach me. Only time will tell if this was the right decision.

A year later, Tara quit. She wasn't happy there. It was time to start living in the present. So Tara talked her way into a six-week marketing analytics internship, working for the globally acclaimed rock star she had idolized for years. Afterward, Tara joined a big tech firm and started in the foreign country where her grandparents lived. Both items had been on her bucket list. When we talked again, Tara felt more satisfied, although still reviewing some decisions.

So What?

Fear of making the wrong decision can be an around-the-clock bully. There is a powerful weapon to counter it: live more in the present. That means letting go of past decisions and, for the moment, future ones. If you must look back, appreciate how far you have come. If you must look forward, allow yourself to be excited about the possibilities and set aside a specific time for worrying!

In the spotlight's glare, every decision looks wrong. If you do the same, it's a sign that your inner critic rules you. Though the critic is your own invention, it has power to hold you back from trying new things and enjoying the experience. And then there's the misery of second-guessing. Instead, start to dream a little.

By the way, if your job suddenly evaporates, it may feel like a crisis. The first thing to do is to chill. Losing your job is terrible, but if you can afford it, make it the excuse to do something you've always wanted to do—at least for a few weeks.

Like interning for a rock star.

THE BOSS WITH A BAD RAP

Even a difficult character has strengths to appreciate.
Make it your business to find them.

Caleb started life in Ethiopia, coming to the United States when he was a baby. His father moved the family again for his UN work, this time to Italy. Caleb was 14 and miserable:

> That Christmas, my parents sent me home to friends. When I returned, I had a rare moment of maturity. I realized that they were doing this to help us. I told myself to stop being a brat! Four of the best years of my life followed. I learned to see other people's perspectives. That's become my key personality trait. I put myself in other people's shoes.
>
> Then my father fell ill with cancer during my sophomore year in college. I was in a bad place. I stopped going to classes and practically flunked out. I moved home to help my mom. It hit me that my dad passed away when I was not achieving. That burden stayed with me.

Caleb finished college, and after a few years in a corporate job, he went to film school. Unexpectedly, his stint in the movie business readied Caleb for working with a difficult boss at the financial institution he joined a few years later:

> In film school, we worked in small groups, rotating through every role. By day 2 of everyone's project, I was invited to be assistant director. I thought, *Maybe some of the skills people think I have I actually have!* I was the only one who could work comfortably with everyone on the team. At times, the student director did not know what he was doing, and I was able to guide him without making him feel pushed around. I learned to speak with people in a way that reduced friction.
>
> I use that today. I had seen the earlier feedback on my boss. The last two folks in my role had had a horrible experience.

Word was, she was very difficult to work for. I'm not sure what the other people were doing. I came here without judgment and with an open mind, understanding that I was the new person. I needed to understand how the ecosystem worked without trying to shape it. I picked up things quickly and didn't need a lot of hand-holding.

My boss was very bottom line and detail oriented, so I focused on those things. I asked the right questions versus being off base for what was not important to her. She had little patience for tangents. She had to trust me with work, and I was able to deliver early. That bought me the benefit of the doubt and a cushion; I had some credit to work with.

A lot of her work personality overlaps with mine. I know when to ask questions, when to interrupt, when to check in versus working independently. I also know how to deflate tension with the right joke at the right time. I rephrase my questions to match a solutions orientation. She feels comfortable with me, and I with her. We get along fantastically well.

Where other people saw a difficult boss, Caleb saw a talented manager with valid needs. His father would have been proud.

So What?

Not every boss is a villain, but some are tough to work with. They're no match for Caleb. He has what experts call *emotional intelligence* (EI). Settling into his role without getting in the way, Caleb's interactions were elegant. Each one helped him learn and adapt.

Caleb didn't e-mail. He called or stopped by. Feedback is much more than an answer to the question "How am I doing?" In-person conversations offer valuable cues from your boss's body language and facial expressions. That's even more important when working for someone with an edge.

How did Caleb find so much to admire in his boss when two others before him did not? He focused on appreciating her strengths. Caleb's admiration for his boss's unrivaled knowledge aligned with his desire to understand the company better. Both liked being in the action. Finding common ground brought them closer together.

Even a difficult character has strengths to appreciate. Make it your business to figure them out.

TAKING ON YOUR

PEOPLE CHALLENGE, PART II

Everyone has the capacity to be a jerk at work. We all have our moments. Some bosses are tough, aggressive, direct, and task oriented. That's acceptable even if it doesn't suit you. Bob Sutton defines "certifiable assholes" as people who are out-and-out rude and who have a sadistic tendency to make you squirm, leaving you feeling demeaned and de-energized.*

Certain conditions exacerbate some people's tendency to get nasty: poor health, lack of sleep, junk food, long hours, not enough breaks, constant job stress. They take it out on you via their brashness, meanness, and hotheadedness. When Matthew came up against that kind of behavior, he withheld judgment. John responded with forgiveness. However, some villains pose greater challenges. Tara had to untangle an entrenched pattern of self-bullying driven by fear. Caleb chose to adapt and focus on his tough boss's strengths. Kayla and Hannu faced extreme bullies. They may be rare at work, but certifiable assholes devastate everyone in their path.

While these difficult situations are unpleasant, life improves once you face them. In all cases, there's a lot you can do to improve your experience at work.

Assess What You've Really Got

When you're having a bad day, food loses its taste and life loses its color. Your dark situation is pervasive *if you let it be*. So pause to evaluate what you're dealing with:

---

* If you're working for someone at the far end of the range, you really should read Professor Sutton's book *The No Asshole Rule* (Business Plus, New York, 2010). If you want to make sure you're not behaving like one at work, take the self-assessment at http://electricpulp.com/guykawasaki/arse/.

- *Assess your situation.* With paper and pen, analyze your professional and personal context. Note everything that's happening at work in the middle of the paper, leaving room for everything in your life outside of it. The intent of this exercise is to gauge the extent of your pain, given everything going on.

  ○ *Work context.* Do you face the jerks every day all day or only occasionally? Draw a circle for you and each jerk with an overlap representing how many work hours you share. Add circles for everyone else at work who interacts with you. Jot down all the forces that are affecting your work, like declining business performance or pressures on your team. If there are positives, add those in so you get a full picture.

  ○ *Life context.* Now add the context of everything else that's important to you: family, friends, communities, religion, activities, and interests. Jot down all the forces that are affecting your life, like a great relationship, young children, or a sick parent.

  ○ *Confirm your intent.* Remind yourself why you're at work in the first place: consider your bigger goals, what skills and experience you hope to develop, and anything else. Write that across the top of the paper.

  ○ *Gauge the relative pain.* Now you can gauge the relative impact of the jerks, bullies, and bad guys on your work life. Assign a number to how torturous the relationship is, from 1 (small occasional pain) to 5 (constant headache) to 10 (unbearable pain). Pain that is greater than 5 is a big red flag.

- *Assess the other persons.* Now use the same approach for the jerks: work context, life context, aspirations, intention, and pain. At a minimum, you'll determine if they are just having a bad stretch or are certifiable.

Find Your Fear and Face It

Your discomfort and difficulty may not be about the other person at all. If this relationship triggers a fear or a need threatened in you, look inward:

- *Find the patterns of your difficult situations.* Look at this relationship and reflect on other situations that may be just like it when you are not at your best. What typically happens? What are your behaviors, and what is being triggered in you? Get curious about those triggers, including personality types that bother you (and why).

- *Dig into the source of your fear.* What does this situation say about feelings and thoughts you don't express, the beliefs and mindsets you hold true, and what is really at stake for you? Keep digging until you recognize the fear pattern. If you don't feel fear, look for what makes you angry instead. That's a signal that an important need for you is threatened. Typical fears and unmet needs are often about recognition or status, certainty or control, autonomy or independence, relatedness, and fairness.* You'll know you've found it when you feel the fear both physically in your body and emotionally.

- *Challenge your mindset.* Just naming your fear will ease its grip, but you can do more. Identify the belief or mindset you're holding that empowers fear. That belief has nothing to do with the other person. It's your choice to keep or replace it. Challenge yourself to adopt a different mindset. For example, *I'm about to be found out* can be replaced with *This is about the other person's insecurity.* In consequence, your experience of the difficult situation will improve as your fear recedes. It never goes away, but it no longer paralyzes.

- *Imagine your new behaviors.* With a change in mindset, different behaviors naturally emerge. Visualize that behavior, using a situation when you had a different mindset without the fear present—for example, *I feel more compassion for my boss.* That mindset might lead you to behave with greater kindness.

- *Turn the tables.* You can use the same approach to better understand what's going on for the other person too. Start with his or her behaviors, noticing without judgment. Reflect on what the person may be

---

* David Rock, "Understanding David Rock's SCARF Model," https://conference.iste.org/uploads/ISTE2016/HANDOUTS/KEY_100525149/understandingtheSCARFmodel.pdf.

feeling and thinking but not expressing. Imagine that person's deeper beliefs, mindsets, and unmet needs. A fearful person acts out. If it's too late for compassion, at least you will have a better understanding of the person's irrational behavior.

Make the Best of Jerks

You might choose to work with difficult bosses or colleagues who have a lot to offer. If they're not certifiable, you should adapt your behavior to bring out the best in them. But if their behavior is unacceptable, take charge of your own protection:

- *Grade that jerk.* Look for these red flags: obsession with detail to assert control; temper explosions or unpredictable mood changes; inflated self-importance; inability to listen; attempts at manipulation (including lying); superficial charm and fun designed to usurp control; and gratuitous cruelty and rudeness. Check whether colleagues feel the same way you do. If several of these flags are consistently present, you've identified a certifiable asshole and it's time to take action.

  ○ *Create the file.* Fully document every interaction and get witnesses.

  ○ *Decide what you're prepared to do.* When you stand up for yourself, you're going to need support. Sometimes, the bully has friends in senior management or human resources, so be aware of the politics.

- *Go to your new mindset and behaviors.* Without fear, you're more able to think creatively and influence the other person's response.

  ○ *Contradict the cues that trigger you.* Don't start with the assumption that everyone is out to get you or that you've done something wrong. Start in neutral, or if you can, assume positive intent. Don't misunderstand: this ain't positive thinking. You're looking for what is actually positive. Don't make up stuff.

  ○ *Listen actively.* Listen for content and not tone, but also for what people don't say and feelings they don't express. If you're thinking about what to say next, you're not listening. Likewise, lay off the e-mails if you're on a conference call. Stay focused and present.

○ *Confirm your next steps.* Briefly synthesize the conversation and summarize what you plan to do. It may feel awkward, but it's a lot less awkward than realizing you haven't got a clue right after the meeting. Even gracious people lose it when you ask for the same instructions again.

• *Manage what you can control.* A creep's behavior is not your responsibility. Don't for a minute believe that you're the cause or that you deserve it. That's the definition of abuse. But you can manage the experience better.

○ *Focus on your growth.* Confront the person's feedback to you and look for what you can use. Implement what makes sense. Nothing stops you from acting on good advice.

○ *Set your boundaries.* This takes a bit of courage, but muster your inner protector and put that voice on the loudspeaker. Communicate when things are not working for you—without blame. Make a clear and fair request for what you want.

○ *Scout out other people to work with.* Get to know the managers who are peers of the jerk. Some will be energy drainers, but others will be energy boosters. Don't take your friends' words for it. When you can, move. This is one place when the adage "Grow where you're planted" is misguided. If you don't feel valued and respected, find a better pot to grow in.

Protect Yourself from Real Harm

• *Get help right away.* Let's say the other person has just stood on the table in the meeting, pointed at you, and cursed you at the top of his voice. That's nuts! What if he just criticized you publicly in a cruel way? Both times, this person's behavior was irrational. Get help!

○ *Enlist your boss and mentor.* This assumes, of course, that the boss is not the bully but, rather, someone who can help. If your boss is a conflict avoider who tells you to just get on with it, find someone else. This is what mentors are for. You're the better person for recognizing that you should not be handling this situation on your own.

○ *Call in the big(ger) guns.* If all else fails and your pain is high on the scale, reach out to someone—the boss's boss or human resources. It could even be a senior colleague from another area who has survived or witnessed incidents like yours. At this point, you're willing to risk exposure.

• *Set up barriers to protect yourself.* Short of a restraining order, make sure you're never alone with the bully.

○ *Enlist support.* Get buffered by someone with more power. Frame this as a company issue—because it is. Find someone who is able to put the company's interest before friendships.

○ *Use your voice.* Imagining life without this day-to-day energy drain may be enough to give you the courage and energy to walk away. Before you do, make sure that someone in management has heard you out. You have an opportunity to improve work life for your colleagues even if you choose to leave.

○ *Prepare to walk away.* Sometimes, the situation is too far gone to save. In that case, start lining up your next job.

The working world is not as civil as we'd like it to be. If you're the jerk, you're having an impact you probably don't want to have. Give some thought to your behavior. Self-awareness helps you naturally adjust.

In many instances, villains roam office hallways relatively consequence free. Some creeps turn out to be Dr. Jekyll on occasion and Mr. Hyde most of the time. You may face a monster like that—someone who makes work intolerable and unsafe. Luckily, more and more people are standing up to rid the workplace of these guys.

If that's you, you're a superhero.

7

When You Need a Sponsor

The term *sponsorship* is now officially a buzzword. Aren't mentors and sponsors the same thing? A word on the distinction: you want both, but it's sponsors who make the difference in your career.

A mentor is wise and experienced, a good person to teach or guide you. He or she doesn't have to know you personally. Often, mentors are assigned; with good intention, they meet you just once or twice! Most important, finding growth opportunities for you is not in a mentor's job description. Mentors fulfill their responsibility when they pass on insight and advice based on their experience. They might tell everyone else the same stuff too. And they don't, ever, need to stick out their necks for you.

The person who takes risks to increase your odds of success is a sponsor. Because he or she really wants you to succeed, your sponsor gets in the game beside you. Believing in you more than you believe in yourself may be all it takes, but he or she also will share ideas, coach, connect, support, defend, grease the skids, and advocate for you. Most important, your sponsor is on your team, providing growth opportunities to help you develop and advance. Even if your sponsor is a peer, he or she is respected and well connected. But your sponsor is probably at least one level up, with more reputation capital than you now have.

Kate wanted someone to guide her post-medical school residency, but her first mentor was too busy to do the job:

I looked for a mentor in cardiology and eventually found someone; it didn't turn out to be so great. She was world renowned, she had mentored others, and my research was in an area of mutual interest. But she was incredibly busy. We ended up meeting infrequently. I needed someone to take me under her wing, to show me the ropes. That wasn't happening.

I was very productive working with her—publishing a book chapter, articles, and original research manuscripts—but I didn't get the guidance I needed and wanted. I felt lost and a little angry. I thought I had chosen the wrong person.

Kate was unsure where her career should head next. At that time, her hospital hired its first full cardiologist-professor on an education track. That doctor was living Kate's career dream. Taking a chance, Kate reached out:

She e-mailed back, "I would love to meet with you. Tell me what works!" I showed up with lots of questions about her career. Then I told her about my ideas for educational projects. She had ideas too. We kept meeting. She encouraged me to apply for grants and helped me edit them. Our relationship happened quickly, without formality. She invited me to do things at the medical school. She started to open doors. She invited me to teach her class. She invited me to give a presentation at our national meeting, saying, "Now we have to make sure you do a really good job. Let's practice your presentation so you come off looking great."

When I turned 35, she brought me two bottles of champagne and gifts for my kids! We help each other out clinically. She was receiving a prestigious award from the medical school and needed someone to cover for her. I did it, no problem. She has been phenomenal in helping me figure out what kind of educator and what kind of doctor I am. She sees me following her once she retires.

What Kate first described was a mentor, but she wanted a sponsor. The second time around, that's what she found. As Kate learned, sponsor relationships evolve organically. Start early to make your connections, as these stories demonstrate:

- *What difference does a sponsor make?* Joshua's low probability for success in life rose exponentially when he met his sponsor.

- *How do you cultivate potential sponsors?* Realizing that sponsors make the difference, Francesca mastered apprenticeship.

- *What kind of sponsorship do you need?* Jason's relentless coach taught him to persevere, especially when the chips were down.

- *How do you balance sponsorship and independence?* A CEO helped Tracy leap forward, but their relationship turned out to be a double-edged sword.

- *What happens when you're in conflict with your sponsor?* Eva was caught between two sponsors who had competing demands.

- *What's in it for sponsors?* As Rick learned, when you sponsor the right person, you get much more than you paid for.

These stories confirm that nothing is a given: strangers can become bosses, bosses can become mentors, and mentors can become sponsors. Or not. Sponsors are not fixtures in the organization. They take care of their own careers first. That's why you must cultivate more than one relationship.

It all starts with working together. The person who becomes your sponsor must have a reason. Excellent work is a requirement, but it's not enough. The sponsor must benefit and also want to help you.

That might, but might not, happen on its own. It's up to you to change the odds.

BUT FOR THE LOVE OF SPONSORS

Sponsors fan your desire for greatness. They help you dare to dream even bigger. They see more than you see in yourself.

Joshua came from the inner city, shaped by the reality of being black, economically marginalized, and undereducated. Born in Indiana, he was the eldest of three. His half-brother was just three weeks younger, and the boys were close. Their father was a cook, in and out of Joshua's life. Were it not for mentors, who knows what path his life would have taken:

> My elders lit the fire in me. They were heavy-handed and strict about their values. My mother's reprimand helped me understand choice: "Just because other people are doing it doesn't mean you should do it." My uncle said, "If you have completed this task, go find another." They were not as tough on my brother and sister. My sister wasn't successful in escaping the inner city. My brother wasn't successful either. He was murdered when we turned twenty-one.
>
> But at each stage of my life, I had a mentor who taught me to be responsible, to be accountable, to be curious, and to stick with it. For example, in the fifth grade, my African-American computer teacher would bring artifacts from his international travels. He planted the idea of culture and diversity, enhancing my appreciation for difference to this day.

In the seventh grade, Joshua decided to become an engineer. That boyhood aspiration led to a college scholarship, an internship with the company providing it, and an honest-to-god sponsor:

> The company provided room and board and mentorship for college. Because I insisted on electrical engineering, I was the last student in the program to be placed. I met Linda, the head of HR, by luck. She came from a broken home too, and she saw some of that fire in me. Linda and her husband opened their home to me for the next six years. She made that internship life changing.
>
> When it came time to do my senior-year project, my invention worked, and people said, "Man, this is really cool! This could be sold." It took me several months to complete the engineering design. I was burned out, but Linda told me I had to apply for a patent. The company's legal team would help me acquire it. At the time, I didn't realize the importance.

Joshua's ambition, purpose, and perseverance sustained him. But Linda's sponsorship made the difference to his limitless outlook:

> Never turn down an opportunity you don't have. If someone says, "We want you to lead this team, and we think you can learn on the fly," you can respond by saying, "I don't have the skills. I'm not ready." Or you can say "Yes" to have much greater impact. If you're scared and don't want to do it, that's selfish.
>
> I'm not making these choices because I'm great. I hope a kid will read this book and realize she doesn't have to be born great. She can become great if she listens to the wisdom of people who came before. By 45, God willing, I will make CEO. My target is $19 million in net worth. I plan to retire on a few million and give away the rest. Then I want to help a lot of people learn what I didn't learn early.

Joshua's start paved the way for him to join a large utility company in engineering—grateful to Linda, who opened a door to greater possibility.

So What?

Joshua's faith taught him that God is always present. His mother taught him to own his choices in life. His mentor taught him to love learning. But his sponsor taught him to stretch higher—and she helped him get there.

What if Joshua had not insisted on electrical engineering? What if he had not met Linda? What if he had not followed her advice or not succeeded? Happenstance played an important role in Joshua's life, but everyone gets their share of luck. It's what you do with it that matters.

Sponsors fan your desire for greatness. They help you dare to dream even bigger. They see more than you see in yourself. Most of all, sponsors create the opportunities for you to achieve that goal. They want it for you as much as you want it for yourself.

Hats off to Linda, the unsung hero who took sponsorship to new heights.

THE MASTER APPRENTICE

Time is their biggest constraint. Potential sponsors will offer a quick chat, an elevator ride, or an invitation to observe a meeting. Take it.

Because Francesca's parents met working at a hip New York retailer, she regards herself as a product of fashion retail. Family connections launched her into a fashion internship, but Francesca took it from there:

> I was concerned that people would judge me. I wanted their perspective to be based on my performance. So I worked nights on things I wasn't asked to do. You have to constantly be thinking about what more you could be doing.
>
> We were researching a consumer market segmentation strategy. I added an additional consumer segment and presented an additional report. The findings were adopted. Then I sent an e-mail with initial thoughts and suggested next steps, without being asked. That project helped me prove myself.
>
> I feel it's my responsibility to provide the answer almost before it's asked. It goes back to how my parents raised me. I anticipated their next question. In my review, my merchant talked about my ability to see what was going on. She said that I was extremely proactive. She appreciated that I had always reached out first.
>
> One of the most challenging things in the fashion industry is making a career out of it. I've met so many strong and established women who have advised me to build on my relationships.

Returning after college, Francesca was mentored more than the others because she built relationships and delivered results. However, nothing lasts forever, and Francesca found herself at a crossroads:

> My boss had given me stability. She helped me develop merchandising skills. She had advocated for me, getting me into

the right meetings. When she said she was leaving, I felt abandoned.

Her exit coincided with a task that I owned for the first time. I was concerned about going into disorganized chaos. I did the best I could, but I felt unprepared. My motto is, "Just figure it out," but you don't know what you don't know. Without someone teaching me, I wouldn't develop. I was not being set up for success.

There was no plan to replace her. At the end of the day, I realized there were factors outside my control. If the company would not invest in helping me develop to get where I wanted to go, I had to leave.

Francesca's first mentor relationship dated back to her internship. Because the two had stayed in touch, Francesca reached out:

She had always said, "Keep me posted if you're thinking of leaving." I expected her to say, "You're not ready." I was surprised when she said instead, "I have an opening."

The process went so quickly. I had wanted to stay for two years, but this offer and opportunity outweighed everything.

Francesca left to join that mentor, now her sponsor, in a new role in a new company. Over the next two years, Francesca became a senior manager. When her sponsor quit to join a startup, Francesca followed soon after.

So What?

Francesca knew that to be successful, sponsors were a requirement, and so she made it her business to apprentice. Potential sponsors have the skills and know-how you need. Reach out with genuine admiration and a request to learn. Most people are flattered and willing to help you grow. Time is their biggest constraint. Potential sponsors will offer a quick chat, an elevator ride, or an invitation to observe a meeting. Take it. Anticipate their needs and deliver above expectations. That is Francesca's surefire lesson to cultivate sponsor relationships.

Finally, take the next step by keeping in touch beyond work. As people leave for new jobs, your network will broaden. The fashion industry's revolving door is not unique. Everywhere, people routinely switch companies.

That's why cultivating sponsors is no longer just a nice-to-have. Like Francesca, become a master apprentice.

WILL YOU BE MY RABBI?

Rabbis help navigate the politics. They teach, coach, counsel, and love you. They also pull strings on your behalf. They protect you.

Jason is a force of nature who is going places. We all know people who advance effortlessly. Well, that's *not* Jason. For some, advancement takes effort. And tremendous support. Now, that *is* Jason.

Jason's father was his first rabbi and a relentless coach. Jason knew a golden opportunity when he saw one:

My dad was super-loving and an awesome coach. I saw that if I did the things he taught me, I could be really successful. My father said, "There is no such thing as can't—you *can* do it. We'll do it *together*. We'll attack it." In high school, I struggled to find a way to afford college. I tried to play football but got hit. I tried soccer but wasn't any good at it. But I was the fastest runner. My dad said, "Run as fast as you can. Give it everything you've got! You won't get a heart attack. Don't worry, you'll pass out first!" He helped me until I became decent. And I got a full scholarship to the college I chose.

Starting early, he programmed me to think about banking. At night, he cleaned toilets at the bank, and in the day, he introduced me to bankers. My first year in high school, I began interning.

On my first day in my first full-time banking job after college, I was the first African American in that role, and someone handed me mail for the mailroom! I didn't even know these things happened. But my father taught me to be tough. Even now, he'll ask, "What are you doing today?" I tell him, and he says, "Not enough!" My dad taught me that I could create my own destiny. I've been given opportunities others have not gotten, but I have to go get what I want. It's my job to maximize my potential every single day.

Sooner or later, everybody faces a really tough situation, and that's especially when having a rabbi makes a difference:

> The firm asked me to move to an underperforming office. They told me to improve the unit and work together with a co-head for a few years, until I was ready to manage on my own. He was opposite to me in every way. I had never dreaded going to work until then. I was miserable. It was hard to get out of bed. I was frustrated, and I struggled to find the positive in the situation, but it was contentious. He felt threatened. I felt stifled.
>
> Instead of becoming defeated, my goal was to do the best I could to help my co-head be successful. I learned the nuggets that helped him succeed. I put together a business plan to improve profitability. Gradually, it worked. The right people took notice. Six months later, the division CEO called. He said, "Jason, you seem to have done the work." The other guy had lost focus. He fell off the wagon.
>
> People matter above all else. Table stakes are that you have to do really good work. But people have to want you to succeed. They have to see you as you. I worked really hard to get senior people to support me.

The division CEO had been watching over Jason. The CEO of the bank had noticed too. Jason advanced to managing director and eventually co-head of a large division.

So What?

Jason understood that it was up to him to deliver. He said, "I understand that your boss may be awful, but you need to figure out what to do. No one is going to give you anything." But they can help. Rabbis help navigate the politics. They teach, coach, counsel, and love you. They also pull strings on your behalf. They protect you. Jason knew that, and so he sought out rabbis every step of the way.

In cultivating rabbis, stick to the message that you're trying to achieve positive impact. Do great work and watch your words. No complaining. Jason advised, "Sharing your blind ambition will not go well, but asserting that you want to develop is a good thing." Be like Jason. Get help, give help. Everyone needs help to be successful.

Even your rabbi.

BREAKING UP IS HARD TO DO

It's emotionally tough to gain independence from your sponsor.
It's like leaving home all over again.

Tracy's family is complicated. Her parents divorced when she was not yet born. So she has a mother, father, and sister but also a stepmother, stepfather, stepsister, and two stepbrothers. In particular, women inspired Tracy to dream big:

> I've always seen my mother as being a hard worker. I didn't realize until I got to college that we didn't have money. I didn't see her struggle and sacrifice. She always found a way to provide for her children even though it meant working two jobs. I wanted her to feel that her hard work had paid off. That work ethic drives me.
>
> After college, I worked at an automotive company. There were so many powerful and strong women leaders there that I aspired to become one. In particular, one senior vice president was the person with final say. She set the pace. When she spoke, people listened. That's the person I wanted to be.

Although Tracy started her career in banking and rose to vice president, she felt called to restart in healthcare:

I had an experience in the healthcare system with my grandfather. It was eye-opening, terrifying, overwhelming. There had to be a better way. So I got a master's degree in healthcare. I applied for a fellowship at the healthcare system, and I couldn't even get an interview two years in a row. So many people in banking told me it was impossible because I wasn't clinical. That motivated me. I hate hearing that I cannot do something.

When the boss from my hospital internship became CEO of that healthcare system, she negotiated for me to come. It signaled that God had a bigger plan for me. From day 1, I've been her right hand. She is an African-American woman too, in her late forties and successful.

From the beginning, she created opportunities for me to grow with her. We have a relationship that no one else has. There are people who don't like me because of it. And once I started full-time, it was difficult to get C-suite management to see me as someone else—*not* the CEO's fellow. I struggle with getting them to respect me as a leader in my own right.

The directors perceive that she protects me. I don't think she does, but if I cannot be seen as separate, my best opportunity may be elsewhere. Still I'm loyal to a fault! Relationships matter so much to me. And I'm afraid of failure. It goes back to the struggle.

Actually, management did see and did value Tracy's remarkable leadership. They promoted her to director of cardiovascular services, in recognition of her impact.

So What?

Sponsors create opportunities you cannot get on your own. They may also limit you. Their attention sets you apart; their power can make you complacent; helping them can be all-consuming. Tracy walked an invisible, political tightrope to convince others of her independence without risking a powerful relationship.

It's very hard to change people's perceptions. Once they categorize you, they rarely change. To shift how she was viewed, Tracy had to demonstrate her own leadership *and* bring people's attention to the new evidence.

It's also emotionally tough to gain independence from your sponsor. It's like leaving home all over again. Expect tears. Be sure to honor what your sponsor has done for you. Treat your sponsor with kindness and caring as you say good-bye. Keep in touch. Be thankful. After all, you're standing on your sponsor's shoulders.

And don't forget to be a sponsor to yourself. Appreciate all you've accomplished. Say good-bye to the struggles you've carried since childhood.

BETWEEN A ROCK AND A HARD PLACE

Believing that human beings are interconnected and responsible to each other, Eva did the only thing she could: feel compassion for all.

Eva's grandmother won the green card lottery in her Eastern European country, and she moved the family to the United States. Six-year-old Eva's life fundamentally changed then:

> When you pick up, go somewhere else, into a new culture, your world is flipped upside down. We showed up without English, without jobs, and without our own community. My parents were completely lost. We had no network to fall back on. Everything was an uphill climb. We didn't know the norms, like watching TV to find out when school was closed. I was alone and didn't understand.
>
> I had a very difficult childhood, growing up in a crazy home. My father was an alcoholic and abusive. My mother was a fighter, trying to keep us together. She needed his paycheck. That took a toll on her. I decided to become my own provider.

Eva put herself through school by tutoring children. The mother who hired her then offered Eva an internship in human resources where she worked. Step by step, Eva kept advancing:

> The head of HR was looking for a chief of staff. The interview went brilliantly, and I was hired. I thought, *Someone else sees something in me. I can figure this out.* I got to be at the table, absorbing. I developed in leaps. My trajectory got steeper, and it accelerated; expectations increased. Then the organization reorganized. Another leader came in, and I reported to him.
>
> He invited me to work with him to restructure the function. We were going through the list, putting names into boxes on the new chart. I noticed that my sponsor's name was not there. She had invested and believed in me. I felt I was being pulled apart, eaten alive.
>
> My new boss asked if I was OK with his decision to let her go. In that moment, the leader was testing me. I get why he did that. People need to see your boundaries. He probably needed to know my colors—doing the right thing from a business perspective or letting emotions decide.
>
> My sponsor had been excited about the new organization, texting me in the background. I had to tell her I couldn't share anything confidential. When she was let go, she said, "You knew, didn't you?" It was a slap in the face. I had sort of lied. She was a senior executive who would have fought that decision tooth and nail.
>
> I had to figure out my values and manage politics while still staying true to myself. I thought about the corporation existing to make money, not to be your friend, and I learned to accept it. I have always given others credit for where I am, and yet I worked incredibly hard to get here. My sponsor helped me because I do good work and am worth sponsoring. When she left, I freaked out and thought, *Crap, I don't have her here anymore. What am I going to do now, because I want to be successful?*

It took time, but Eva's new boss became her sponsor.

So What?

Eva was uncomfortable choosing self-preservation. She was put in an emotionally charged situation, in conflict with the person who sponsored her from the start. What could she have done?

Perhaps Eva could have recused herself without impairing the new relationship. That's a tough one. Each player struggled between a rock and a hard place: Eva's sponsor was left in the dark about her job. The new boss had to make difficult decisions. Eva felt pain in in letting someone down: either her sponsor or her new boss. Business realities are sometimes cruel and unfair. It's the way it is.

Believing that human beings are interconnected and responsible to each other, Eva did the only thing she could: feel compassion for all.

IT TAKES ONE TO KNOW ONE

Great sponsors don't have to be white-haired executives.
They simply have to be ahead of you,
and opportunity creators—for you.

Captain of his college soccer team, Rick was drafted by Major League Soccer (MLS). He was thrilled. But two seasons in, he suffered a major injury: his quad muscle was torn to the bone. So when a college friend introduced Rick to media sales, he gladly switched. In his new job, Rick found what he had loved in sports— teamwork, competition, and winning. He quickly advanced into management, without time to learn how:

> The biggest fault of managers is that they did great work to get there, and then they try to be somebody they're not. Usually they try to be tough. That's what I did. For some reason, I thought fear and intimidation were the best ways to manage.
>
> It became difficult pretty quickly. Employees were disgruntled with me. Productivity was not improving. It's easy to be a top-down, fear-inducing manager, but that wasn't working. I started trying other things. Within two months, I

had pivoted. Managers need to respect their teams; they also need to add value. I learned the 80/20 rule: 80 percent positivity and 20 percent discipline.

My biggest fear is to be somewhere where I'm just a number and I don't mean anything. My measure of success is that if someone didn't show up for two weeks, the business would suffer.

Always competitive, Rick became a good manager, then a mentor, and ultimately a caring sponsor:

My high points are when I bring people along on my team. Take the case of someone I've worked with for five years. I hired him when he was 25 because of his work ethic, his resourcefulness to find solutions, and how he transformed himself. The landscape is changing so rapidly today. You hire people for their capacity to learn, not for what they know.

Initially hired for sales, his true calling was operations. That's not what I had anticipated. Selling a deal is easy, but managing it is complex. He was a sponge and learned quickly, whether it was by inviting him to meetings, showing him how to do things, or discussing issues. Then he ran with it. He brought great energy, and I trusted him. Now he manages six others.

He's someone I would go to war with, play a sport with, line up with, every day. We're at a point where we can bounce ideas off each other whether they're in his area or not. We are yin and yang.

When Rick left to follow his entrepreneurial dream of launching a digital marketing firm, his "sponsoree" joined him as equity partner in charge of operations. Rick's measure of success was met.

So What?

Most people look for sponsors at the top, but Rick was still on his way up. Great sponsors don't have to be white-haired executives. They simply have to be ahead of you, better connected, and opportunity creators—for you. It takes a few years to build trust and deepen a sponsor relationship. Don't expect opportunities to shower you right away. But the Ricks of this world want to sponsor good people.

Sponsorship is a two-way relationship that evolves. Sponsors get as much from the relationship as they give, including tremendous leverage, but also collaboration, loyalty, companionship, and the kind of fulfillment often missing at work.

Bottom line: sponsorship makes both of you more successful.

SPONSOR CHALLENGE

Although you may have sponsors unbeknownst to you, don't count on it. And waiting for somebody to step across the line—from praising your work to helping you succeed—can take time.

There's no doubt, though, that you should invest in potential sponsor relationships. After a false start, Kate found a sponsor who pioneered the career she wanted. Joshua's sponsor stayed by his side like a guardian angel. Francesca's first sponsor helped her leave the wrong job for a better one. Jason met challenges successfully through the relentless coaching of a sponsor. Tracy's sponsor enabled her to switch industries and start at the top. Recognizing the value of sponsorship in business, Eva gained a new one after her first sponsor was laid off.

As Rick learned, sponsors help others because it makes business sense. But cultivating these relationships is up to you, and it's an important part of your job. Here's how to go about it.

Know What and Whom You Need

What do you need to develop further? Is it new ideas? Connections? A coach? Someone who cares about you? A hero who can save you? Not all sponsors are the same:

- *Decide what you need.* Start with your goals and professional vision and then figure out who you need to help you and what you hope to receive from each. Even a great role model is not all things to all people. Engaging several people is better. That increases your odds of developing a sponsor and decreases the burden you place on each.

- *Identify the people you admire and whose career paths seem interesting.* This is not about friendship. You don't have to like the person or be like the person. You're looking to learn and develop. If you know your interests, find people who share them one or two levels up. If they have a skill you don't have or if they exhibit a strength you'd love to build, put them on your radar. In a smaller company, that will be obvious. In a larger company, you may have to ask around to identify the individuals. Remember to look for people who are not like you too. They have even more to offer.

- *Become worth sponsoring.* There's no way sponsors will invest time in someone who doesn't deliver. You have to meet—and beat—their expectations, and that's just the beginning. They also want to see your potential. Show it in a nice way; bridle your ambition by putting the company first. In addition, sponsors look for openness to new experiences and the flexibility to adapt. Finally, sponsors want loyal supporters. They want followers who make them successful. And that's exactly what you want too.

Be Open to the People You Meet

Unless you delight in meeting strangers, get comfortable with discomfort. Here are a few telltale signs that fear has interfered in your ability to meet new people who could be potential sponsors: making excuses (*I'm shy, and I don't like meeting people*); finding fault or criticizing (*That person wouldn't be a good sponsor*); and never having the time (*I have too much work that's pressing*). If you recognize any of these signs, get curious about what's stopping you:

- *Meet people.* Look for ways to meet beyond your regular transactions or interactions. Try these ideas.

  o *In a business context.* Engage others by asking really great questions. Come to the meeting early or linger afterward. Admire people's strengths. It's not fake if you mean it. Most people like specific praise meant just for them. Make sure you're not feeding someone a line.

○ *In a social context:* Bump into people by walking the long way to your destination. Find out about their families, interests, or work and show genuine interest. Let them do the talking.

• *Identify potential sponsors, starting with your boss.* With an open mind, use these criteria to assess whether your boss (or another senior person) can become your sponsor.

○ *Access to stretch opportunities.* Does he or she believe in your potential? Is he or she willing to take a risk on you? If not, have a conversation to find out why. You may need more time in your role. If his or her reasons are fact based, listen up. If you feel sidestepped, that's a no.

○ *Give-and-take.* Is this a two-way relationship with mutual respect and support? Reciprocal relationships are much stronger. Even if your boss is a bit prickly, does he or she give feedback regularly that leaves you feeling stronger and more motivated to get to the next level? Someone who only takes (and drains your energy) is a no.

○ *Shared credit.* Bosses who don't share the credit are never going to go out of their way to help you. Some bosses are strategic, pooling the credit for the person up for promotion. As long as your boss gives credit, that's a resounding yes. Your turn will come.

Cultivate the Relationship

You ought to have a few potential sponsors, which means you must spend time with each:

• *Know what you're in for.* A two-way relationship requires more of your time, your loyalty, and your responsibility. Start small. Before asking for what you need, find ways to be of service to the potential sponsor. Reciprocity is the currency of business. Stay focused on your potential sponsor's strengths. Sometimes, senior people appear flawed. Apart from a breach of values, a few flaws make your potential sponsor human.

- *Plan your interactions.* An interaction could be a long lunch or a quick hallway chat. Each time, your sponsor needs to understand your goals and what you want from it. You're in charge. Have an agenda and start by setting mutual expectations for the interaction. Always summarize next steps. Before leaving, ask for closure ("Did we meet your goals? Any further thoughts?"). It's never all about you.

- *Always thank your sponsor.* Share what you're learning in specific terms. People know the difference between authentic and generic. Don't gush or wear down your sponsor. Your sponsor is not family.

Find Opportunities for Independence

If you work with your sponsor closely, separation will be difficult, but important, when the right time comes—when your sponsor has received real benefits from sponsoring you. Gain independence with grace:

- *Raise your hand for small projects.* If your organization has task forces or other projects outside your job scope, ask to be assigned. It's a natural way to broaden your network and find new mentors who can become sponsors. Your sponsor will be proud that you took initiative.

- *Move on.* If your boss is also your sponsor, look for natural ways to rotate out, even temporarily. Ask your boss for counsel in charting your next steps. Moving to a different market or function helps you build new relationships and demonstrates independence.

- *Stay in touch.* Separation does not mean severing the relationship! Find ways to honor your sponsor. Let your sponsor know how you're doing too. Sponsors are invested in your long-term success. Years into your career, you'll see more ways in which they've helped you. Pick up the phone.

Pay It Forward

You can be a sponsor—and it's worth doing. The rewards will be far greater than what you invest. Once your potential sponsoree beats your performance expectations, put your neck on the line:

- *Open the best doors.* People grow through exposure to new experiences and situations that help them build new skills.

  ○ *Withhold judgment.* Determine how to build on the person's strengths and communicate your confidence in him or her. This part is simple: make it clear you're on the same team.

  ○ *Align on opportunities.* Some people ask for too much opportunity; others are too tentative. Both need your intervention. If the person's eyes are bigger than his or her stomach, have an honest and caring conversation. If the person is hesitant, build his or her courage by expressing your confidence.

  ○ *Take a risk.* Find the right growth or experience vehicle with that person's best interests in mind. Some sponsors fail to give someone a stretch assignment because they attach the provision that the sponsoree must succeed 100 percent of the time. Who succeeds all the time?

  ○ *Push the person out of the plane.* With a parachute and safety net, of course! You're in this too, so jump. It's up to you to increase your sponsoree's odds of success.

- *Let everybody know.* Make sure that your sponsoree's performance is visible. Your case should be more than opinion. Show evidence of improved business performance.

- *Help your sponsorees become independent.* Keep in mind that you don't own your people. They should not be seen as bag carriers. Their independence makes you look better and contributes to your advancement. It speaks to your confidence and leadership.

Some people have to fight their way to the top without sponsorship because of bias. But why go it alone if you don't have to? Joining forces with sponsors exponentially increases your chances for success. And being on a team wholly dedicated to your success is pretty great.

When You Dare to Challenge

Choosing to lead by offering a counterview can be heart-stopping. Sharing your perspective in a team meeting is the beginning. Then there's holding your own with senior executives, taking a stand at town hall, or walking onstage to speak to your industry colleagues. Standing out, whether privately or publicly, is intense.

Anne is no stranger to the spotlight. She exudes a confident presence. She started life in Canada, where her father ran small businesses in a remote area. When her parents decided to split, her mother, a diplomat, raised Anne in Japan. That experience offered Anne exposure to the world and early independence. She was proud of her mother, who advanced to serve as ambassador to troubled countries. It was natural for Anne to launch an unprecedented training program in the consulting firm where she worked:

> It was the biggest thing I ever did and my first large-scale project not directed by a "grown-up." My friend shared his idea, and I came on board immediately. It was important to have the idea, but really important to execute it well. Our volunteer team created a brand-new training experience for 100 peers. We had to recruit and engage 20 senior and midtenure people to facilitate.

We had a shared vision and did a good job of dividing up the work without ego among senior and junior people on our team. It took months to prepare. I was working on a project in Brazil, and I used my 10-hour flights to get it done. The last two weeks, I worked around the clock. Invested in the vision, we spent a lot of time rallying others to get them excited to show up. It was risky to ask people to attend on a weekend! We knew success depended on people arriving with a mindset open to learning.

Well, at the end of the two days, we wrapped up and thanked everybody. We got a standing ovation from the entire group.

That was when I was first seen as a leader in a different way from just executing what people asked me to do. Each morning, I had led a brief meeting to tell the senior leaders what I wanted to get out of the day. I treated them as my staff. One said, "Junior tenure people don't talk to partners that way. That was amazing!" A few helped me get my next job after that experience.

I look back and think, *It was a really good decision. There would have been no way that senior people would have recommended me for my follow-on job!* It was a game changer.

Management assumes that every young leader is like Anne, poised and able to take a stand with top executives.

That's simply not the case.

Even for professional actors, it can be frightening to step out of the shadows on to the stage. Few people are naturals. They prepare tough questions and answers and rehearse. But here's the thing. Speaking up is the least of it. Saying it in the right way counts, and that includes everything from the emotion you convey to your tone, the speed and rhythm of your cadence, and your pauses. Knowing when to remain silent is important too.

And voice without presence is insufficient. I confess: I hate the words "executive presence" and "personal brand." They rankle me. You're not a can of soup. You're not a packaged executive. Your value comes from how *you* bring yourself to work and how *others* see you. Are you regarded as a leader with confidence, someone to follow? That starts with your intention for how you want to be seen. It extends to the way you hold yourself, your walk, how you stand or sit, the space you fill, your energy, and the connection you make with each person in the room. That's presence.

Taking a stand combines voice and presence. It uses everything you've got. Doing that well signals to the higher-ups that you're ready for more. Don't believe me? Watch well-known speakers. If they're any good, you feel moved to answer their call for action.

Check yourself out by standing in the shoes of management. Your silence might be misinterpreted as disengagement. Your hesitance could project lack of confidence. Your discomfort could mean lack of potential for advancement. The way you sit could signal arrogance. Speaking up too brashly could be misinterpreted, as could interrupting, speeding up, or talking too much. Feel overwhelmed? Happily, voice and presence are learned skills, as these stories show:

- *What's actually stopping you from speaking up?* Growing up with a significant speech impediment, Martin never thought people would want to hear from him.

- *What will it take to get you to step up?* When told that she should consider leaving, Joy chose to stay and prove them wrong.

- *How do you take a stand on your own behalf?* After he realized that no one else would take the responsibility, Jared stepped up to fight for himself.

- *What are the steps to leadership?* With a strongly held desire to experience the world, Seckin started in Turkey and worked his way up from there.

- *How do you build the muscle to step out with greater comfort?* An independent spirit, Bruce mastered how to challenge with extraordinary results.

Learning to challenge is a rite of passage at work and in life. It's a universal need. We want to be valued and respected. We want to be counted.

Here's the hardest part: standing in the spotlight to take your share of the credit. Everyone is watching and listening, on social media too. It takes courage to be seen and heard. But no matter where you are on the spectrum from wild enthusiasm to sheer terror, it's nothing short of thrilling. You're crossing the line to become a leader.

No matter what your job title is.

AT A LOSS FOR WORDS

The real confidence destroyer is self-judgment.

The head of HR in a financial investment firm bubbled with joy when she suggested Martin for the interview. "You'll love him!" she said. "He's one of a kind!" You see, Martin had turned a showstopper into a temporary detour:

> I've had—since I was four or five—a speech impediment. I didn't think much about college or a career because I didn't see that it was possible for me. I figured I'm not somebody who would get to talk to people.
>
> But I became the sort of person who talks almost to prove to myself a willingness to put myself out there. Just to say something and not allow it to prevent me from speaking.
>
> In the mock trial club in college, I got more of a hint that I might be able to be a person in the world who could have conversations in a professional context.

The issue lingered for a long time. Other people worry about sounding stupid at work; Martin worried about getting his words out:

> My fear is if I make it clear I have this impediment, I will be found not to be qualified or capable. In my first year, I was genuinely convinced I could be fired any day and that my hiring was a fluke. Now I know it's not true.

I was given responsibility early on. After a few months, it became hard for me to maintain that image of myself as not being able to go someplace. I had started picking up the phone, able to say, "Hi, this is Martin." It had always been very hard to say my name. That happened gradually. It's sticky; it's hard to change even with so much evidence to the contrary. In moments, I still wonder whether I have the chops.

How did Martin's metamorphosis happen? Replacing his mindset was the catalyst, but new mindsets don't just switch on:

For me, it was realizing how long term the process would be—it's very easy to get frustrated—to feel capable. It's like going to the gym to exercise. You won't have big muscles quickly. You have to keep working at it, and it will happen over time. I really don't believe there is some great insight. All the Hallmark stuff is true—you know, *you are good enough*—but you won't be able to internalize it by reading it on a card.

You'll need to continue to work to convince yourself of something that other people already know. Often I've been convinced I've said something in a way that was not eloquent—and I've worried about it and asked someone if it was OK, but no one ever said anything other than "You're great." Certain insights I have are just habitual and wrong. Applying analytic thinking can be helpful to pick something apart, like the variables in a meeting, but don't apply it to your own performance. You won't perform well that way.

I see people joining with the same fears. I can assume that some of the worries I have now will appear unnecessary too, as I grow. I've seen this movie before.

For someone who used to believe that college and a career were not in the cards, Martin left me with no doubt that he was more than up to the challenge.

So What?

That's mindsets for you, deeply embedded beliefs that shape our horizons. A speech impediment poses a physical obstacle, but a limiting mindset is more formidable. When Martin replaced his mindset—*People don't value what I have to say*—his experience improved. But mindsets are stubborn. There's no on-off switch for them. You have to work at it. So focus on appreciating—*enjoying*—the process of evolving.

The real confidence destroyer is self-judgment. Martin held on to his self-image long after he'd changed. There's building new muscles, and then there's getting used to the new you. As you practice, ask people around you to let you know when they see you changing. That alerts them to pay attention that you *are* changing. Their evidence will be powerful; pretty soon, you'll stop seeing yourself as a person who cannot, should not, stand out.

Baby, that's just not you anymore!

SHATTERING CAREER-LIMITING SILENCE

Don't kid yourself. Anytime you want to get to the next level of performance, there will be pain.

Joy's father fought high blood pressure and kidney disease; her mother donated a kidney to save him. Together, they gifted Joy with the belief that ambition, grit, and love would meet any challenge. School was her first opportunity to test that belief:

> I was a top student at my neighborhood elementary school. Then I transitioned to junior high, where students came from all over. It was a very painful time. Seventh grade was the most difficult year in school ever. Many tears were spilled.
>
> I was so frustrated because I couldn't keep up. I was a B student—not what I was used to. I could have dropped out. Fifty percent of the minority students did. But staying in that school prepared me for the type of challenging environments I would have later on. It forced me to take myself to another level. Challenge became my norm.

Joy's dream was to design jet engines. She hit the jackpot, interning at an aircraft company while in college. Soon she learned that it would take 20 years to move beyond designing one small part. So when a consumer goods company called, Joy answered the phone. She started upon graduation.

It's hard to imagine that Joy would be anything but successful. However, a training session to help African Americans excel sent her into a nosedive:

> My report card had me as the lowest performer in the pool. The training coordinator said, "You're probably not going to do well here. Your manager must have told you—you're not a good fit. You may want to start looking." When I didn't speak up, it showed that I was not engaged in the training—not interested, not bringing forth any new thought or train of thinking. It was not a question of brains but how I had engaged.
>
> It was horrible! I cried all the way home.
>
> The coordinator had said that white managers don't feel comfortable giving feedback to their African-American subordinates, but I went in the next day and asked. My boss said, "What are you talking about? You're doing very, very well." He gave me examples, and they were all positive. Still, maybe he didn't feel comfortable. I second-guessed him.
>
> I noticed that my work style was very different. I'm an introvert on the extreme side. In meetings, I was not the one speaking up with an opinion. I would think about it and talk to my manager later.

Deep down, Joy lived in horror that she wasn't a good fit. But for the next six months, she worked very hard to prove the report card wrong:

> I built a lot of relationships with people I would not have necessarily reached out to. I ran my issues by them and got coaching. I had been an island.
>
> About a year later, my boss gave me a critical project to lead. If it didn't go well, that would be clear feedback. But he started including me in meetings, and I thought, *Clearly, I'm a strong contributor to the group, and they value me.*

A year after that, my director and some external partners were meeting. I was the most junior person in the room, and I was adamantly opposed to what the group wanted to do. I spoke my mind. The purchasing manager told my director, "Joy is someone to be afraid of!" and my director said, "She's the strongest person on my team." That's when I thought, *I'm pretty darn good.* I was on Cloud Nine.

Joy is going strong today, eight years at the company and a brand manager.

So What?

Joy needed that intervention to provoke her to face the fear holding her back. She could have left for a more harmonious culture somewhere else. Instead, she accepted the tough feedback and challenged herself.

Everything you do in a group situation—whether you speak or remain silent, take an action or do nothing—is a signal. Most of us are so focused on the discussion that we forget we're transmitting. All the time. Unless people know you well, they're not judging just your performance but your readiness for more leadership responsibility.

Don't kid yourself. Anytime you want to get to the next level of performance, there will be pain. Get ready to head into the uncomfortable zone where learning happens. Joy had to build bridges and reshape her network with people who could help. That took all three of Joy's strengths—ambition, grit, and love—plus courage.

One last note: This isn't a one-time thing. There will be more than a few heart-racing moments. Every day, there are opportunities to strengthen relationships or start new ones. Each meeting is a new opportunity to challenge. But with practice, it gets easier, like riding a bike—impossible the first time but eventually great fun.

STANDING UP FOR YOURSELF

You might hear "no," but you're better off asking. Both men and women who ask receive more than those who don't.

Jared was always responsible, the oldest of six. He was wired to work hard with his head down—ambitious to advance—but with a strong need for stability:

> I was homeschooled until seventh grade, interacting mostly with adults. When I wanted to go to a real school, my parents sent me to a private school for two years and then to a public high school. Those experiences—being able to be successful in three environments while maintaining a strong sense of myself—gave me confidence. I crave continuity and stability, but those transitions were not scary.
>
> My dad was an independent software consultant. As I was growing up, there was a lot of instability. That's why I've always had a big corporate job. I want to know that my company is going to be around tomorrow. Knowing that I have a stable core enables me to be open to other experiences. It helps me feel in control.

After two years working in a corporate environment, Jared ran into a pay and promotion freeze. He had been a good soldier, working hard and believing that all was well:

> I was getting great feedback, and I knew I was valued. But profitability was bad, and I had not been promoted. I felt betrayed! My performance had been compared to people two levels higher. A 10 percent raise would not have killed the company. I realized, *I have to take care of myself now.*
>
> It felt awkward. I had never pictured myself in this situation. It was tough to accept that no one was going to take care of me. I went to see the head of the office and said, "I value the great feedback and that clients value me, but it's not

showing up in my paycheck. Adjusted for inflation, I'm making only $2,000 more than when I started."

I could tell that he was surprised. He said, "You're right.
I'll look into it. Follow up with me if you don't hear back."
I felt in control as I left. He knew I wasn't happy; I had
successfully communicated that. I also felt angry—that was
how I overcame my awkwardness.

I did follow up. I had been ready to leave. When I received an off-cycle raise and promotion, I stayed. The disruption wasn't worth it.

Learning to stand up for himself served Jared well. In time, he advanced
to vice president in corporate communications—in a move to another
financial institution.

So What?

Not everyone feels comfortable speaking up about pay and performance.
It's disruptive, and that could be destabilizing. But it's part of the job.
Strong performance earns you the right to speak up. Of course, you must
do it well to avoid backlash.

Make your case strong but fair by arguing your value to the business.
Management doesn't have to take care of you, but they want the business to
thrive, and you're part of that. The stronger your case, the more likely you'll
prevail.

It's the sad truth that speaking up about pay or performance is harder
for women. Rehearse the conversation ahead. There's a fine line between
getting what you deserve and being misperceived. Present your point of
view with openness, neutrality, and positive framing. If you show how it's
good for the business and fair for you, you ought to find a ready audience.
You might hear "no," but you're better off asking. Both men and women
who ask receive more than those who don't.

Jared grew up that day. In taking a stand on his own behalf, he risked
instability, and that worried him. But in taking responsibility for himself,
Jared gained independence.

That's a pretty great trade-off, if you ask me.

THE REWARDS OF INDEPENDENCE

It takes courage to ask why things are done the way they are.
But it takes even more to do something about it.

Seckin grew up in Istanbul, an only child. His hardworking parents often came home late from the bank. Accordingly, Seckin was a latchkey kid. In return, he received a precious gift: independence:

> I learned to make decisions and accept the consequences. I learned to cook for myself and not to make a fire at home! Like making fries.
>
> I did it the way my mother did it. I remembered that she did not put the oil in the sink, but I forgot where she put it. I had a brilliant idea to throw it out the window into the garden. We were in an apartment. Our neighbor had her laundry hanging, and I burned it. I had to give two months of pocket money.

Independence stirred Seckin's curiosity and sense of adventure. He went to college in France on a scholarship and then to the United States for his MBA, gaining global experience afterward in consulting. When Seckin returned to Turkey, he joined a financial services firm in product management, with the difficult challenge of delivering growth in a stagnant market:

> I thought it was weird that banks offered our product or the competitor's, but not both. So I started to analyze why. I brought examples of products from other countries to our bank clients. I helped them launch the new products in Turkey.
>
> Then I expanded this approach to other countries. I relied on data that no one was using. Senior management gave me more countries to manage. Ultimately, with a team of seven, I covered over 20 markets. I learned how to lead by example,

how to manage the team. I gained an internal reputation for best practice.

From there, Seckin's boss's boss in Europe invited him to apply for a U.S. management role. She had just transferred to New York when she made the call:

> Frankly, I said, "I'd like to, but I don't know the American market at all." She told me that it would be a fair competition. If I didn't get it, I realized I would have more to learn. So I applied and went to New York to the interview. I am not nervous in interviews or customer meetings. I prepared notes. I asked myself very challenging questions. I was happy and excited, feeling blessed. But when I got back home, I told my wife they could easily get someone from New York instead of moving us and dealing with a visa process.
>
> After a customer meeting in Ukraine, I got a call from New York. I got the job! I was happy but stressed. I never believed they would give me that role. It would have been more consistent to transfer me to Europe.

Seckin then stepped up to his biggest leadership challenge yet with the help of his new team:

> I was now responsible for a product sales team, and I wanted to meet them, learn their expectations. I wanted to work hand in hand, knowing their aspirations, work styles, everything. I had only one thing in my mind: to be genuine and to be myself. I tried to pass on my high positive energy, to show that we were in it together.
>
> My team told me that I was transparent with no hidden agenda. Past managers did not try to have the team shine. I did this with respect, combined with intellectual curiosity, to learn from them. I am not ashamed to admit it. They have been in the market longer. If you will explain to me, I will be very attentive and fully listen. I always want to learn.

The more you meet with others, the more perspectives you get. You realize you are not right or wrong. You become more open and stop having just one idea that you radically support. Your judgment evolves.

Step by step, Seckin reached a senior position—never giving up on his desire to experience the world.

So What?

Seckin faced every leadership challenge as an opportunity for learning and creative problem solving. Curiosity is a gigantic breath of fresh air. It takes courage to ask why things are done the way they are. But it takes even more to do something about it.

Seckin also had a secret weapon: his teams. They helped him scale the business and move to a market he knew nothing about. Seckin absorbed everything his teams offered and questioned everything. Fantastic combination!

A learning mindset is the neon-lit billboard for this story. It propelled Seckin to challenge the status quo. It's also why Seckin reviews his week on Fridays. He said, "I question what I could improve. In 10 years, I want to be successful at work. But if I only work, I will not be. I could have failure in my relationships or physically. Being *very* successful would be better than *extremely* successful because of that." A happy workaholic like his parents, Seckin also made sure to pay attention to having a full life.

Naturally, learning to make margaritas for his wife was in his weekly improvement plan too.

THINKING FOR YOURSELF

Before you challenge, find ways to reduce your risks. Offering a solution is one. No one likes a person who only criticizes.

Bruce's voice is confident, independent, and persuasive. I was curious to learn where that came from. Born in a small New England town, Bruce described his childhood as "entirely regular":

I've always wanted to accomplish things and be challenged. I'm competitive. My little brother was fairly athletic. I wasn't into sports until I saw he was good at it! I've always pushed myself into situations where I was uncomfortable.

I had a lot of opportunities growing up. School was easy. Teachers would teach, and I'd be doing my homework during class so I'd have more free time for whatever I wanted to do later.

I remember my mom saying, one day, that she was never wrong and that I was a pain to challenge her. I told her, "You have to present the facts or logic if you want me to go along." Even back then, I always spoke up.

In high school, Bruce followed his parents to work for the same pharmaceutical company. HR persuaded him to study computer science in a college near headquarters. So he did, with a part-time job on the night shift. Bruce moved into information technology upon graduation.

Fifteen years later, Bruce was the youngest vice president in the company. He didn't advance simply because he worked hard. Taking a stand set him apart:

We were merging our company with another. IT consultants came in to present their recommended approach. Their pitch was to take over our entire infrastructure operations. Our management wouldn't have to worry about the new company after the merger. I thought, *There goes my job!* I suppose fear made me speak up!

My approach was different. I believed we could do it ourselves. My plan was a positive: it cost less and enabled better collaboration. That was a turning point in my career. They got rid of the outside vendor and put me in charge of the infrastructure integration. The next week, we flew to Germany. That was my first time outside the United States and the first time I had to present. I wondered if someone would figure out that I didn't know what I was doing.

As infrastructure team leader, Bruce reviewed the overall integration plan. He thought the consultant's plan was ridiculous, impractical:

> Everybody was saying, "You have to get behind it." I kept looking for the person with common sense who would realize that it was not possible in the time frame. When I didn't find that person, I was compelled. I called the senior guy. I gave him my background and then raised questions about the critical path. I told him what I thought. He started to listen. They changed the schedule, and he made me responsible. He still remembered that call 10 years later!
>
> You can't be satisfied that somebody else knows what you know and is in a position to ask questions you could ask. It might be just that you don't know the bigger picture or all the facts, but don't be afraid to voice your view to help. I'm highly sensitive to people's perception of me, but I don't let it hold me back from doing the right thing.

You might be thinking that twice is enough risk for one person. Bruce asked to join a senior meeting and spoke up a third time despite being warned not to by his boss:

> An IT supplier was pitching the dream of new tools, making it sound all too easy. The very senior meeting chair asked for people's reactions. Everyone kept their heads down. Most were just hoping not to be called on! I spoke up and said we already had the tools and the solution. The hard work was coming together to use it in the right way to get the value.
>
> The chair looked down the table and asked who I was. I explained, and then she said, "I'm going to lean on you and make sure you deliver." I'm always looking to surpass people's limitations on me.

The meeting chair, also CEO of the company, gave Bruce a new role reporting directly to her.

So What?

Bruce's ambition and independent thinking are energizing. Now if that attitude is something you'd like more of, listen up. I'm not advocating speaking out willy-nilly. Be measured and thoughtful. Line up your ducks before challenging the crowd.

Start by aligning your interests with the company's. That makes it a win-win. Ignore what everyone else thinks. Sometimes they're dead wrong. If you think you're right, get clear on your logic and gather the facts. Appreciate that if someone else's case is strong enough, you ought to change your view.

Before you challenge, find ways to reduce your risks. Offering a solution is one. No one likes a person who only criticizes. Frankly, that guy is a pain! Use a more nuanced alternative to direct challenge, like asking questions. To increase your effectiveness, treat others with respect. Put your money where your mouth is, and something wonderful could happen.

Get ready. Standing out may land you an opportunity you don't yet know about.

TAKING ON YOUR
LEADERSHIP CHALLENGE

As you grow, you're going to take stands. You've probably already done so at least once. Remember the time when everybody else stepped back, and so there you were, standing out? Challenging? Good for you!

The tales in this chapter of daring to challenge hold the tensions between raw ambition and paralyzing self-doubt, a need to fit in and a need to be heard. That's why it's so hard. Inch-deep advice such as, "Just do it" doesn't do it. Anne made it look easy, but she practiced her entire childhood. Martin had to overcome a physical impediment and the mindset that came with it. Joy had to face a career-limiting fear. Jared, Seckin, and Bruce learned to challenge by focusing on the opportunity.

Standing out is part of growing into a courageous leader with a vision of how things should be. Anyone wanting to make an impact enters this arena. Here are your next steps.

Understand What You're Choosing to Do

If taking a stand feels risky and uncomfortable, it is. Before avoiding one, think strategically. Explore your opportunity in terms of your aspirations, career, and what draws you in:

- *Analyze the spotlight.* Before taking your stand, nail your day job. Remember, that's the core of your evaluation. What's the second thing? Still your day job. Then assess your stand-out opportunity, with four criteria:

    - *Right thing to do:* Does this help the company—and should it be done?

    - *Energizing:* Is it exciting to you, with significant potential for impact?

    - *Visible:* Will the impact be visible to senior management?

    - *Probability for success:* Can you deliver on this extra work and do it well?

- *Psyche yourself up.* In other words, perform a Jedi mind trick on yourself. Adopt a positive mindset that gives you courage and confidence.

    - *Uncover your limiting mindset.* It's holding you back from standing out (as in, *Speaking up will get me fired*). It's often entrenched, hiding beneath another mindset that feels justified (as in, *Junior people should show respect by remaining silent*).

    - *Observe it by standing in the shoes of a third party.* Get curious about how that mindset helps you but limits you. For example, it may be stopping you from blurting out half-baked ideas, but it may also be stopping you from ever speaking up.

    - *Reframe from fear to ambition.* Choose a different mindset that enables different behaviors (such as, *I can make this great idea happen*). The mindset you choose is one you have in different circumstances, when fear isn't present. It worked for you there and can work for you here.

○ *Visualize your new behaviors.* When you replace your mindset in this situation, different behaviors will naturally result. How do you feel now? Can you see yourself taking action?

Prepare to Stand Out

Practicing presence has an outsized impact for minimal effort. It readies you for action. Don't cram the night before you intend to speak up. Practice your presence repeatedly—in rehearsal and situations that carry less emotion for you—to expand your range of comfort:

● *Use others to embolden yourself.* Seeing yourself through others' eyes will help disabuse you of constraining mindsets.

○ *Set your goals.* State your short-term goals clearly and consider whether you've got the right coach for those goals. If not, find the right one!

○ *Know who you are at your best.* Ask a few managers who know your work to comment on what you do well, who you are when you're at your best, and what you could do to be at your best more of the time. Share this feedback with your coach too.

○ *Do what your coach suggests.* If you stumble, don't blame anybody—not your coach and not yourself. Stumbles are great learning moments. Thank your coach for it.

● *Get your ducks in a row.* You've made your decision so get the facts. Otherwise, it's your opinion versus anyone else's. People notice the individual who opposes the status quo. That's the definition of standing out.

○ *Figure out your stand.* Challenging others is like lobbing a grenade into the meeting. There are many other ways to take a stand. Consider engaging one by one ahead of the meeting, connecting with the meeting chair by phone and e-mail, joining or leading a task force to develop the recommendations. Draft your messages in bullet points and have your elevator pitch ready.

○ *Do your homework and make your plan.* Don't assume everyone else is wrong. Ask around, get the facts, and check your thinking. If your facts stack up, turn it into a business case that considers the challenges, alternative views, and solutions. No one wants to hear complaints or problems. Clarify what would have to be true to take this recommended direction. Find a trusted sounding board.

● *Rehearse in the rehearsal room.**To warm up, practice in front of a mirror to see yourself in action. Then take a cell-phone video of yourself, or better yet, ask friends to help you. Go well beyond your comfort zone. Practice standing at the front of the room to compose yourself before speaking. Practice speaking loudly and softly, quickly and slowly. Experiment with different emotions such as being authoritative versus friendly. Expand your range to increase your impact.

● *Practice regaining your composure after an adrenaline rush.* Start using your mindfulness practice ahead of time. You're going to need it in the moment—and right after. To recap:

○ Sit up comfortably—head on spine and back straight, with your body at rest (untangle your legs and arms). Close your eyes and turn inward. For a few minutes, take a deep breath in on the count of four, and breathe out deeply on the count of six. Do that a few times.

○ Reflect on what you hope to create. Set your intention—for example, *I will be an active contributor to the discussion.* Repeat this practice in a quiet space before walking into the meeting (the washroom works well!). Hopefully, you feel calmer and alert.

● *Get ready, get set.* Prepare open-ended, exciting questions that get other people engaged without cornering them. Examples include: "What does great look like?" or its opposite, "What are the 'black swan' events we're missing?" Be ready if someone throws the question back at you.

---

* Thanks are due to Claude Stein, a voice coach and gifted facilitator who taught me this term. If you've been an actor or performer, you know. For everybody else, imagine a safe place where you can experiment, where you are showered with support, and where you can only succeed.

Step Forward

Speaking up is just the tip of the iceberg. Taking a stand involves your words, voice, stance, delivery, and ownership—your whole being:

- *Be in the moment.* As you enter the situation, remember your intention, feel your emotion, and purposefully form connections to the others. Take your time. You want to be alert and focused, able to shift in the moment.

  - *Gain your composure.* When you feel strongly about an issue, it's normal to raise your pitch or speed up. It's also normal to show nervousness through unsettled physical movements. None of that helps your case. This is where mindfulness comes in. Use it.

  - *Get used to the headlights.* The first time you're in a tense situation, you may feel shock. You can make this heart-racing situation easier with a mantra you've practiced, like "I've been thinking" or "Here's a different way to look at it." Or take a few deep breaths.

  - *Engage others with respect.* Listen actively, paraphrasing to show that you're hearing what's been said. Look for ways to connect the dots between what others are saying. Position your perspective in the positive. Paint the picture of what could be, and listen to the responses you receive.

  - *Regain your center.* After speaking up in the meeting, use the same rhythmic breathing to slow your heart rate and direct your focus.

- *Stay with it.* Once you've taken your stand, you have a responsibility to help the organization move forward. Own that.

  - *Respond with lightning speed.* Become superb at handling the follow-up, in the moment or right after, to resolve a misunderstanding or answer a question. Use a line such as, "Here is what I understand from what you've said. Please check my thinking." Be confident in the fix.

  - *Figure out the next steps and take the lead.* You've started a chain reaction. Now take the lead in reaching a better solution. It probably involves working with others, so welcome the opportunity.

- *Give yourself some credit.* You've survived the rush, and you'll do even better the next time. Your heart will soon resume its natural pace, and the thinking part of your brain will restart.

Stepping forward and standing out make you a more compelling, more inspiring, and more human leader. That's when you're in the game. There is a seat at the table for you. People are watching and listening.

And in *this* game, your chance for positive impact has just skyrocketed.

LOVE FEAR HOPE DESPAIR
PURPOSE PRESSURE
MISTAKE REVIEW
BRING PEOPLE ON BOARD
BULLIES JERKS
TAKE A STAND
RISK SELF-DOUBT
SUPER   ENERGY
MEN   R S NSOR
LOVE FE   DESPAIR
PURP   ESSURE
MISTAKE REVIEW
BRING PEOPLE ON BOARD

9

When Risk Taking Feels Like Jumping Off a Cliff

When asked, most executives wish they had taken more risk early in their careers. Easy to say when they're at the top! What stopped them? You too probably take less risk than is good for your career or your company.

How do you know which ones to take? You don't ever really know. Some risks are invisible. Sometimes, not doing anything is the biggest risk. Everything turns out to be a risk! That's why exposure to risk taking helps, as does learning from people who took bold risks. It's great when they succeed. We learn even more when they crash. We get a thrill in both cases, and we get a better understanding of the line between acceptable and crazy.

Jessica learned to take risk in steps, doing her dream job: news journalism. She accepted a risky assignment to interview two media moguls:

> I had a wonderful editor who encouraged me to go after this story of an unraveling relationship. Had I stepped back to ask, "Why on earth would this person talk to me?" or "What on earth is he going to say anyway?" then I probably would not have done it. But with the suggestion planted, I went for it. I decided I was going to get this billionaire mogul to give me the whole story. I was definitely scrappy about working

the angles to get the interview. I faxed a letter and used my connections. A long shot, but it worked!

I have a tendency to say way too much in an interview. I remember thinking, *Be quiet and let him talk.* There would be great stuff if I let him meander. I was recording *and* taking backup notes. I was nervous, but it was a killer interview! Then I called the second person and got his version. I remember sitting in a tiny chair in his massive office. He was taken aback by what the first mogul had said.

With the help of my editor, I wrote a story that ran on the front page. It wasn't my first front page, but it was my story with the biggest impact to date. I was nervous about potential fallout. I still get nervous to this day thinking about it. Nervous and excited.

Jessica's early exposure to risk inspired her to take more. A few years later, she left her prestigious job to start up an online tech publication with deeply reported articles and industry scoops:

I had begun to question my goals. I left because I had a desire for a product like this, to have more impact on the news industry, to become a better reporter, and to operate a news organization of consequence. My thoughts went from it being a hobby for fun to something I could not stop thinking about.

I own my company 100 percent, and I am betting that it will become a publication in a modern way with the impact of the business newspapers. I'm trying to have a team of people writing smart stuff, making the world smarter. I love news. I love being on the team, meeting people, and networking. This is the life I want.

Steady experience taking risk helped Jessica walk out of an established and well-respected institution. For her, it was a good trade-off. What about you? These stories can help you stretch:

- *How can risk taking enhance your work experience?* Simon moved from Paris to New York for an exciting development in his career, only he hadn't yet found the job.

- *How do you choose which risk to take?* Unemployed with rising debts to pay, Brandee had to choose between two very different job offers.

- *How can you make risk less risky?* Jenni was ready to give everything up to join her new wife on their passion project.

- *What if your risk is genuinely risky?* To succeed in his dream job, Robert made a big investment others argued against.

- *How can you make risk painless?* Kevin's first startup took off like a rocket and then flamed out, which is when his second chapter began.

At work, risks are waiting for you with no guaranteed outcomes but chances to soar. The first time you take a big risk, you're far from your comfort zone—maybe all the way to the terror zone. Sure, sometimes risks take you south. No one looks forward to that. But if you avoid all risk, you'll never do a thing.

Imagine yourself on a conference stage at the pinnacle of your career. The interviewer asks, "Looking back, what is your one regret? What would you have liked to tell your younger self?" You'll pause. With a satisfied smile, you'll say: "I have no regrets. I told myself to take more risk. And I did."

HEADING GLADLY INTO THE UNKNOWN

Meet a heck of a lot of people. Not everybody pans out, but you're not playing for a high score. Low scorers can win.

Simon was an extravert, a lucky break given his place in line as number three of eight children! In France, the best students compete in prestigious preparatory schools to succeed in the national competition for university spots. Simon got into prep school, which was his first—small—risk:

> I am not more stupid than others, but I had to work and work to catch up. For six months in school, I was thinking,

People are way better than me. By the second year, I was doing OK. During the final exams, I was playing the game with everybody, and I saw that I could win the match.

After that experience, my work has been driven by the conviction that if you want something and you work hard, you can do it. You have to understand the code and the game. You have to trust that you can play. You can lose three or even five rounds, but there is no reason you cannot catch up.

When it came time for business school, Simon chose a riskier three-year program in three countries, speaking three languages! Students had to find their own work by persuading companies to give them a job. So Simon grew adept at taking risks:

It was mind broadening. The hardest thing is to understand how to interact. Others don't think the way you think, behave the way you do. To be accepted and make friends, you have to adapt to the culture.

I did a nine-month internship, always working on a computer. Afterward, I wanted to do something different. There is a website for people who need sailing crew members. I found a company that wanted its boat conveyed from France to Brazil. It was 40 days on the boat with a guy I didn't know, with nothing in common other than our passion for sailing.

My mother and my girlfriend's mother were scared, but people think it's crazier than it actually was. We had some tough moments, but we made it work.

Simon got comfortable with risk. When he married, his wife and he wanted to move. They agreed that when one got a job offer, the other would follow. His wife received a transfer to New York, and Simon was delighted. He turned down his consulting firm's invitation to transfer, too. It was a chance to explore other industries and start fresh. As Simon waited for a work permit, he began to network:

I wasn't scared. I had never been to the United States before, and I was excited to discover the New World. The labor market was pretty good, so there was no reason not to find a job. It was all new. Everything was possible, and I love meeting people!

I arrived in New York, a little French guy, and I contacted people I knew—business school mates, my cousin, former work colleagues. I asked questions but also presented myself. You have to so that people spend time on your request. It's harder for people to bounce off your idea without something concrete. I said I was exploring media, sports, entertainment, luxury, consulting, and consumer goods. It was not the time to close doors. I did it consciously, as I didn't know what would come out of it. That first circle of 10 gave me access to new people or ideas for networking. I met some people in financial services because that's what I had been doing before. I got an offer, but I turned it down.

In the second circle, I had 30 brief discussions. From there, I went into the third circle knowing exactly what to ask. You can get very specific, and you get interviews in a bunch of companies. I was close to 100 contacts but ready to learn more.

Eventually, someone from a consumer goods company offered Simon a strategy job with a promise to move into marketing. A few years later, Simon advanced to global brand manager for a new product launching around the world. Promise kept.

So What?

Once Simon turned networking into a game, playing the game was fun. Gamification can make a challenge feel less risky. Start by packaging your experiences in a way that makes you interesting. Craft the pitch: industries and roles that interest you and why you're a good bet. Practice your delivery with friends. Then cast a wide net, asking for referrals who become your second circle. Their contacts become your third circle. As you progress, you'll gain insight into what you really want.

Part of the game is making the mother of all trackers to monitor progress. Include the people you meet, e-mails sent, salient facts, and contact information because you'll never remember everything.

This game works, by the way. Not everybody you meet pans out, but you're not playing for a high score. Low scorers can win. Play well and you'll have at least one intriguing job offer and a few long-term work relationships.

Game on!

AFTER THE FALL

Set fear aside for the moment and consider your long-term horizon.
Which opportunity creates more positive energy?

Brandee's story of risk taking started with her great-grandfather, who was a bootlegger. Her grandfather died young of a heart attack. Understandably, her father played it safer—working in finance for the state government. But, the eldest of five daughters, Brandee was a risk taker:

> In the fifth grade, I saw boys picking on a boy who was overweight and challenged. The biggest bully spiked him with a volleyball. I felt horrible. I had felt empathy for him before, but I never had the balls to act. The tipping point was seeing the boy's bleeding nose. I punched the bully so hard his nose split open.
>
> Well, I was walked to the principal's office and had to have lunch with him. He said, "I think you did the right thing. You didn't do it for yourself. You were sticking up for someone." I told my mom, and she agreed. From then on, I felt really confident. And the boys were scared of me.

In time, Brandee earned a doctorate and became a pharmacist, working in retail, mail order, and nursing homes. The work bored her, so when her best friend suggested a contract job in a pharmaceutical company, Brandee jumped. That was a great move, but the contract ended four months later:

My manager said, "We love you. We think you're great. But we don't have a job for you." I cried myself to sleep every night for a month. I thought, *Oh, my God, I made a mistake. I had a great job before. Maybe I should call them up and ask for it back.* My husband was in law school, and we had just bought a town house. I was afraid of not being able to pay our mortgage. We had student loans. Money was the scary thing, but returning to my uninspiring job was even more dreadful!

I was willing to gut it out to find a job I wanted. I interviewed at two companies. I got a really good offer for a full-time job with more money at the first one. But I really connected with the hiring manager at the second. He offered me a short-term contract job that same day.

The first company felt like a morgue. The energy was stifling. If I wanted the safe bet, I would choose that. That would have been a fear-based decision. But I didn't want to be part of a toxic environment. It didn't feel right. And I had gotten used to discomfort.

Part of what got me through was listening to myself. I wanted to achieve through inspiring others. I wanted people to bring their ideas to the table. I wanted to be a visionary.

Brandee accepted the contract job without assured long-term security. A few months later, it became a permanent position. In time, Brandee advanced to become a medical director in her pharmaceutical group, driving strategy through cross-functional collaboration—visionary stuff.

So What?

Fear drove Brandee to want the stable, higher-paying, secure job. Longing to be inspired propelled her to the other. A contract job was clearly less optimal in the short term, but a longer horizon helped Brandee make a love-based decision. Of course, a breadwinner with young children at home might choose the safer bet—not because of fear but out of love for the family.

If you're simply afraid of the risk, that's fear talking. Set it aside for the moment and consider your long-term horizon. Which opportunity creates more positive energy? What new possibilities might be revealed next? What joy does it stir in you?

Before heading for safety, consider that.

LIVING AND WORKING IN TECHNICOLOR

What's on your bucket list? How could you test that?
Plan a rapid prototype experiment to limit risk.

After two years in investment banking, Jenni walked away:

> I absolutely hated it. I had no control over my time. Saturdays I would work a full day. Sundays I would go to church, have lunch, and then work till 10 p.m. I didn't like the work. It required tons of concentration. It was repetitive.
>
> My Taiwanese parents wanted me to make money, but I almost lost my life doing that. I want to either make an impact at work or have my work make an impact in the world. So I took almost a year off to do volunteer work overseas.
>
> It was scary because I worried that I wouldn't get another job. When I returned, I lived at home. My parents said, "Get out of the house! At least go try to find something!" My friend helped me write a cover letter and get the job at this tech company.

Five years later, Jenni considered her next risky decision. The company offered a one-month sabbatical, but she wanted more time to make a film with her wife about being LGBT. Planning to quit, Jenni told a friend who encouraged her to ask for a leave instead:

> I pitched the break as a passion project. Something terrible usually happens to gays in movies created elsewhere in the world. We wanted to show stories of hope. There were no role models, especially people of color, to give kids a vision of what life could be.

We started interviewing LGBT leaders in the area. A dozen interviews helped me crystallize what we would do: blogging, filming, and traveling the world to give LGBT leaders a voice.

Taking a year off work to make the film was inherently risky. And Jenni did not have either money or experience to make a film! That said, the experience inspired Jenni to ask for more from work and life:

> It was just an idea. But when you hold on to an idea that other people get behind, it becomes so much more than you thought it would be. At the end of the day, somebody is going to tell you it's a horrible idea, the worst idea. You have to get over it. You put your heart in something. Someone says, "You're being selfish." That hurts. I think that the people who make a real difference in the world have to disappoint someone.
>
> I have this amazing fortune. You ask yourself, *What am I on this earth to do?* The answer is just in front of you. For me, it's my experience—being an Asian American, raised religiously, and coming out.
>
> My biggest dread would be to spend the next 30 years climbing the corporate ladder. My ambition has not gone away. I still care about my career and want to make director. I was deferring too much to my boss. For example, in a meeting I did not add anything to a conversation because everyone was more senior. Now I realize I know things they don't know. I had to embolden myself.
>
> It's something I struggle with: I bind myself and think I can only do this much. My boss never made me feel like I couldn't advance. I had to be assertive enough to make it clear that this is what I wanted and work toward it.

When Jenni did assert herself, she made director—twice, in the movies and at work.

So What?

Jenni's experience taught her how to mitigate risk. Pursuing a passion project is a much smaller risk than quitting a good job. By designing and testing the project before pitching it to her management, Jenni reduced the risk further. That test helped make her case. During the sabbatical, Jenni shaped her vision to integrate social impact into work in partnership with her wife. She learned that the biggest risk would be waiting too long.

What dreams do you have? What have you postponed that you wish you could do? How could you test that? Plan a rapid prototype experiment to limit risk. It might lead to something wonderful.

The universe might just hear you.

A FIGHTER AND AN UNDERDOG WALK INTO A BAR

He also knew that if he kept doing what he didn't want to do, he would surely fail.

Robert was a C student in middle school. His dad said that Robert's brother was book smart but Robert was street smart. Those words fired up his competitive drive. He moved to the top of the class and in college took his first risk, which naturally led to more:

> I majored in finance. Television seemed like a dream. But I wrote a spec script with friends, and we read it in front of the class. It was empowering to get people to laugh. I developed a style and voice that made my papers engaging. It gave me confidence to find something I really did well.
>
> Because I had had a lot of success in school, I took the risk of trying to get into television. I wanted to be a sitcom writer, and I became a television intern. It was blind ambition! I was neurotic. I overstudied and overprepared. I have a curiosity to take things apart and understand how to rebuild them in a better way.

Funny how things work out. Five years in, Robert was a bored television assistant, going nowhere. He had to take more risk:

> I was in my late twenties without a career and without the confidence I had in college. In the wake of another failure, I applied for an MBA and put down a deposit. To make some money, I took a temp job at a small entertainment company.
>
> Three months later, they were starting up a TV management group. I told the head guy I wanted to run it or I'd quit. Fear drove me. I knew I had something he needed. I didn't love business school, and this was my last chance. I had nothing to lose.
>
> He gave me the job, and I stayed.

Robert got a few shows on the air and parlayed his achievement into a better job at a bigger company with higher stakes:

> In every job I feel like I should be the best again. Competition should be part of the culture. People get used to pumping out the same things and don't try to push the envelope. That bothers me. Complacency drives me crazy!
>
> Well, the creator of a show I grew up watching came to pitch an idea. We didn't buy it, but I ran after him to invite him to lunch. We had lunch and talked for hours. I asked if he would ever do a remake of his first show. He said, "No, that's crazy. But what about—?" We dogged down the rights. The script came in. People hated it.
>
> There was a point where everyone said, "No way are we making this pilot!" When I know I'm right, I'm gonna fight to the end. I don't care if you fire me—you better hear me out or I'll get really upset. If you don't understand, you aren't seeing my vision. If you're not hearing my opinion, then what's my value?
>
> I got a meeting together and got the pilot greenlighted. We had conflict all throughout. I had fights with my boss, my boss's boss, the president, at times heated. I willed this thing to go. At some point, they got on board. They got jazzed.

Robert wholeheartedly believed the show would be a success. And it was.

So What?

A lot of industries are inherently risky, including the entertainment business. In that environment, Robert took even more risk to fight for his show—committing fully. That fueled his competitive juices and creativity.

Although Robert had the courage to take big risks, he wasn't fearless. He worried about things not working out, just as the rest of us do. He also knew that if he kept doing what he didn't want to do, he would surely fail. That makes him a dreamer but not a romantic. Robert said, "I don't believe you don't give up on your dream. At some point, you do give up. But other dreams would make you happy."

Call that pragmatic dreaming. Fully commit to your dream; keep the runner-up in reserve.

FAILING FOR A LIVING

Don't trivialize failure. It's more painful than anyone lets on.
No amount of sugarcoating lessens the hurt.

Kevin is the ultimate entrepreneur, son of a commercial mariner from Hong Kong. Today, he is a sought-after advisor with an MD, a PhD, and a record of successful venture capital deals. Back in ninth grade, Kevin started his first company—by accident:

> We set up a website to play computer games and ended up getting a lot of traffic. Someone wanted to give us a few million dollars to fund it, so we took the meeting and then the money! I was running the company and hiring people. I didn't know what direction I was going in. I failed.
>
> When the company collapsed, I had to lay off the staff. It was bizarre to fire people 10 or 15 years older. It was depressing. I didn't think I could mess up any more than that, but it helped me. I ended up taking a more nontraditional path.

It was one of the reasons the hedge fund owner found me, and we created a relationship. More doors opened to me.

My mom was not amused when I worked at the hedge fund during high school. She wanted me to go to medical school. Then when my fund made a lot of money, my mom was upset that I left for medical school!

Despite the pain of failure, risk taking drives Kevin. When his wounds healed from the failed website, he had a new and better idea:

I was getting my undergraduate and graduate degrees at the same time. I started doing some healthcare policy work, and from there I started a medical device company. The whole healthcare system was so dysfunctional that I had to try.

It took a lot of work to build something worthwhile. It was very frustrating—it was very difficult to raise money or create revenue! People assumed it went really well, but it was the opposite. We ended up being acquired by an Israeli company working on the same thing.

Risks are scary, and failure is painful. Still, Kevin believes it's worth it, at minimum for the learning:

When Marissa Mayer was being considered for Yahoo!, I asked my friends, "If someone offered you that job, would you take it?" My philosophy has always been to take it. You'll learn a ton no matter what.

One of my biggest fears is the perfect storm where everything collapses at once. A defense mechanism is that I take on a lot of projects because I have a high fail rate. I don't want things to fall apart and leave me with nothing. At the university, I was taking eight classes and refusing to drop any. At the same time, we were working on the company and not getting traction. I was in a messy relationship. Eventually the school forced me to drop a class I would have failed. I was depressed, but I wouldn't get help. It's hard to admit that I need it.

Culturally, many Asians keep their dirty laundry a secret. You don't show you're vulnerable until you cannot keep it together. A lot of this is in my own head. I believe people are viewing me in a certain way, and I'm constantly trying to live up to that expectation.

Kevin dreams of changing the way healthcare is delivered. Fired up once more, Kevin joined a leading tech company to work on cutting-edge healthcare projects—his biggest risk yet.

So What?

When risks go south, failure can feel catastrophic. Don't trivialize failure. It's more painful than anyone lets on. No amount of sugarcoating lessens the hurt. That said, Kevin learned to recover in order to try again.

To help you recover, turn to friends and, if you have one, a sponsor with relevant experience taking risks. If depression settles in, please get professional help. Failure is a genuine loss. Skip the grieving step at your peril. The passage of time will lessen your pain, but the right support speeds up the process.

Keep in mind that your next dream—one that's well worth doing—is just around the corner. Odds are very good that you'll fall in love again.

---------------------- TAKING ON YOUR ----------------------

RISK CHALLENGE

Risk taking is a fantastic and necessary part of your development at work. Choose a job, take an assignment, meet a new boss, accept a move—every job-related decision carries a risk, even in stable companies. We're not talking about betting-the-farm risk, which puts the company in jeopardy or your life on the line. Some people cross that line, but only the survivors look smart.

You can find a happy medium between suicidal thrill seeking and 100 percent safety. Build your risk-taking capability in steps. Jessica learned to take risks at a prestigious, secure job before taking the leap. Simon learned to turn risk taking into a game. Brandee used a love-based rubric to accept more risk. Jenni mitigated risk by taking a sabbatical. Robert understood how full commitment was less risky than going halfway. Kevin tolerated a high failure rate by keeping more irons in the fire.

No matter what your starting point is, you'll increase your comfort with risk taking by gaining experience. Consider these four recommendations.

Make Your Decision

Come to grips with what really matters to you. It helps to have a colleague or friend be your coach. He or she will push you past lazy thinking and obvious answers:

- *Find your courage.* Ground yourself in your strengths from the start by looking back on a high point experience. It could be an achievement that you didn't think possible. Maybe others didn't believe you could do it either. You operated at your best. You felt proud, confident in your value. Notice how you feel in this place of greater courage. Make your decision with that grounding.

- *Clarify what you want.* You can't have it all at once, so choose what's important to you on this list: money, prestige, flexibility, hours, travel (or staying put), learning, variety, great colleagues, innovation and creativity, skill-building, impact, or something else. Take two items on your list and choose the one you prefer. Keep trading off until you find the most important things you won't give up. For example, flexibility might beat money, but learning might beat flexibility. That's what you want more. Can your current position provide it?

- *Begin to shape your goals.* What are you looking for? You don't have to be politically correct. Your goal doesn't have to be forever. It doesn't have to be worthy of a billboard. It just has to be big enough to stir up *your* conviction, courage, and self-motivation. If you're starting from scratch without an idea, involve your friends to dream a bit. Learn about dreams other people have. Get started by declaring something even if you're not sure.

- *Stand in that future's upside.* Three years from now, what do you hope you'll have accomplished? What new options does that mission create? If the job turns out to be what you hoped for, what becomes possible for you? And what else? And what else? Keep asking until your upside explodes into ridiculously grand possibilities. This is not the time for practicality (or thinking small).

- *Compare that to today's downside.* Imagine that you stay in your current job. Can your current job be a stepping stone to that future? What happens over the next three years? Maybe your first thought is, *Phew, I avoided a risk, and that's a relief.* Keep going. If you feel thrilled or energized, look closer. You might feel otherwise—bored, depressed, stale. Where does that lead you? Compare the upside of the new challenge with the downside of not acting. How does the risky decision look now?

- *Do one final check before jumping off.* It's deliciously evil fun to imagine the worst. Surround yourself with friends to gather multiple perspectives. Describe your pending decision. Then ask each person to offer up a worst-case, nightmare scenario. It has to be one that would keep you up at night and have at least a 1 percent chance of happening. (Martians are not allowed, as fun as that might be.) Determine how to mitigate each risk.

- *Confirm your decision.* Assume you go forward. Sleep on it. Take the time to let it sink in. Envision your decision as having taken effect. This is your last chance to make a calculated risk.

Commit to Your Decision

Sometimes, your risk feels incredibly bold. Make it stick by declaring it to yourself and your network—out loud and with conviction:

- *Declare your decision to yourself.* If you've committed to skydiving but are paralyzed at 12,000 feet, sit back down. Return to the decision in a few months and revisit the process. You may get a second chance. If the opportunity is gone, learning your risk profile will help you jump next time around. But if you're ready to jump now:

  - *Do the equivalent of burning bridges.* No doubt about it: the possibility of failure looms no matter how well you prepare. If you always have an option to retreat, you won't fully commit. So face forward because it is your only option.

○ *Choose a growth mindset.* If you're seeking perfection, you've already begun to undermine yourself. If you're seeking positive impact, you'll most likely have some. If you're seeking to grow, you will no matter how it goes.

○ *Set a daily intention of learning.* Intention helps you pay attention to what is important. It sharpens your focus for the day, in a chaotic meeting, or at the end of a tough week.

- *Tell your network.* Get some support and counsel for the journey. Be thoughtful about whom you turn to and what you say. You don't want naysayers to drain you, and you don't want to overshare, but you do want to declare yourself.

Build Your Resolve

You're about to board the plane for your jump. There are a few things you can to do make this trip great. Pack a safety kit, for starters:

- *Start before you leave.* Learn everything you can about the opportunity before you officially start. Move up the learning curve before you leave your current job. If you've prepared well, by the time you start, you'll feel ready.

- *Meet everyone you can.* The best opportunity to meet new people is before you jump. That's because you have more leeway to ask questions. Make it your business to expand your network. You never know who will become an ally, mentor, or sponsor, so treat everyone without judgment and with respect.

- *Set up your support.* Stepping into the unknown stirs up fear. Find a partner, buddy, or support group to lean on. No one ever said that you had to go it alone.

Do or Do Not

There is no try! You're either doing this or moving on. If you've made the decision and still nothing is happening, pause to consider the power that you've relinquished to fear:

- *Name it.* Sometimes, naming the fear that stops you from acting disarms it. If that's not enough, write a letter to it or remind yourself to leave fear at home while you move forward. If fear paralyzes you, please seek professional help to gain the support you deserve.

- *Hold up the mirror.* If you've never gone skydiving even though you wanted to, how does it feel to forgo adventure—again? How many times do you want to sit on the sidelines and watch other people do what you want to do? Summon that internal coach to help you leave the safety of the plane.

- *Reboot when you need to.* If you're having second thoughts, return to the fundamental question: *Why do I want to do this?* Remember what motivated you, what others said, and how you felt. Retrace your logic. Check how you feel now. If those motivations and conditions are still in place, you know what to do.

- *Remember to breathe and enjoy it.* This is the part folks forget. You're now officially on the adventure. That's exciting!

What's the worst that can happen? Usually, what actually happens is far less frightening than what we imagine.* You'll fall down. It will hurt. You'll feel some negative emotions for a while, like embarrassment. It won't be easy to bounce back. But you will.

Keep in mind that losing streaks do not last forever. (Neither do winning streaks.) Take a break but then pick yourself up, dust yourself off, and go back into that arena to make something great happen.†

---

* Find Daniel Gilbert's research on why we make bad decisions in his book *Stumbling on Happiness* (Alfred A. Knopf, New York, 2006) or just watch his TED Talk at www.ted .com/talks/dan_gilbert_asks_why_are_we_happy.

† Teddy Roosevelt had the gift of inspiring people to greatness. If you're in need of some inspiration, read this excerpt from his 1910 speech "Citizen in a Republic": "It is not the critic who counts; not the man who points out how the strong man stumbles, or where the doer of deeds could have done them better. The credit belongs to the man who is actually in the arena, whose face is marred by dust and sweat and blood; who strives valiantly; who errs, who comes short again and again, because there is no effort without error and shortcoming; but who does actually strive to do the deeds; who knows great enthusiasms, the great devotions; who spends himself in a worthy cause; who at the best knows in the end the triumph of high achievement, and who at the worst, if he fails, at least fails while daring greatly, so that his place shall never be with those cold and timid souls who neither know victory nor defeat." A shout-out to Brené Brown for her book that draws its title from Roosevelt's speech: *Daring Greatly* (Gotham Books, New York, 2012).

10

When You Have to Be a Superhero

There are times when you look back and think, "I have no clue how I did that. That was [amazing, the greatest thing ever, a miracle]!" You thought it couldn't happen. But when something stirred inside, you knew you were going to do this. It was a ridiculously impossible assignment. You stood up to the organization and changed its course in some way. How it happened is a mystery, but you were unbelievably courageous—a fool, more likely a hero.

Take Shannon's case. She's been looking after herself since she was 17 years old. That's when Shannon left home in the middle of the night, after another violent fight with her father. Taking along her mother and twin sister, Shannon stayed with friends. She then found a job to support them.

So Shannon is one to take on tough challenges without regret, as she did a year into her recent job in digital marketing at a leading pharmaceutical company:

> I took this project by the horns! The program had been run by 10 people. People had been fired or promoted as a result of working on it. The team had been dismantled. Now they were trying to hire new team members. I was pretty much on it by myself with some external support.

We had to be more creative—not just repeat the old way of doing things. I told them we had to go big or go home. That made some people uncomfortable. I prefer not to just phone it in but rather, take a big risk. Either it's phenomenally successful, or it's not. Strategically, I felt we would have mediocrity if we just fiddled along. We had to catch up. So I pushed the envelope.

With the strength of 10, Shannon finished what others couldn't—turning the digital marketing program into a great success:

It was pure, unadulterated hell. I just didn't let go. Even when it felt like things were not going to get done, I worked through the night and didn't let anything drop. You want to bring everyone with you, but you have to get work done. I had to manage expectations and politics. It was a high-stress environment. I slowly started winning them over with smaller risks. For example, I hired a creative agency completely the opposite of what they were used to.

I've always been very scrappy. As soon as there is an opportunity to achieve things, I want to get 100 percent. It proved to senior leadership that I could do a good job and could be trusted to run this all by myself.

Shannon presented the project to the CEO. The *New York Times* wrote a story on it. And she was promoted two months later.

The heroes in the five stories that follow, like Shannon, displayed fortitude, courage, and belief in a mission much bigger than themselves. Hopefully, they will persuade you that taking on superhero challenges is worthwhile:

- *How do you become a superhero?* Born on a tiny island far away, David's journey eventually took him to New York and a profession he had only dreamed of.

- *What happens when you stand up to leadership?* Alessandra found skeletons in the closet, but only she was brave enough to do something about it.

- *What do you do when both work and life threaten you?* Two demons plagued Elizabeth: a mysterious kidney disease and a boss she called "the Devil Incarnate."

- *How do you take the ultimate stand?* With a radical market strategy in hand, Sam overcame resistance from the entire organization.

- *What happens when you battle the supervillains within?* As James experienced extraordinary success, fear threatened to destroy it all.

Superheroes fully embrace risk taking. Most show early interest in adventure and newness. They thrive in crisis. Because they're purpose driven, superheroes make huge personal sacrifices without much reflection. Their reward is the highest high you can get at work.

They're like the rest of us in some respects. Do you want work without risk or challenge? (Hint: That gets old pretty quick.) Do you want stability over everything else? (Hint: Those days are gone.) Even if you prefer to hang out in the comfort zone, someday you may need to be a superhero.

When that time comes, you'll be ready.

THE QUIET HERO

The superhero's journey is less about what you accomplish, though the trials are impossible by definition, than how you face the obstacles in your way.

Life started for David in Jeju, a tiny island in South Korea. When he was five, a Mormon family from Iowa City met him and provided a new start. But everything seemed to be a struggle:

> My adoptive parents told me I was gifted and had abilities, but I didn't do well. I was always middle of the pack. The most frustrating part of life was the conflict between my potential and what I could do to perform.
>
> Being diagnosed with attention deficit disorder (ADD) gave a name to my frustration and how I could cope. I began to take medicine. It's a gift and a curse! It gives me the ability to hyperfocus on what I'm passionate about.

Even then David faced a mountain of obstacles: finishing college after dropping out, finding a job, and shifting from IT into web development. Through hard work and serendipity, David found his way into a pioneering systems project for a top finance firm, his biggest challenge yet:

> I had a lot of fear as to whether I could hold my own. My previous jobs were in little companies without exposure to the professional community. I had a sense of trepidation about whether I could compete. My education was not about the fundamentals of being a good developer. It took a lot to come up to speed. I read math, computer science, and algorithms textbooks every day on my way to work.
>
> But I'm opinionated and vocal. I spoke up right away. We were struggling with a component of the software where we had to process a large amount of data quickly. Costs could rise exponentially because of a few more seconds in processing. I came up with an algorithm. It was a bit complicated, but it was beautiful in terms of its efficiency.
>
> Being listened to by peers, having my ideas discussed and respected, boosted my confidence. Being exposed to people of different age levels and experiences helped me get over my fear. I was not behind anyone. I could challenge and assist engineers who had double or triple my experience.

David began to soar. He started working on a new business project that the firm was investing in with the goal of spinning it out. Its scope was beyond anything David had envisioned, one that aimed to beat the existing competitor:

> We grew so quickly. We started with four, and we're up to a couple of hundred developers now! It's exciting that we're able to explore, learn, and progress.
>
> It was definitely my most complex project yet with hundreds of thousands of lines of code. I realized that I can not only compete but *exceed* many of my peers. I'm a very good problem solver. I'm exceptional at pattern recognition, and I'm able to think abstractly.

> I want to gain respect as the person who can figure things out. I would like to be one of the smartest people in the world!

A modest hero with a strong sense of self, David overcame every trial he faced on the way to vice president.

So What?

David didn't start out to become a superhero. No one could have predicted where David's journey would lead him. If anyone tells you it ain't so, don't listen.

The superhero's journey is less about what you accomplish, though the trials are impossible by definition, than how you face the obstacles in your way. You'll need raw talent and strengths, including ambition, curiosity, and creativity. You'll need dedicated focus on an audacious mission with a stretch goal. You'll need tenacity, perseverance, and resilience. In other words, you need grit, and a lot of it.

David had all that and more. Every challenge helped him face entrenched fears that he was not good enough. Each one taught him more about using his own strengths.

That's why the hero's journey zigs and zags. Stops along the way are not detours. They're essential to your growth.

THE CITIZEN LEADER

Alessandra didn't expect the leaders' strong resistance. But by broadening ownership for the change she envisioned, she prevailed.

Hard-driving Alessandra grew up in Naples, Italy. Her parents worked in medicine, but Alessandra wanted something else. She left three companies before she finally found what she was looking for in the fourth:

> I joined a consulting firm to learn about general management. I decided to try consumer goods next. As soon as I reached my sales target, the company left me without a challenge.

So I joined another consultancy, but when I was about to turn 30, I realized it had no plan to develop female leadership. That's when I came here. The shock of changing to a slow, industrial environment was great, but I put a lot of energy in, and after two years I was promoted. After three, I got into this leadership program.

Ambitious and committed, Alessandra fought for what she believed in—even though she stood alone:

I discovered that a product line had a bad cost structure compared to competitors. I found a 30 percent gap and thought it was a tipping point moment. I gathered the leaders, two levels higher up, presented my analysis, and suggested what should be done and why. For the first time, somebody had pointed out the elephant in the room. Normally, the group would be very vocal. This time, they were silent. It felt like I was pitting one group against another.

Afterward, a leader I had trusted called me to his office. He said, "You have to change the way you communicate. You are young. There was a lot of expertise in the room. You should not tell people what to do." I felt knocked out. I lost my faith in what the leadership team could get done. It was clear they did not want to act. They always had excuses. Somehow, there were factions they did not want to break.

I was put in a corner for the next two weeks. It felt horrible going to work. Some people boycotted me because of the way I communicated and my intent to do something. I felt sad and also angry. My dreams of being in a place that valued innovation and teamwork were falling apart.

Still I kept digging, involving more people in the discussion. Somehow, I generated a big wave. Every time somebody challenged me, I went back and improved my fact base. My case got better, and more people became owners. It became my personal mission! The global CEO kept asking about this analysis. My boss was away, so I had to present it. Then the CEO reraised the issue and made the change.

He also recommended Alessandra for the global general manager program. A true superhero, Alessandra achieved what others saw but could not make happen.

So What?

Alessandra didn't expect the leaders' strong resistance. But by broadening ownership for the change she envisioned, she prevailed. Each new voice strengthened her case, and ultimately, the crowd caught the attention of the CEO.

Had the global CEO not intervened, perhaps Alessandra would have been silenced or ignored. We cannot know. Regardless, she learned that the organization is a network with different factions and hubs. Though collaboration slows it down, it creates ownership. Size does matter. One person is a dissenter, but a group is a groundswell for change.

Alessandra's courage comes from her mission to improve things. She told me, "I would like to know if there is a way, globally, that this generation can change things faster than before. Is there a river where we are all going with the flow in the same direction?"

Sometimes it takes a junior woman, a citizen compelled to do the right thing, to wear the superhero's cape.

THE COWBOY SHERIFF

You feel frightened, helpless, stripped of dignity. You can wait for a superhero to save you, or you can become one.

Travel was a fixture in Elizabeth's life. That was fortunate, as it helped prepare her to embrace ambiguity and change:

> I started to travel at a young age. My dad was invited back to China, to Guangzhou for three years. We stayed in Ohio with our mother, but we would visit China now and then. I flew to Canada on my own at 15. In college, I went to Ireland to study. I also went to Ecuador by myself and worked for the Salvation Army. I was thinking about what to do,

and somebody showed me a photo of Iceland. I went the next day.

Travel set me up to cultivate curiosity. The more I got, the more it wasn't enough. I got comfortable meeting strangers and having random conversations. It's also a mentality to make every moment count—you have only one life.

So when life and work clashed in an epic battle, Elizabeth was ready. One of seven grads nationwide invited to join the rotation program for a consumer goods company, Elizabeth chose an office in the one city she had never visited. She was alone when she fell gravely ill. Over the next few years, Elizabeth battled for her life:

> I was leaking protein through my urine, and no one knew how to stop it. The doctor was experimenting. He treated me as a guinea pig, giving me so many medications I could not tell cause and effect. I was in and out of hospital emergency rooms. I had a crippling disease, and no one knew what started it.
>
> In *The Shawshank Redemption*, a character said, "I guess it comes down to a simple choice, get busy living or get busy dying." I didn't have energy to get off the couch, but I was still breathing and realized I could smile.
>
> It's humbling. I know I'm not invincible; I have an expiration date. I can go down in the blink of an eye.

At the same time, Elizabeth continued to work on an account sales team led by a long-standing bully:

> She was "the Devil Incarnate." I had just been diagnosed and had to go to the doctor. She said, "OK, we're just in the busiest time of the year, but if you have to go, go!" I was crushed. I felt guilty, coming from a traditional Asian family where doing well at work is important.
>
> I was also young and making a bunch of mistakes. She criticized every single one, including a document that never went to the client. She called me into the office, slammed

the door, threw my papers in the air, and said, "What is this shit?!" I looked down for a second. She snapped her fingers in my face and said, "Look at me!" I left her office, snuck behind an office cabinet, and cried.

She was a bitch! The next day, she e-mailed me a to-do list, and then she stood over me as I tried to get what she asked for. I felt small and trapped. It was awful to feel stripped of dignity. She treated me like I wasn't worth human respect. I had to remind myself every day, *You're alive. You choose your attitude.* When people are that ugly, it exposes what you think about yourself and your need to grow a backbone.

When I finally told my mom, she said, "That's not right. How dare she?!" The rest of the team had not called HR. They were afraid of retaliation. I wasn't afraid. I told a senior person in our office. The head of HR flew in, and the bully was fired.

Elizabeth's disease went into remission. She landed a great new job elsewhere and started planning long term, even more boldly.

So What?

It would have been natural for Elizabeth to give in. Instead, she retained her power, battling a crippling disease while standing up to a bully. That's what a superhero does.

Everybody faces threatening challenges at work sooner or later. Negative events can trigger it: the business tanks, management executes a layoff, and out you go. You feel frightened, helpless, stripped of dignity. You can wait for a superhero to save you, or you can become one.

When the worst has already happened, you have nothing more to fear. Focused on what was in her control, Elizabeth saw that she could and should take action. Her downside risk was limited. Her new husband had health insurance. She had accepted the consequences. Elizabeth said, "When your health is affected, it's *never* worth it. Get the hell out, even if you're in your dream job!"

After cleaning up Dodge, that's exactly what Elizabeth did.

THE CRISIS AVENGER

Once convinced of the right thing to do, be willing to fight.
To overcome the obstacle before you, be willing to flex your plan.

Growing up in Australia, Sam watched his father go from bank teller to finance entrepreneur, from rags to riches. His attraction to risk taking was reinforced by a love of adventure that included bungee jumping:

> I love to go canyoneering—following a river down from a mountain. It's a wonderful way to explore nature and test yourself. A couple of times, I came very close to not making it. Once, I had a broken leg and couldn't escape a waterfall. My encounter with a life-and-death experience put work into perspective. It's not life threatening. People who have encountered death handle stress better and have greater confidence.
>
> I've always been fascinated by people who have beaten the odds. My father helped me realize that you can sit at a table where everyone agrees with each other and disagrees with you—and you're still right. Your idea needs to test out in the real world, but it might not test out in the boardroom.

When Sam was asked to lead a new innovation team in the consumer goods company where he worked, he jumped:

> My new boss said I seemed to be good at figuring this stuff out. I know now that the company leaders had no idea what they wanted. It was an important global business, large but least profitable, on a downward spiral, and neglected. The situation was so dire that incremental change would not turn things around. There had to be something radical.
>
> It feels arrogant, but the vision and strategy was clear to me on day 1. Really, all roads led to one answer. I took a big risk, but I was able to counter every obstacle in our way. It was oddly motivating to have a challenge that I truly believed in. My contrarian nature found a productive outlet.

I fought the organization for about 18 months. We operated in the area between management actually saying "Yes" but no one saying "Stop." I knew I was right, and I would find a way through the forest to get there, even if I had to drag the organization behind me. It was absolutely exhausting.

A senior executive approved the new strategy after each of the three levels below had approved it. Then Sam turned to his next assignment—and more obstacles:

My project went to the execution team. I was disappointed that they didn't see what they were being handed. It was like handing over my baby. I started to focus elsewhere with more responsibility. I saw a different business challenge, but with a similar solution.

The new team voiced all of the same concerns. I felt like we had learned nothing as an organization. It was crushing. If you put enough people in the room, you're going to get something really stupid. I learned that if you're going to make sacrifices, make sure it's for a cause you really value. People will never tell you that you were right and they were wrong. It was not a fairy-tale ending.

Six months later, I ended up in New York with a new role in global marketing. I want to focus on finding and fixing challenges, not just be a cog in the machine. I would like to be a free agent, battling crisis 100 percent of the time.

Sam's superhero strategy delivered massive profit improvement. His career advanced continuously, with less than two years at each level.

So What?

Having a huge impact on the organization is thrilling, as Sam learned. Once convinced of the right thing to do, be willing to fight. To overcome the obstacle before you, be willing to flex your plan. Sam advised, "It doesn't matter what plan you have as long as you're heading in the right direction. Don't get stuck on the plan."

Battling years of inertia and active resistance to change takes its toll. Sam was able to persevere and recover by taking on intense physical challenges like rock climbing. He said, "Everyone has a finite amount of frustration that can go into their bottle. You have to empty it to start over each week."

The most telling sign of a superhero is what he or she values most: being a free agent. Sam prized that more than anything—except for the next thrilling crisis.

THE DEMON SLAYER

Love is James's superpower. Hope for making things better
flows from it; so does optimism for the future.

Abandoned by his father and mother, James almost didn't make it out of the neighborhood:

> My father was out of my life before I finished elementary school. My mother suffered from mental illness and drug addiction. One day, my grandmother sat me down and said my mother had been discharged from rehab, but she didn't come home. She had been my dream defender. I'd say, "Mama, I want to be a firefighter," and she'd say, "Baby, that's great." No matter what, she was supportive.
>
> After that, I stopped believing in the whole idea of dreams generally. I was about to give up when people came out of the woodwork and said, "How can we help?" They saved me from hopelessness. It helped me put traumatic loss and hardship in perspective. I realized early it should not have to take a divine conspiracy to help a frightened, lonely kid.

James's résumé tops most, including a prestigious education; internships in the law, investment banking, politics; and great jobs. Perhaps it was his extraordinary experience of life that caused James to step off the "right track" and launch a mission-based startup:

Everybody with wealth and authority thought it was a terrible idea. We thought it was a great idea. If enough people tell you you're crazy, you're probably on to something. We did it on our own dime, camping in cow pastures in Montana, cold-calling local businesspeople, asking if we could help. They're solving a problem on the ground—how can we make our community better?

I believe I have a stronger version of *I'm awesome*. The measure of this life has to be about much more than personal success.

After graduation from business school, James's trauma resurfaced. His inner demons returned to destroy everything he had built:

The startup took off. I gave the school's graduation speech. I was on the cover of a magazine. However, I was deeply aware of the cracks in my "vessel," in pain and hurt and lack of forgiveness and fear and weakness, things I had been ignoring to keep going. I was struck by how much my personal issues affected my organization. For the first time I was forced to face it. I realized I had to take myself seriously to deal with the gap between our company's success and how I was processing the stuff in my history.

Holy crap, what's going on? It was one of the worst years of my life and one of the most important. I had nowhere to run. I did not have another job or school to go to. There was no going back home. This was real Life with a capital L.

James plunged to the depths. To save himself and the company, he turned to friends and prayer:

I believe things last as long as they need to for you to learn what you're supposed to learn. I saw that most of my freak-outs were driven by fear. So much was about self-worth. Close friends said, "How are you doing?" but I could not tell them the whole story. Then they said, "I'm there with you, not just for you," and I realized I wasn't alone. People are working through the same things.

I woke up in a cold sweat at night and wrote down everything I thought I was afraid of. They looked a lot smaller in writing. I needed tools, some perspective, and the space to allow myself to do the work that I needed to do. And then I started to put one foot in front of the other—tackling fear, loving it. Love is a practice. Self-love is a practice.

If you almost die, very quickly résumé virtues become irrelevant. If I die today, what's the life I want to live and be judged on? There is no logic that I should be here. I'm scared shitless every day. I'm never going to be fearless. People who say they're not afraid are total liars.

The trials James faced prepared him to take on superhero challenges. More than four years in, his startup is going strong and he is too.

So What?

In facing his internal supervillains—childhood trauma, adult fears—James began to untangle deadly patterns. Religion helped him, and good friends supported him, but love saved him. James's favorite question when helping others is, "What would you do if you weren't afraid?" Courage is the ability to feel afraid and do it anyway.

Love is James's superpower. Hope for making things better flows from it; so does optimism for the future. Love, hope, and optimism counter fear, but they also make profound change possible. James saved himself, yes. But his mission is much larger—to inspire business's next generation and change the course of America.

Superhero stuff.

SUPERHERO CHALLENGE

You may not feel ready to be a superhero. However, your mission is vital, and your back is against the wall. You make the decision to move forward. You face fear and steel yourself for the fight. With a fierce belief in the goal, you'll stop at nothing. You draw on resources you didn't know you had. With your team, you achieve what no one thought possible.

Superhero experiences are peak experiences. They entail long hours, unending stress, and extraordinary effort. And yet most top performers would like more of them. It's what they'll tell their colleagues, friends, partners, and children.

The people in this chapter were regular citizens who took on superhero challenges. Shannon could have kicked the can down the road, but she chose not to. David challenged himself to invent an elegant solution. Alessandra stood up to her leadership team. Elizabeth took on the office bully. Sam led a transformation, and James took on nothing less than the battle between love and fear, good and evil. Amazing.

The superhero challenge is the extreme version of all the other challenges combined. These recommendations will help you mitigate its severity.

Embrace the Mission Fully

Purpose may be present but disguised. You may know it, but not believe. You may believe, but not feel ready. Assess the situation with eyes wide open. The mission requires your full commitment to succeed:

- *Assess the assignment.* Test it in the following three ways.

  - *Explore its source of meaning.* Is this your chance to do the right thing for your company or community? Is it an opportunity to serve alongside great people? Is it a way to accelerate your development? One of these should be enough to greenlight your project.

  - *Take the energy test.* Is this challenge something you hardly have to think about because you're so fired up? Or do you agonize about it because you think you should do it? There has got to be a "want to do it" in there. If your heart rate speeds up just thinking about it, that's a good sign.

  - *Assess the fit.* Your background, work experience, leadership style, and personality may make you the ideal candidate. Without hubris, is this a challenge that you're particularly well suited for? Or is this something that anyone could do? If you're just a warm body, the other two tests must be positive to take you over the hump.

- *Assess yourself.* Superheroes may work part-time, but when they're on the job, nothing else matters. That's how you need to be, so gauge your commitment, which needs to be 100 percent—or more.

  ○ *Estimate your capacity.* Get ready for life in the high visibility, high risk, fast lane. If work-life balance is more your thing, be warned. Throw balance out the window and find ways to expand your capacity.

  ○ *Measure your optimism.* Superhero challenges take full conviction in what you're doing despite all the unknowns. Skeptics will ask questions that raise doubt in your own mind. You'll need conviction to find ways around those obstacles to reach the goal.

  ○ *Establish your base of support.* Superheroes need a few good people on their team. Likewise, identify well-placed supporters who believe in this cause and in you. Syndicate your decision with them.

Be a Superhero Every Day

You're about to take on challenges bigger than you, requiring capabilities you may not yet have. This isn't jumping out of a plane. You're heading into space. You're an astronaut now!

- *Believe in the mission.* When you do, everybody else will be more likely to believe in you. That's the essence of leadership and the one thing you can never let go. You get to declare the vision, but you also have to believe in it so much that others feel safe following you.

- *Sustain yourself despite the pressure.* This is a pressure cooker situation that threatens to boil over regularly. Make sure you're working on what really matters so that the priorities don't overwhelm you. And take care of yourself. Health is now a requirement of the job.

- *Get used to making mistakes and recovering quickly.* With a project so complex, there is no way you can avoid every mistake. Get great at apologizing, repairing, and moving on. And find a coach a few years ahead of you, someone not stuck in the system. Your coach can help you navigate the beneficial, but also ugly, politics.

- *Learn from everyone.* People will be judging you and offering advice of every kind. Listen well but don't feel obligated to follow every rule. You're going to disappoint someone while in service to your mission.

- *Recognize other people's experience.* Stand in their shoes and be a truly great listener. Take the time to build your team too. People stretch to higher performance if they find meaning in what they're doing together.

  ○ *Assume positive intent.* Most of the time, people are not out to get you. If you genuinely help them and treat them with respect, they may return the favor. Others have to get through a few stages to believe—from surprise to skepticism, curiosity, and excitement. Stay with them. Skeptics may become your most loyal supporters.

  ○ *Drop the emotion.* Get curious about what others say. If they spout fallacies, use your fact base to counter them. It will be more likely that they don't have the facts, in which case share yours without emotion. It's a balance between the passion you feel and the logical thinking you need. Too much of either and you lose people.

- *Face the office villains—and your fears.* At some point, you have to confront the resisters, blockers, and naysayers to bring them on board or find a work-around. Before leaping into battle, understand them.

  ○ *What you're trying to do is hard.* The people who have tried and failed were not idiots. We all forget that, criticizing those who don't agree or block us. Find out what they did and why they think it failed.

  ○ *Use the fears checklist to uncover what is triggering you.* To recap: feeling invisible or ignored; feeling like a fraud or unworthy; feeling uncertain and lost; feeling like you are losing control or letting people down; feeling loss of freedom or autonomy; feeling powerless; feeling rejected, or abandoned; and feeling like you are the subject of or a witness to gross unfairness. When you've found your fear, get curious and reframe.

- *Tap your sponsors.* Your chances for success increase exponentially with a few senior people on your side. Everybody passes through the valley of despair. This is a great time to get some support—your sponsors can help you face fear and untangle old knots.

- *Behave as if you're always in the spotlight.* Because you are, even when you don't feel much courage or confidence. Turn to a trusted team member when you need to vent. There is a reason that Batman has Robin.

- *Accept the unknown.* The biggest risk you'll face is failing to recognize when the plan is wrong. Stay focused on the goal and be flexible. You will make detours and side trips to accommodate others, and you'll also be wrong a lot of the time. That's OK as long as you're generally headed in the right direction.

Know Your Exit Strategy

You're facing twin dragons who guard the treasure: organization resistance and self-doubt. These dragons never die. If you capture the treasure, you'll receive countless invitations to do it again elsewhere. Keep in mind that it's hard to be a hero for long. Eventually, your winning streak will end. Or the dragons might overpower you, and then it's better to abort the mission. In both cases, you need an exit strategy:

- *Assess your danger.* During a war, we risk life for the cause. But work is not war, even if it feels that way. If you feel like you're fighting to the death, seriously consider leaving.

  - *Check for warning signs.* If you're too far gone to know, ask someone to intervene. If you're burning out, do something about it. If you're in over your head, tell someone and get help. You do not have to go down with the ship.

  - *Commit to your walk-away point.* Predetermine the point at which you're better off walking away instead of completing the mission. Answer the question, "I will walk away if [event] happens."

- *Prepare to ramp down well.* Early on, talk to sponsors to identify your options for what's next. It's tempting to focus just on today, but remember your future.

- *Navigate your career.* You may have found that superhero work is exactly what you want. Or you may have enjoyed it as a one-time experience. Before you get the next request to be a superhero, have the necessary conversations to set people's expectations.

- *Ride out of town.* Win or lose, heroes attract a lot of invisible arrows. You could save the town and still not be welcomed to stay. Prepare for the possibility of leaving before you have to. Your experience is invaluable to your next workplace. They will be delighted to embrace a proven superhero.

Peak experiences are exhausting. Take a breather after the dust settles. You'll feel low from the crash as you withdraw from an adrenaline-fueled existence. Life without adrenaline feels flat and dull, but you must rest. The best way to do that is to be in calm waters—on vacation or in a more routine role.

Use this time to reflect on what you've learned about yourself. Renew your energy. If you can, slow down entirely. There is great joy in being present and open to what's happening here and now. It's also a gift to others, who want more of you.

Soon enough, you'll swing into top gear, which may or may not entail being a superhero again.

SLOVE FEAR HOPE DESPAIR
PURPOSE PRESSURE
MISTAKE REVIEW
BRING PEOPLE ON BOARD
BULLIES JERKS
TAKE A STAND
RISK SELF-DOUBT
SUPERHERO ENERGY
MENTOR ADVISOR
LOVE FEAR HOPE DESPAIR
PURPOSE PRESSURE
MISTAKE REVIEW
BRING PEOPLE ON BOARD

11

When Everything Sucks

Sometimes work sends you to the bottom of the well unexpectedly. You didn't ask for this. What a lousy surprise. It's impossible to climb out, but remaining is unacceptable. Your first instinct is to quit, but that won't help your career. Still in shock, you try to think. As luck would have it, setbacks pile on. You get sick. Your relationships sour. You have trouble sleeping. You stop exercising. You eat more. You drink more. Everything sucks.

People tell you, "Think positively." They've got to be kidding! When the forces of darkness arrive, they pulverize positive thoughts. Pretending otherwise is like using a feather as a weapon. Unless that feather has some superpower, you're screwed.

Being in the suck happened to Lev when he was 10. His Russian mother, a blacklisted journalist and screenwriter who reported on the collapse of the Soviet Union, had started a new TV show to expose government crime. She was a single mother, Lev her only child:

> Mom was threatened, and so she applied for teaching and research fellowships in the West. We came to New York City. The day we were supposed to return to Russia, Yeltsin was impeached. I remember because we were watching TV at JFK airport. I told my mom that she could return but that I had decided to stay. I was raised to have a voice, and she listened. Reluctantly, she agreed to stay with me.

We settled in New York illegally and learned to get through various troubles, like couch-surfing as a step up from wandering the streets. We were fortunate because I was the youngest refugee case the lawyers decided to represent. The head lawyer's father got us an apartment and sent me to private school.

But just like other immigrants, I was falling through the cracks. My paperwork was in limbo. When I went to college, I got lucky again. Colin Powell visited our campus, and I was invited to meet him. I told him our citizenship papers had been lost for years. Immediately after, I got an invitation for our interview and exam.

I can handle crisis well because I know what real crisis feels like. I know how to create a safe space where you can have the time and energy to identify a problem and solve it. Just doing things won't solve the issue; it only makes you feel good that you're busy.

That's the suck. Crisis shaped Lev's professional vision to help other immigrant students achieve bigger dreams. As the dean of a university program for gifted students, he is achieving it:

In this program, we have 120 spots for 1,800 applications. There are more tears than anything here. Kids distrust the government system, and I show that it works. They start to realize a future that they could not have imagined.

For example, I inherited a Greek student in his junior year. I noticed that something in his file did not add up. He had a 3.98 GPA with a math and classics background. We're supposed to place the students in summer internships, but he always worked in his local supermarket. I called him in to discuss grad school. He said, "Those places are not for people like me." During our conversation, I phoned a neighbor who had been a classics don at Oxford for 60 years.

Lev and his neighbor persuaded the student to get his master's degree. He went on to earn his PhD.

We're drawn to stories of triumph, especially when the hero or heroine is the little guy who uses wit and integrity to make it through the suck. The term itself is army slang for a situation gone very, very bad. Civilians at work know it too. These stories can help you change your odds:

- *How can you get ready for it?* Trained in the military, Marjorie learned to embrace the suck in combat, great preparation for her work.

- *How do you know you're in it?* As Geoff experienced, sometimes you miss the usual signs, and before you know it, you're drowning in quicksand.

- *What do you do when things explode?* Jonathan's startup was running smoothly until disaster struck.

- *How do you get through the suffering?* Pushed out of the startup she cofounded, Samantha was caught in a downward spiral of rage and humiliation.

- *What does it really mean to push through?* When work and life imploded, Scott had to take action or lose it all.

You get to decide when "everything sucks" based on your own pain threshold. It's not a lifetime sentence. You'll toughen up. You'll get stronger. Embracing the suck can lead to wonderful things, not the least of which is a new lease on life. No one said you'd have to like it. And after the first crisis, you'll be better able to make it through the next.

And there will be a next one if you plan to continue working.

PREPARING FOR THE DAY

Practice for the day when you're thrown into the deep end.
You don't want to find yourself in the suck without the means for survival.

Marjorie was proud of her American upbringing in a blue-collar town. Her parents taught their nine children the values of citizenship and service. Then in September 2001 the terrorist attack happened. It spurred Marjorie to choose the military—leading at the front line—instead of attending grad school:

My older sister had joined the military to pay for college. She was in Germany when the Berlin Wall came down. At seven, I remember watching President Reagan on TV saying, "Tear down this wall!" I was thinking, *Wow, my sister's over there. This is huge!* She brought back a piece, and I was allowed to touch it. It made me believe that the world can be what we hope it to be.

That's why I had such a call to action. We had to stand up for ourselves and others. I didn't want to sit on the sidelines. I had to be part of the story because America was going to change. Everything was going to change.

Marjorie served 10 years in the Army Reserve, including two combat deployments. Advancing to frontline commander, she encountered the suck often. For example, right when her husband returned from a 15-month deployment, she was called up. They had wanted to start a family, but instead, Marjorie headed to Afghanistan:

I thought, *Can't we just have a break?* "Suck" is what you don't want in your life. No one wants to be told they have to live for three years away from their partner. No one wants to be told cancer, or they didn't get promoted. It's bad. You can bitch about it and you can complain. It isn't what you wanted, but hell, you can't deny it. Get comfortable embracing the suck. You're there. You feel uncomfortable, but you have to do it.

If you're driving a convoy and you're ambushed, all of a sudden people are shooting at you. Some people might think you have to stop and find the enemy who is shooting. Others might want to back up and go away. But in the military we learned that you stomp on the gas pedal and push through. If you push through, the likelihood of your survival is exponentially higher. It feels counterintuitive, but that's how you survive.

After completing her military service, Marjorie was recruited by the board of a large nonprofit. After 18 months as president and COO, expecting to become CEO, she landed in the suck:

When I walked in the door, I thought I would stay for 10 years. The board had created my position as part of the succession plan. The CEO had been looking to retire in three to five years. Then her story changed to five to seven years. She had a case of "Founder's Syndrome." I started to see boomers *not* retiring, everywhere. She was not going anywhere, and I knew I was going to leave. I didn't know when, but I wanted to leave the organization as tight and as well as I possibly could.

The needle doesn't move for me—in life and in stress. I stay where I am naturally predisposed to be. I thought, *I'm not going to battle. I love my job and my work, but I'm going to let her figure this out.*

It wasn't about becoming the CEO. I didn't need the prize.

So Marjorie shifted her measure of success to leaving the organization in better shape. And when she left, Marjorie felt like she had prevailed. Resilient, she turned to her next chapter in a life of service.

So What?

Embracing the suck is critical for soldiers—and for the rest of us. Practice for the day when you're thrown into the deep end. You don't want to find yourself in the suck without the means for survival. Marjorie said, "You need to arrive *before* you arrive."

Physical training is good preparation. It strengthens you physically and mentally: you learn that you can do more than you thought you could. At work, taking on stretch challenges is the equivalent.

Ongoing renewal is paramount too. At a low point, Marjorie received a live Christmas tree from her husband, lights and all. Without thinking, she stuffed some lights in her pocket and returned to her containerized housing unit. She said, "The lights reminded me that I was loved. When you're going through the suck, be conscious. Get your Christmas lights and hang that shit up."

It's easy to just let life go by. But when we land in the suck, priorities sharpen; we pay closer attention to what's important.

That's a good thing.

A SIMPLE TWIST OF FATE

Ask a problem question and get problems.
Ask for new ideas and get solutions.

Geoff's life changed in 2001, when his father was let go and struggled to find stability at work for the next decade. There were entire years when Geoff's dad was unemployed:

> That's when I shifted my mindset. I realized that, for the things I wanted like college, I had to do it on my own. I might need to support my parents. That had me in a scramble to get ahead, to feel financially stable as fast as possible. It was a tremendous amount of stress. Today, the economy has rebounded. I feel I have options, but I'm still paying off student loans.

Motivated to look for a dependable career (engineering), a stable industry with steady growth (consumer goods), and an established company with strong values and good prospects, Geoff turned down 10 offers until he found what he needed. Happy ending?

Not quite. Within months, management was debating whether to close the plant where Geoff worked. With reduced staffing, the frontline managers—Geoff included—were stretched to the breaking point:

> I was working a hundred hours, seven days a week. At first it was exciting, but as people left, our workload increased. I had an overwhelming feeling of being burned out before the year was up. I set four alarms to wake up and get out of bed. I downed two five-hour energy drinks a day. It was so bad. I remember coming home to get ready for the third date I had with the woman I later married. I fell asleep and missed it entirely.
>
> I was living with a roommate, but I didn't want to talk to anyone after work. I would go to my room and lock the door. I was physically drained, and I didn't have emotional energy

either. We used to joke that we would bring beer to work because we enjoyed being together, but now, no one asked to go out. We were all exhausted. We even had a fatality.

One of the guys told me about a recruiter. I had been networking to find opportunities inside, but I went to see her. She said, "Look, you're early on in your career. Go back to your company and have more conversations." I didn't want to hear that. I had had a lot of conversations; nothing was being done. The recruiter threw up a roadblock. I didn't see anything changing.

Stymied, Geoff tried another route. He reconnected with the person in HR who had recruited him. Their regular conversations became his lifeline. Eventually, a new plant director arrived and asked Geoff to join his transition team:

The plant director and his production director coached me to view this situation as more of an opportunity instead of an overwhelming burden. They taught me to step back and look at the overall picture, not getting caught up in the intricate details. They asked, "What can we do to turn this plant around?" They showed me that I had the tools. They were open to my input. They helped me see that making the changes was within me.

An early initiative was establishing a process for cleaning the machines. It seemed impossible. They said that with my strength to connect, people would trust me. All I needed to do was design the right process. I took six months to put it together for the machine operators. We had tremendous improvement in efficiency. It was thrilling!

Putting my ideas in play and seeing results got me out of my funk. It was night and day. I knew we would have a great impact. I knew people would follow me. I was more excited to get up and go to work. I felt more energy at the end of the day. As I started to grow and the plant started to turn around, the production director said, "Look at the opportunities you have. You are entirely capable of doing them. You are smart enough to figure it out. You know."

That experience changed Geoff's fortune and his outlook. He advanced to production director in time. Better yet, he dreams of running his own company someday.

So What?

Of course Geoff knew that the plant was in decline. He just didn't see that he had slid down with it, sinking into helplessness. Once you're helpless, you stop trying. You believe that nothing you do will change the situation. If you ask the same questions, think the same thoughts, and do the same things, you'll get the same result. That's your red flag. It's time for new questions.

The new plant and production managers asked creative, inspiring questions that shifted Geoff's thinking from problems to solutions. Instead of looking for the root cause of the problem or blaming somebody, management asked for ideas. Then they supported their young team to implement changes.

Ask a problem question and get problems. Ask for new ideas and get solutions. Brilliant. The effect on Geoff's energy was almost miraculous.

PUTTING OUT THE FIRES

Be sure that your guiding principles are not just good for a poster.
They'll come in handy when you land in the suck.

Jonathan's start in life was promising: he was a bright kid with a terrific education. He also had the good fortune to land in the suck early on:

> My first year in college, I played on the lacrosse team and was influenced by the group. I adopted their world view of being cool. One night I got hazed, got drunk, peed in public, and got in a ton of trouble! It was truly embarrassing. My parents

and I had to talk to the dean. That was the best thing. It snapped me out of my teenage arrogance and got me to appreciate school. I started focusing on interesting things: history, race, and politics.

Then I went to work in government partnerships in a finance firm. The financial crisis happened, my group folded, and I was moved to mergers and acquisitions. That work and the people were not inspiring. I remember flying on a private plane to Miami with the head partner, just us. He was totally focused on his wealth. If I ended up like him, I'd be a real loser. I thought, *You couldn't pay me to be this guy!*

I was going to private equity next, and I realized it wasn't what I wanted to do. I decided to leave.

Jonathan and a friend started up an innovative digital media company. Three years later, they landed in the suck unexpectedly. The company's second employee had been steadily plagiarizing. Jonathan's decision would have been straightforward had that employee not sacrificed blood, sweat, and tears from the beginning:

> It had crossed my mind, like *How did he write three articles in the last hour?* But we were trying to reinvent the business, trying a hundred things an hour! As the company got more serious and had more standards, he was lifting, writing, and not crediting. Intentionally hiding what he was doing.
>
> I felt responsible for what he had done. He was like my brother. The signs were all over, but it was something I hadn't cared about. But 40 other people were in the way of serious harm. The process was the way it was. I had fired people before. It was about coming to grips with it.
>
> That weekend, I felt bad. You know the way you feel it in your stomach when something is wrong? You can't ignore it. I felt uncertainty about how we would bounce back, what this meant for the business in an uncertain time. We were not on super stable financial footing. We couldn't just double down on reporters. It was hard to figure out what we would do next.

There was no time for grieving. For all of us, careers equal life. I had to tell the company what had happened. It was as big a shock for them. As a leader, I carry the energy for the company. If I'm down, everybody is down. I knew that the only response was to give them the game plan: "We did the right thing, and we're moving on."

The company survived, strengthening Jonathan's capability to lead through the next crisis.

So What?

The decision—firing a good friend and dedicated employee—was wrenching, but the company was on the brink. There was limited time to make decisions. On Monday morning Jonathan would have to act without a sure plan. When you're in the suck, push through, and figure it out later.

Sticking to a long-term mission helps you through it. Curiously, Jonathan had held on to the guiding principles taught by the investment bank he had rejected: Attract and retain intellectual firepower. Don't ever drop the bar. Work hard and collaborate. Be purpose driven. Those deeply embedded values saw Jonathan—and the company—through a company-threatening crisis.

Be sure that your guiding principles are not just good for a poster. They'll come in handy when you land in the suck. Guiding principles exist to drive daily actions, especially when business is not 'as usual.' So if you don't have any, figure them out now.

BRINGING YOUR A GAME TO PLAN B

We all wish for working lives without pain.
That's not realistic. But in the fullness of time, wounds heal.

Samantha had wanted to lead a startup since she was a kid. Her first one was in ninth grade—a nonprofit to help underprivileged kids. Even before that, Samantha was already building the skills of an entrepreneur:

We moved from Texas to the West Coast, and then nine months later, we moved east! I was 10. My parents did a great job making these moves into an adventure. In the West, I had no friends; in the East, I was popular. I realized this was fickle and stupid. That year was transformative.

My parents raised my brother and I to think we could do anything but that it wouldn't be easy. I joined the soccer team, and the girls hated me. When I wanted to quit, my parents made me stick it out for the season. We learned we would try things and sometimes fail.

As an entrepreneur, you know you'll be an idiot and fail at some things in order to get where you want.

A few years ago, Samantha and her friends planned a pioneering online business. Well-placed people loved the concept and paid attention. But even before it got out of the gate, there was trouble. The team could not agree on the strategy, the economic model, or even the website look and feel. As the team fractured, conflict almost destroyed Samantha:

> Everyone knew it was doomed to fail, except for the people in it, me included. I overlooked clear problems. I really didn't want to quit. I couldn't imagine letting go. I was sensitive to how it would look. Other people told me we would have conflict, and I felt we could handle it. When we initially had some, I got several legal threats and was pretty scared. My parents said, "Be thoughtful, and do what's right. Don't provoke. These just may be threats." It became "the strongest one wins."
>
> I didn't quit until June, when I woke up to find that I was locked out of the company website. I felt humiliated in front of all the people I had brought on. I also felt the loss of everything I had built, my life savings included. I e-mailed a hundred people and told them what had happened. I was in such pain that I needed other people to be aware of what I was going through. I won't pretend it was quick and easy.
>
> I spent three weeks curled up on the floor, staring at the ceiling. I wondered how I could face people. My cofounder, Hannah, helped me through. She encouraged me to devise a new business plan. We recruited our entire old team. We had

a furious brainstorming session and shaped the new brand.
It began to feel real.

Samantha and Hannah put that new plan into action. They launched a new business that had more success in its first month than the original. By the third month, things were humming. After four months, Samantha had her confidence back, vital to a CEO and cofounder. She realized they were going to make it.

So What?

This is a story of pushing through when there are casualties. Let's not brush by that. The difficult image of Samantha curled up on the floor evokes her strong feelings of humiliation, despair, rage, and grief. But Samantha prevailed. By honoring her loss, she could move forward to recovery. With the next goal set, her energy returned in waves, as did her competitive spirit.

If you're grieving, start by acknowledging your deep disappointment. Name what you're feeling. Surround yourself with real friends. Be careful not to wear them down by oversharing, and they'll stand by you. They each have something you need: empathy, ideas, coaching, counsel, connections, a hug.

Try to resist the urge to double down, losing yourself in work. Working feverishly slows down recovery. It's distracting, but it's also a form of self-punishment. Instead, ease up on yourself and renew. When you forgive yourself and others, your scars fade.

We all wish for working lives without pain. That's not realistic. But in the fullness of time, wounds heal.

ESCAPING THE BLACK HOLE

You can't fix a bad situation at work without helping yourself holistically. You've got to face the $64,000 question: Why am I here?

When he was young, Scott began a lifelong obsession with science and engineering:

> My earliest dream was to be an astronaut. I was four when the space shuttle *Challenger* exploded 73 seconds after liftoff.

Most parents would try to shelter their children from those risks, but I wanted to become the first man on Mars.

In college, Dr. Richard Smalley, the Nobel Prize–winning scientist, gave a talk on the need for a hydrogen economy, and I was sold. I wanted to work on the "single most important problem facing humanity today": new sources of sustainable energy.

Joining an automotive company after graduating, Scott followed that dream. He was assigned to help commercialize zero-emission electrical vehicles that could be powered from any energy source. The challenge was enormous:

This was leading-edge technology with a lot of opportunity for new inventions and solutions. It was revolutionary—freeing up some dependence on oil, making our air cleaner, and fighting climate change. It was taking the stuff from rockets and putting it into cars.

But the program kept getting delayed, postponed, and pushed back. If you don't hit the targets, you miss the gateway. I remember being at the supplier when the program was canceled. Someone said, "Don't be discouraged. It will be our life's work to develop this." I was excited but terrified. It's a story I could tell my grandchildren, but we were in the middle of a recession. I had no idea where I was going to go. If I went elsewhere and said I was a hydrogen fuel cell researcher, they would say, "What's that?"

So I sacrificed my dream for my family.

Scott transferred to a new role as the liaison between the power train and manufacturing functions. Three years later, he was burning out. Landing in the suck, Scott had no option but to embrace it:

I had a lot of stress being a middleman. It was like getting punched in the face by both sides. I was stressed at home too. All the earning pressure was on me.

I wanted to take a winter vacation for my birthday, but my wife told me to go alone. I was gaining weight. I was having panic attacks at work. I was stressed at home. We fought about money. My doctor told me to diet, exercise, and go to therapy. The therapist told me to diet, exercise, and try breathing techniques.

My supervisor relied on me heavily, but I had to move on. I'm driven and ambitious and capable of more. I started looking for jobs internally; my mentor invited me to work for him. Then I looked at how I spent my time and my commitments: to be a good provider and earn my engineering master's. Also, I made a commitment to my health. I told myself every single day that I was going to exercise. Instead of going out to lunch, I went for a walk and ate a sandwich at my desk.

I did think about suicide. Many people succumb to the overwhelming feeling of insignificance. The love I have for my kids stopped me. And thank goodness for my therapist. As much as we American cowboys want to be the rugged individual, everyone needs help once in a while.

Scott secured a better position to provide for his family. He achieved his academic goals. He restored his health and fitness. But instead of growing together through this dark period, he and his wife grew apart. Their marriage ended. Step by painful step, Scott took back his life.

So What?

This is what it looks like when everything sucks. Scott pushed through, not all at once and not overnight. There is no medal for making it to hell and back on your own. Sensibly, he got help—doctor, therapist, and trainer too. They're paid to tell you the truth and help you face it. When you're in so deep you can't see yourself, hired professionals shine.

You can't fix a bad situation at work without helping yourself holistically. You've got to face the $64,000 question: *Why am I here?* Scott had a vision and set goals. He achieved important milestones in small steps—like running the marathon and filing patents, regaining self-respect and self-confidence. His first dream gone in a puff of smoke, Scott shaped a new one—making cars safer for people and the environment.

He hasn't given up on space either. Scott dreams that if he lives to 80, he will buy an affordable ticket for a trip into space on a rocket ship.

———— TAKING ON YOUR ————

SUCK CHALLENGE

Pushing through the suck at work takes grit.* Many popular expressions describe it: the nauseating "Suck it up," the ironic "Grin and bear it," the laconic "Man up," and the suspenseful "Grit your teeth." Each adage amounts to the same thing: just hang in there because time will pass, and if you're still standing, you've survived! Lucky you.

That's unhelpful advice. I cannot imagine telling 10-year-old Lev to suck it up, although he was heroic. When Marjorie landed in the suck for months on end, advising her to take it like a man would have been offensive. Geoff gritted his teeth, but that got him nowhere. When Jonathan and Samantha were slammed, suggesting that they grin and bear it would have been cruel. Sucking it up was the last thing Scott should have done.

I'm certain of this: You will land in the suck sooner or later. You don't get to choose when and where. If you quit right away, you'll lose the opportunity to learn. Better to stay for the learning and then decide. Hopefully, these recommendations will be more useful.

Prepare for the Day

It's worthwhile to prepare for the unexpected, awful work equivalent of being in the suck even if you don't know what form it will take. Preparing builds self-confidence and self-esteem. Preparation can win you the game:

---

* Angela Duckworth is the expert on grit, having dedicated much of her academic research to her mission to use psychological science to help kids thrive. She defines *grit* as passion combined with perseverance. By "passion," she means sustained goals and not intensity of emotion: sticking to it until you finish what you've started because the goal is important to you. If you're intrigued, read *Grit: The Power of Passion and Perseverance* (Scribner, New York, 2016).

- *Take physical training seriously.* It teaches you to deal with discomfort of a physical kind. It also helps you see that your limits are not what you thought they were. If you're someone who rarely exercises, listen up. This is not about going to the gym. It's learning to rise to a challenge. Train in something that interests you. Try running, biking, hiking, yoga—anything. The key is to find something where you'll dedicate real time and endure some physical hardship. Then sign up for an exciting, big goal that you're not really sure you can accomplish. When you do accomplish it, you'll be stronger and more able to manage stress.

- *Use everyday challenges to prepare.* You face all kinds of daily crises that are great sources of training. Instead of viewing them as annoyances, recognize them for what they are: "micro-suck" experiences that help you prepare for the big one.

  - *View daily hassles in this new light.* If you have young children, this is your chance to shine! Kids provide great training, although interactions with partners, parents, friends, and pets will prepare you too. You have countless opportunities to practice remaining calm and alert, focusing on finding the solution without allowing distractions to sidetrack you.

  - *Practice living outside your comfort zone.* Take an adventure vacation! You don't have to be on *Survivor* or *Amazing Race*, but forgo the beach for something on the wilder side. Adventurers swear by white water rafting, scuba diving, rock climbing, or wilderness survival. Or do something completely new to experience the wild side in relative safety. Pick a spot that intrigues you and go there to face the unfamiliar.

  - *Go to the edge at work.* Set an uncomfortable challenge that stretches you. For example, make building your network the bold goal by doing it in the extreme—aim to become a consummate networker, known to others as a polished connector.

- *Practice mindfulness to train mentally.* Even a few minutes a day helps you gain mental alertness and focus. Although it's a daily practice, it also helps in the chaos of crisis.

○ *Adopt a favorite mindfulness app.* Accessing alertness and calm is easier if you practice every morning or evening. If sitting quietly just won't work, try a substitute for mindfulness. For example, prayer or reflection at night before going to sleep also works.

○ *Make up your own mindfulness practice.* There's no magic to this. You can practice mindfulness almost anywhere. Take going to work. Eliminate all distractions on your trip: no reading, speaking on the phone, or making lists. Just be present. If that doesn't suit you, try another way. Some people walk or jog slowly as they meditate. Others drink a glass of water intently, observing how it feels. Even looking out the window works if you focus on that one activity. The key is to choose to focus, gently resetting your attention each time it wanders.

● *Set up your emotional support.* Who you gonna call? (I couldn't resist, but sadly, there are no *Ghostbusters*, male or female, here to get you out of the suck.) Line up your people now. Decide who among your family members, friends, and work colleagues would not judge or say, "I told you so" but stand by you. Figure out who will be your rock and strengthen that relationship now.

● *Prepare to lead.* When you land in the suck, someone has to be the leader, and I'm hoping you'll take charge. Prepare for that day by strengthening the following three capabilities.

○ *Technical.* Leaders need to create the plan, make good decisions, take responsibility for outcomes, and delegate effectively. Be sure to get that training with live experiences.

○ *Meaning.* Leaders create meaning for others through values and vision. They also bring their full selves, appearing more human. So know your values and practice living them. Be clear on your purpose and create the vision that others can help you realize. Be vulnerable: in other words, don't be a robot. Let people know what you're thinking and feeling (within reason).

○ *Connection.* Focus on the others: what they need. Transmit positive emotions and energy; it mobilizes others by creating a safe environment. People who feel you care about them are more likely to engage. Think about how you show up at your best. You probably do all these things in that state.

Embrace the Suck

Accept the suck when it happens. Only then can you can push through, even when your body and mind are screaming in revolt. You can't press a button to change the channel or eject:

- *Get complaining out of the way.* You can't bottle that stuff up, so vent and move on. Your anger and resentment have a purpose—to jump-start your adrenaline—but don't let it work against you. Negative emotions color what you see. They're like quicksand, pulling you down.

  ○ *Let it out, once.* Have your say—to friends or family—and then put it to bed. No one but a therapist will hear your story a fifth time. I've mentioned this before, but if things are exploding, a therapist may be just what you need.

  ○ *Write your nastiest e-mail.* Leave the recipient field **blank** and then press **save**, or better yet, **delete**! It's cathartic to let it all out. As a policy, do not fill in the recipient field for at least 24 hours. Cool down. Reread your e-mail and have a good laugh. Ideally, your need to send it will have vanished.

  ○ *Keep a special journal at home.* Pour your heart out into pages that will never be read by anyone but you.

- *Assess the situation.* Determine whether you're really in the suck or whether you're just in an uncomfortable situation. Are you in crisis mode, past learning, past growing? Really? Any one problem can make work suck, but that's not necessarily cause for leaving.

  ○ *Ask questions.* Is it bearable? Can you adapt? Are you meeting your development and impact goals despite the severe discomfort? What is the likely time frame for pushing through? Try to understand what's temporary and what's not. On a scale of 1 to 10, how much pain are you in, 10 being unbearable?

- ○ *Talk to the experts.* Find out if other people view the situation as you do. Gather advice to determine if there are actions you can take. See if the situation can be moderated.

- ○ *Recover your energy.* Are you healthy? Are you in a stable relationship? Are you engaged outside of work? All things considered, are you generally satisfied with your work situation? Do what you can to embrace the situation with equanimity.

- ● *Adapt the mindset that enables you to make decisions.* It's natural to do it, but denial wastes time. Even if time isn't of the essence for survival, use it well by shifting your mindset from victim to owner. You're in the suck now. OK. What is in your control?

Push Through

Pushing through means owning your situation and taking leadership action. Clearly, one set of advice won't work for every situation, but there are some common threads that may help:

- ● *Tap your lifeline.* Solicit the support you need. In other words, get out of your house or office. Just when you want to isolate yourself is when you must reach out. If you're an individual contributor at work, don't fly solo. Talk to your boss or other senior people who have the know-how and diplomacy to help you get through.

- ● *Make every day count.* There is more you can do than you might imagine.

  - ○ *Set reasonable, small goals for your day.* Establish an intention in addition to writing a to-do list. An example of an intention is appreciating what is good about the situation. Adopt a positive mindset. Instead of *I'll try not to blow up at people today,* shift to *I see and appreciate the strengths colleagues bring.* The words you use matter.

  - ○ *Take it step by step.* Look for immediate solutions first, holding off on the last resort—quitting—for now. A lateral move or temporary assignment may get you through the suck. After you've found and rejected internal opportunities, it's time to leave. If you do leave, do so with grace.

- *Sustain your energy.* You could be in the suck for a brief period or many months. In the latter case, it's essential to find ways to sustain the extra energy it takes to push through.

  - *Do intense workouts.* Exhausting yourself physically helps drain negative emotions like anger and resentment. The release of endorphins increases your feeling of contentment and helps you shift from denial to acceptance. Make sure you fully focus. Get a trainer if you can afford one. When you're pressed for time, walking around the block may do the trick, but it has to be fast, with arm swinging too! If the weather isn't right, walk up the stairs until you feel tired. Watch your heart rate, so you don't overdo it. Then walk down slowly.

  - *Get a talisman to remember that you are loved.* Figure out what your "Christmas lights" are to remind you that you are loved and valued. It may sound hokey, but do it because it works.

  - *Restore your spiritual energy.* Some people turn to their faith, reporting that belief enables them to accept difficult times more easily. Others draw on sources of spiritual renewal such as music, poetry, and being in nature. Whatever resonates for you, build it into your day and week.

  - *Practice gratitude each evening.* Get a journal for this purpose and write down one new thing you are grateful for that day. Make it specific. You're retraining your brain to scan for what to feel thankful for.

It's odd. Harsh circumstances have the power to deplete and destroy, but they can help us grow enormously. We don't want awful experiences, and we don't ask for them. But they do serve. We have the capacity to grow through the lowest points at work when all seems lost. In those moments, we pay more attention. We resolve to live life more fully. We face an opportunity to lead at our best.

When you find yourself in the suck, don't blow your chance to shine.

LOVE FEAR HOPE DESPAIR
PURPOSE PRESSURE
MISTAKE REVIEW
BRING PEOPLE ON BOARD
BULLIES JERKS
TAKE A STAND
RISK SELF-DOUBT
SUPER ENERGY
MENTOR SPONSOR
LOVE FEAR HOPE DESPAIR
PURPOSE PRESSURE
MISTAKE REVIEW
BRING PEOPLE ON BOARD

12

When Work Doesn't Feel Worth It

When work doesn't feel worth it, people lose interest. They phone it in. They feel listless, lethargic. They're sad, depressed, drained. Some quit. Others slowly fossilize.

Snap out of it! Finding yourself in the dumps is a superb opportunity to make changes. Once you're down, there's nowhere to go but up.

Take the story of William, a West Coaster who dreamed of working in fashion in New York. He made it happen after school, working at a fashion magazine. But that experience turned out to be worse than *The Devil Wears Prada*! With no room to grow, William quit. From there, he went into fashion design before settling on a career in beauty. While it sounds glamorous, William went through another rough patch. Assigned to a big beauty brand, he no longer felt that work was worth it:

> In the role before this, I had a voice. It was my product and my visual and a two-way street with my senior managers and the ad agency. That was completely cut off in the next role. It's not allowed at my level in this brand. I was considered too junior to have this conversation with the agency. I didn't even sit in the room!

That was frustrating. If I showed up or didn't show up for work, the company would still move forward. They told me coming in I had to have resilience. I thought I was up for it. But it's tough.

William underscored that he didn't want to *be* the voice, just to have one:

At school, we learned about making your mark. That's an old person thing to say! You work hard for 30 years, and one day, you're the head of whatever? Well, if you hire me, it means you're interested in what I have to say and offer. When people say, "I don't care who you are, it's what you deliver," I love it. With proper guidance, the more ownership I have, the happier I am. I want to have my opinion heard, my data used, and a dialogue.

My view is that, if I am not learning the skills, what's the point of being exposed? In your twenties, you're a sponge. Learning is key to what I need. If you're not experiencing, not speaking up for yourself, and not observing, then you're not learning. My tolerance is for a year or less.

William had a point. He worked in a competitive field in a competitive city where you advance or you lose. Things don't come to you. You have to ask for them. William knew that he had to beat performance expectations to earn the right to ask. But in return, he wanted to feel useful and included. Without that, William felt no different from the next guy. Not the most motivating message for him, right?

There are so many ways to lose momentum, but as these stories show, you have options:

- *How can you make the best of it?* Stuck in a project put on ice, Charlotte decided to take action.

- *When should you wait it out?* Elliot loved publishing, but he couldn't move beyond the grunt work stage.

- *How do you stay engaged when the novelty wears off?* Gary began every job with excitement, it didn't last long.

- *When do you know it's time to leave?* Eduardo thought he landed a great job, but 18 months later, he couldn't drag himself out of bed.

- *What do you do when you can't stand another day at the company?* Stacy-Marie found out the hard way.

I won't sugarcoat it: some jobs lead to dead ends, and some are deadening. In the moment, it's hard to know if you've got a lifetime sentence or if the wait will be over soon. You don't want to be duped, and you certainly don't want to miss a fabulous opportunity because of impatience. You're between a rock and a hard place without an answer.

But you don't have to do *nothing*.

Everyone in the following stories faced ambiguity, uncertainty, and change. In some cases, the organization itself changed. However, that doesn't mean it's OK to hang out in standby mode. You're an agent of change too. You can always quit. But before you do that, take some time to figure out who you are and what you really want. Otherwise, you'll land another job in another company with surprising similarities to the one you just left.

Your issues will feel oddly familiar in no time at all.

SHOULD I STAY, OR SHOULD I GO?

*It's up to you to be resourceful in finding internal options.
Talk to everyone to learn about possible
new roles and opportunities.*

Growing up, Charlotte was no stranger to unexpected bad news. The first time it happened, she was small:

> Dad took over my grandfather's family business when I was three. A dozen years later, he got in trouble with bank fraud and went away to federal prison. He had tied our family assets to the corporate assets, so we lost everything we had. That was a defining moment. We went from having everything to having nothing. My mom picked up and got her CPA. We visited my dad every week. The hardest part was

when he returned home. It was years before there was normalcy in our lives.

To help out, I went to work. I learned that there will never be a point in my life when I'm not in the workforce. I also learned the value of deep relationships and knowing who cares for you. My school was incredibly supportive, offering my sister and me scholarships. I've never forgotten that my teacher said: "People expect a lot from you, and that's why we do things for you two." That drove me to do more and be more.

Nobody needs to know everybody's dirty laundry, but at the same time, everybody's got some. I'm empathic to people who work for me. I know I don't know what's going on for them behind the scenes. I'm also more open in sharing my intentions. My dad told people what they wanted to hear. For me, the truth is not always good, but it has to be told.

After trying politics, getting her MBA, and experiencing what small companies are like, Charlotte joined a large company to develop her business skills. Five years in, she was asked to help launch a new revenue stream. She took on the project gladly. But a year later, Charlotte had lost her zest:

Everyone was behind the new line of business. We charged hard for six months. Then we were told to hold because our division was going to be spun off. It was a complete surprise. And when the brakes were pulled, they were pulled hard and abruptly.

More surprising was how long we were held. I was in a freeze pattern for the next nine months, with no date for when we would rev up again. I looked internally for a new project or new role.

The holdup could not have come at a worse time. At 33, Charlotte had wanted to start a family. She assumed a stable work situation would make it easier to advance after returning from maternity leave:

I talked to people to find out what I should do and what skills to build. I journaled every night. I thought about who I am, where I am, who I think I want to be, and my place in life.

I vetted a few opportunities and proposed those to my manager. She came back and said they didn't want me to do those things. She gave me an eight-week project that I finished.

Then I went through the process again. I tried to get another role, but was met with political resistance. People didn't want me to move out. I went through a mentoring process to negotiate options that wouldn't upset others but would help me grow. I talked to very senior people in order to get definitive closure. It was like playing bumper cars. For the first time ever, I was very unhappy at work.

It opened my eyes to outside opportunities. I'm happy to be a team player, but nine months was generous. I entered the second round for a few roles outside, exploring cultural fit and whether I could be happy. I wanted to know if it would be a good move.

Eventually, Charlotte joined a consumer services company to help launch a new business line. In her first year, she won two awards: the President's Award and the company's innovation award. Looking back, Charlotte was thrilled with her decision. Looking forward, her first baby was on the way.

So What?

When the project was put on hold, Charlotte was patient. When things didn't get back on track, she hired a career consultant to understand if it was a me problem, a company problem, or a timing problem. Charlotte used the waiting time to gain self-awareness. She learned that feeling disconnected was a systemic issue: her project was neither a core business nor company priority.

It's up to you to be resourceful in finding internal options. Talk to everyone to learn about possible new roles and opportunities. If they don't exist, you're right to look further. You know the real score inside more than the shiny new things on offer outside, so be careful when comparing options. Know what you're looking for. Charlotte wanted professional growth in a culture that valued community and belonging, openness, and clear direction.

When everything at an external opportunity checked out, so did Charlotte.

STUCK ON PERMA HOLD

No one stops you from growing in place.
If they do, get out of there fast.

Elliot's dad, a senior advertising executive in a radio company, left a promising career to become a pastor. That was a life-shaping decision for Elliot too:

> People at his company thought it was a really big risk. But they say money is not the most important thing—do work that's meaningful to you. That's how I think about it. Look, life wasn't super dramatic. Our parents didn't share a budget with us, but we weren't starving or scraping by!
>
> I planned to go into journalism. In my senior year, the career department offered me a chance to apply to a publisher. I hadn't thought of books, but I got in and loved it. It's fun to work on a book that becomes a runaway bestseller. A few years ago, we published one that sold a million copies. Seeing the book take off showed that my grunt work wasn't lost, even if I couldn't see what would become of it.

Highs are wonderful, but they don't last. Two years in, the company reorganized and promotions were delayed. That was a difficult time. The pendulum was swinging between hope and despair for Elliot:

> I had been working really hard, finding new authors and meeting with agents. My business card read: editorial *assistant*. I felt people would think I was out of my league. I felt resigned that my promotion wouldn't happen. I just kind of

went through the day and tried not to let things drop. I'm a pretty big rule follower.

If I made a connection with an author or read an exciting book, then I had hope. It reminded me that I loved my work. Then I felt something would break eventually. My boss would follow up every month or so. The answer from on high was, "Yeah. We know, we know." I thought, *I'm qualified. Friends got their promotions. I'm doing the work that comes with the title.* I felt I was falling behind. I worried what that would mean for my career.

Then we had our annual review. I'd be promoted then! My boss ran it up the flagpole. It would be my first real promotion, so I didn't know how it worked. I thought, *It's going to happen. Everything is lining up.* And it didn't. My boss said, "I've been trying. I'll go talk to them again." My wife was supporting me through it. She said, "Maybe they'll promote you two levels!" I knew that would never happen.

My dad always said, "Don't worry about scratching your way to the top. Do a good job. Care about it and try to be someone people can trust. Things will happen." That perspective felt strange last year. We were raised to go to college, work hard, and believe that things were going to go right. Then you do grunt work for years, you don't like everyone you work with, and you don't feel excited about what you're doing.

Almost three years in, Elliot got his promotion. It turned out to be the doubleheader his wife had forecasted. She had a field day.

So What?

Waiting is miserable. Every month you wait, colleagues are celebrating their advancement. Having to wait two years seems like forever when it's a huge chunk of your work experience. I get it.

It wasn't that Elliot would not be promoted. It was just that he had not been promoted. On good days, he did what he should have been doing: *growing on his own.* No one stops you from growing in place. If they do, get out of there fast. Chances are, you'll surprise yourself by how much you can grow if you do your job and then some.

When the time came, Elliot was surprised. His promotion came in a new imprint. He said, "I didn't think that I would have so much influence. Ten years out, if this imprint is successful, I'll be growing alongside it."

For some, the wait is not worth it, but in Elliot's case, the investment paid off handsomely.

BREAKING THE CYCLE

Be wide open. Serendipity can lead to something exciting.
A happenstance conversation can open the door.

Gary and his parents moved more than most, four times by age four and another five times by high school. Moving doesn't stress Gary; he simply picks up and goes. The practice helped him at work, moving to renew creative freedom:

> The job started out awesome! But I was naïve about what creative design meant in the real world. They didn't want much. I was shut down over and over. I was too edgy, too clean, not conservative enough. They told me, "That's not the way we do things here." I felt so *not* creative.
>
> My best friend had moved away, and a friend of his had a friend who knew about a job at a large retailer. I happened to be with them on the weekend. Monday morning, I applied. They liked me, and so I took a chance and moved. I wanted to challenge myself, to feel like I was contributing and growing creatively.
>
> For three years, the new job fed my need to be creative and explore the retail space. Once I started designing the same stuff year after year, work started to weigh on me just as it had before. I started feeling it again, like I was going through the motions. I was really vulnerable and couldn't

shake it. I was doing myself and the company a disservice by treating it as an obligation and not a privilege.

Each day, I woke up dreading work. I would look for reasons to leave at lunch or focus on just one task, the one I enjoyed the most. Then I'd scramble to finish the rest at the last minute. I began to think I didn't want to do design, but it was all I was trained to do.

As the newness faded, Gary fought the urge to move on. He questioned his dream to set up a design company in a storefront and live the hipster life above it. Half-heartedly, he looked for internal job postings. Fortunately, Gary's bosses intervened with a new request to test social media:

I heard "opportunity"—make this into something nobody expected. My energy returned. The key word for me is "opportunity," the unknown. Sometimes people look at that as scary, but I looked at it as something with possibility.

No one had expectations, so whatever I did could not possibly be wrong. I could say, "I'm just figuring this out with everyone else." I had freedom to explore and design, without a committee to approve everything. No one knew what social media meant, but we needed to be there. It was fun and new and flashy, and it came with perks like interviewing and filming bands.

Gary's temporary role continued to evolve and expand thanks to two great bosses who understood his need for creative challenge. It didn't hurt that luck was his good friend.

So What?

Gary started every job with excitement that always wore off. Unaware of the pattern, Gary found that the solution was to move on. That made sense when the job had no creative room. Flexibility and ambiguity energized Gary, along with new creative challenges. He just didn't assume it was possible in the job he had. Sometimes, there is more room to grow than you know.

Be wide open. Serendipity can lead to something exciting. A happenstance conversation can open the door. A small opportunity can turn into something bigger over time. Gary believed that any career plan should nail down no more than 70 percent, leaving room to respond to chance.

Sometimes you cannot see opportunity because you're not paying attention. If it's not happening for you, consider moving to a different seat—disrupt your routine. At the very least, you'll discover a new view.

WAKING UP

You recognize work that is worth it when you feel it.
Your body knows before you do. Your emotions know too.

Eduardo's mother and father emigrated from Brazil, taking any job they could find: construction, janitorial, housecleaning, factory work. Passionate about automobiles, Eduardo wanted to learn the auto body repair trade. However, Eduardo's father had a different aspiration for his son. Accordingly, Eduardo became the first in his family to go to college:

> I remember my first day vividly; it was scary but exciting. Looking back at my high school years, I realize I didn't fit in. I was always very nerdy. I always felt out of my comfort zone. In college, I could bond with people who were smart and engaging. I wanted to set the pace so my sisters would have the opportunity to go too.
>
> I didn't know what I was getting into. An accounting professor suggested that I work on something practical before pursuing my passion. The best option was working in accounting in New York. So I did that.

Taking a consulting job, Eduardo worked hard for a year and a half. Imperceptibly, his energy was replaced by an inexplicable malaise. Eduardo had checked out, becoming a cog in the machine, feeling more like inventory than a human being:

> I didn't really see how my work benefitted anyone other than the partners and CEOs. The partners were nice guys, and we

worked closely together. But they showed up infrequently and took all the credit. I wanted to work with people who had my best interests at heart. I knew I was being paid to produce work. I was proud of my craft and did it well, but I just didn't want to do a lot of it. I did what I needed to do but nothing more. I don't know why I showed up.

It was a downer because I felt I was letting my teams down. It seemed they didn't care about me, and I didn't care anymore either. I wasn't engaged in what I was doing. People knew. They didn't want to work with me.

It kind of sucked. I was having a hard time coping with the stress. I let things go.

Then Eduardo was assigned to a new project that excited him. He started working hard again, but it wasn't enough to alter his performance record or outlook. When asked about his low utilization, Eduardo said he had been sick, which was true in the sense that malaise brought him low. It had extinguished the fire in his belly:

> It's hard to say how you know when you're in the wrong job. I woke up one day and asked myself, *What am I doing here?* I was actively researching tech companies and working really hard. It was my last hurrah.
>
> Toward the end, I knew I wanted to make a jump. I did think twice about developing more where I was. Then I met with someone at the tech firm where I had interned in college. It was a new adventure. Technology was moving so fast that I thought I would miss even more by not leaving soon. My parents thought I was crazy, but I went against their advice.
>
> Everyone I now work with really loves it. We're all smart. We could easily leave and work somewhere else. But we stay here because we can help people experience the world. Everyone shares that sense of purpose.

After three years in his new job, Eduardo still feels curious, engaged, and energized. And glad he switched jobs.

So What?

Rest and a new assignment alleviated Eduardo's malaise but didn't eliminate it. That's a red flag for sure. Still, it was a hard decision. Staying on, he would continue to develop, advance to manager, and earn higher pay, with a potential option to switch to tech. His parents would have preferred him to stay. Eduardo leaned toward jumping sooner.

Why? The clue is energy. The current job left Eduardo feeling drained. In contrast, Eduardo's energy rebounded as he attended technology meetups and interviewed people in the field. His positive emotions—derived from a sense of purpose, feeling valued, working with like-minded colleagues, belonging—were missing in the first job and present in the second. Now Eduardo was shooting for the moon, dreaming of running a small tech company.

You recognize work that is worth it when you *feel* it. Your body knows before you do. Your emotions know too. Listen to them. If your energy has drained, return to square one—your pursuit of purpose at work and in life—to renew.

TIME TO GO

The old model of work—where you give your all
in exchange for a protective environment—is no more.
That's not a bad thing. It's liberating.

Stacy-Marie grew up in Trinidad, inheriting ambition and the desire for purposeful work from her mother, who had been a finance professional until Stacy-Marie's father pressed her to stay home with the children:

> I saw how much she resented being home, how stifled she felt. We went from having neither parent at home and completely fine to having Mom around and mad at us all the time! That informs how I think about priorities. I don't apologize for enjoying my work. When I'm with family, I am with them. I also choose not to have children partly because I'm more interested in the challenges outside.

Becoming a journalist, Stacy-Marie rose in the ranks to become editor of the newspaper's innovative startup with a three-year runway to prove itself. Ten months in, management decided to shut it down. Someone had leaked the decision to another paper before Stacy-Marie was informed. She was up in arms:

> I lost it! I sent a scathing e-mail to the top people, saying, "I don't care that you did it to me, but you did this to my team. You thought that a media splash was more important than people's livelihood???" I do not regret what I did. I was permanently soured on this culture.
>
> The first and most important thing was to make sure my eight team members were OK. I got everyone a job. They were fine, but still I was really angry. I knew it would be unhealthy to join another organization. I wasn't arguing with the business reasons but the psychological ones. My boss was unwilling to fight. You treat us the worst and fire us first. Why should we be loyal when we are mistreated?
>
> Then I quit. I had a contract, so I was not being laid off.

Stacy-Marie was so stressed that she threw out her back and suffered migraines almost daily. It felt lousy at the time, but that experience turned out to be a gift:

> I had never been able to separate myself from work. I had always done impressive things. Where I grew up, people look at your school or your company. I had to figure out what it meant to be Stacy-Marie versus Stacy-Marie-impressive job title. It came to me by force! Somebody said, "What do you do?" and I didn't know how to describe myself. *I'm trying to figure that out*, I thought.
>
> I went to museums, did yoga, made jam, canned tomatoes, and wrote. I spent hours reading. My husband was working in Trinidad and Haiti, understanding and supportive. I was by myself, but I could own being by myself.
>
> I learned that I love to figure out how to solve wicked hard problems. I'm really good at it.

Eventually, Stacy-Marie went to graduate school on a journalism fellowship and returned to blogging about media, tech, and more. With renewed energy, she dove into topical issues, channeling her fierceness for good.

So What?

It sucks to shut down a business, lay off the people you hired, and leave your job! Give yourself permission to be angry. Did you deserve it? Of course not! Were you poorly treated? Yes! When your principles are breached, the company and its work are not worth it. But now that's over. It's time to renew.

Gone are the days when you could snag a cushy job for life. Big companies and startups go under regularly. Global competition is fierce. Some company somewhere is ahead of yours. The old model of work—where you give your all in exchange for a protective environment—is no more. That's not a bad thing. It's liberating. The social contract is changing: you don't have to give up your whole self. In turn, work no longer owes you job security or a career path. It still owes you integrity and values, challenge and professional growth, and a competitive financial reward. You still owe the company integrity and values, performance that meets or beats expectations, and acceptance.

With this new world order, take responsibility for what you need from work. And then hold up your end of the bargain.

TAKING ON YOUR

WORK CHALLENGE

We're right back to the beginning. But for the paycheck, work without purpose is hardly worth the effort. Pretty soon you don't feel like getting out of bed. Whenever someone suggests an idea, you immediately see its flaws. That effectively shuts down the conversation. You're left alone with no solutions. Quitting feels like the only option. If you only had the energy.

It's disheartening. Everybody in this book had the grit to persevere through a rough patch at work. But malaise is like fog. It's easy to lose your way; it's hard to fight what you cannot see.

Now and then, boredom can be a relief after a hard stretch. Boring is comfortable and in some ways relaxing. But these stories didn't stop there.

William found himself silenced at work, with no one to trust. Charlotte was stuck in a holding pattern. Elliot languished without answers. Gary ran out of room to grow. Eduardo isolated himself, spiraling down. And Stacy-Marie felt the sting of unfairness. Fortunately, they took care of themselves and took action.

If you're facing a work challenge of this proportion, you have more control than you may realize. You're not lost, and you're not alone. There's plenty you can do.

Decide Whether to Wait

Why doesn't work feel worth it? Getting past complaining and blaming is going to take some soul-searching. Identify what's permanent versus temporary, what's outside versus in your control, and what are the nasty versus good bits at work. Here are some questions to provoke your thinking:

- *Is this a me problem?* Sometimes, being run-down, worried about something else, or unhappy in a relationship can spill over to work. If that's your case, postpone doing something about work until you address your other issue.

- *Do you want to stay in this industry?* If you generally love what you do, it's worth hanging in there even if the current work is dull.

- *Do you enjoy the environment, people, and activities in this company?* Explore the organizational culture, processes, leadership, people, and deeply held values. Is this a place you want to spend eight or more hours a day? If everything about work generally feels right with the exception of the valley you're in, it's worth fighting to stay.

- *Is this a timing issue?* If you trust that management has your interests at heart and will ultimately recognize you, waiting is worth it, especially if you agree with the company's values, mission, and strategy.

- *What unmet ambitions, goals, and interests do you have?* If you're deciding between if and when, be clear on why you would leave and what you'd leave for.

- *Can you find a way to fill these unmet needs where you are?* Imagine if an internal move, a change in job parameters, a sabbatical, or a difficult conversation would help you improve life at work. Imagine boundaries shifting and, consequently, how you would feel about work then.

- *Is something else a much, much bigger attraction for you?* Like all relationships, this one may not work out if your heart's not in it. Even if you improve work, another opportunity may blow it out of the water. That's the deciding factor.

Make a Clear Decision

Now is the time to step up. Whatever you decide, move on from indecision:

- *Think it through with a friend or mentor.* This is a big decision; chances are, you feel conflicting emotions. You may feel frustrated, disappointed, resentful, afraid, sad, angry, guilty, or all of the above. Talk to someone who won't fall into that deep hole with you.

  - *Ask for empathy, not sympathy.* It's nice when other people feel your pain, but you need sounding boards, people who can offer a different view—even if it's contrary to yours. If you need a hug, fine. You deserve one because you're going through hard times.

  - *Let it percolate.* It takes a bit of time to reach such an important decision. In the worst case, take enough time to know for sure. You may reach the same answer, but you are less likely to go on a self-destructive rampage that will never be forgotten.

- *Face up to your role in it.* This is like a failed relationship. You share responsibility for why work doesn't feel worth it. You chose that company and that job. Figure out why and what that means for you during the breakup.

  - *Avoid blaming and self-punishment.* So you chose the company or role for the wrong reasons: it was the shiny new thing, you had no better option, the boss and coworkers seemed nice, the money was good. Taking responsibility doesn't mean beating yourself up about it. That's the worst thing you can do. We're all flawed creatures.

  - *Make jam, not war.* Find the constructive activity you can lose yourself in to renew. Sitting around the house fuming won't work. Don't feel you have to face reality 24/7. An engrossing project can help refresh your curiosity, give you a sense of achievement, and increase your self-esteem. Build a deck; learn to fly; start a vegetable garden.

○ *Engage in physical activities.* Relieve the stress of leaving or the fear of being jobless by changing your physical state. Take up tae kwon do, jogging, Pilates, anything! You'll feel better almost immediately.

○ *Be kinder to yourself.* You live in a competitive, fast-moving, unforgiving world without a whole lot of kindness. Take care of yourself in emotional terms. Get that hug we talked about. If your mother is unforgiving because you've left your job, call your grandmother or a caring friend.

● *Activate your network.* Please don't wait to create your external network until you've decided to leave. Even if you're an extreme introvert, you need friends, and friends have friends. Work those six degrees of separation!

○ *Start early with friends and relatives, college alums, and people you know from work.* It's harder to network when you're looking for a job. People can smell desperation. Do it well before you need help.

○ *Make your connections meaningful.* A lot of people network at a feverish pitch, racing through business cards. You don't need quantity. You need access to people in different networks. When attending an event, make it your business to meet just a few people you're interested in. It may take a dozen interactions to find someone you want to meet, but then pause and deepen the conversation.

● *Start exploring your interests.* If you didn't experiment with different companies and jobs early on, get going now. Not everybody has a chosen field. Meet very different people to learn what drew them in. You'll either catch their energy or not. Remember the magic number? It takes up to 100 people to unlock new opportunity.

Stay or Go—Intentionally

Most people quit without even raising their issue. That's nuts. You're going to leave, so why not push the boundaries? In most cases, you have more flexibility than you think. You might land a stretch assignment or role that makes work worth it. Be respectful and ask. You'll only sound entitled if you take without giving:

- *Let people know what you hope to achieve.* It really helps to clarify what you want (in contrast to knowing what you don't want).

  - *Involve others, gauging their interest in you and your goal.* Ask others about their careers, especially the time most relevant to your stage. They may give you worthy advice or spark ideas. Most will be curious about you, making it easier for you to share. If they're not, move on and don't take it personally.

  - *Find other people who need to know.* Mentors, sponsors, human resources, even your boss's boss need to know your goals at work and how you propose to achieve them. Your campaign ought to be subtle. No one likes a self-serving, sharp-elbowed self-promoter. If you feel that you're between a rock and a hard place, find someone who knows how it's done around here to coach you or pass along the word.

- *Include your boss on your team.* If your goal is in the realm of possibility, your boss is in a good position to help. Maybe the boss thinks you're an entitled prima donna. The best way to find out is to ask.

  - *Enlist the boss's help.* You may not like what the boss tells you, but it's always worth knowing where you stand. If your boss feels you're not ready for the promotion or challenge you want, find out what you need to demonstrate. If the boss agrees with you, at least you know you're not clouded by arrogance.

  - *Build trust in your relationship.* Deliver on your promises and be straight with your boss all along. Your next step is acceptance. Withhold judgment when your boss expresses a different view from what you expected. When it's your turn, just ask nicely for what you want.

  - *Share what you feel and think but are afraid to reveal.* How else will your boss know what you want? Find a respectful way to share what you're feeling. Why respectful? People don't trust individuals who seem to put their own agenda first. That said, most bosses want you to be successful and happy (or at least cheerful).

- *Learn more skills while you're looking.* You can be actively developing despite being in a holding pattern.

  - *Do the work of the people a level above you.* Ask for assignments or take them on your own—in addition to the work you're expected to do. Some managers find it disconcerting to have a team member stretch the scope of a project. Talk it over so your boss does not misinterpret your actions. However, a good manager wants you to take initiative.

  - *Learn what the people around you do.* No one is stopping you from meeting people in roles you find interesting. If you're uncomfortable reaching out, get past that by asking for advice. Most people are open to genuine requests, especially when it doesn't entail sacrifice. Make your visits brief and be sure to thank everybody.

- *Open up to serendipity.* It's easy to turn down ideas or connections that seem odd. Don't.

  - *Zig and zag.* Not every opportunity you pursue is worth your time, but you learn as much on a wrong turn as you learn on a right one. Be alert as to why that zig doesn't feel right and head for the next zag.

  - *Pause when your instinct is to shut down.* You may be right, but hold that thought and sleep on it. Ask yourself what's right about the idea or what would have to be true to make it right. In the morning, whatever you decide will have had the benefit of reflection.

When work doesn't feel worth it, something has to change. The process of deciding *if* or *when* to leave is messy. There's no one right answer, which means that quitting is not always the best decision.

Be mindful of the part you play in making work not worth it. Wipe the slate clean. See the people around you as if you'd never met. Look for adventures that weren't there the day before. Remove the invisible bars of a cage that doesn't exist.

You have more control than you realize—over yourself. Whether you stay or go, you'll be in a better place where you're once again giving and receiving enough to make work worth it.

Endnote

Congratulations! You've made it through a dozen work challenges, with dozens of stories and recommendations. This is the moment when I pass the baton. Thank you for receiving it. Your experiences facing challenges are as relevant and important as the ones in this book.

I'm no Pollyanna, and I'm not going to coolly lie that everything will turn out for the best. Things don't always turn out as you expect or hope, but one thing is certain: if you don't face your work challenges, it won't turn out at all. You'll use up energy working very hard *not* to face the challenge. Consequently, work will be duller and more stressful, your growth will slow, and you'll feel stuck.

But that's not going to happen. You *are* going to face your challenges, if only to experience more adventure at work.

Not ready? Things are changing so fast that you won't ever be 100 percent ready. You're ready enough, and that's what counts. Run toward challenge. Sometimes you'll succeed. At times, the pressure will feel overwhelming, you'll make a mistake, or your review won't be what you wanted. Somebody will make your life miserable or stand in your way. You'll have to work hard to cultivate sponsors. Risk taking will make you feel anxious. Maybe being a superhero is not your thing. Perhaps work sucks, drags you down, or lacks what you need—now. These challenges all serve.

You know what to do. Start with deeper reflection on your hard questions. Get curious about your thoughts, feelings, mindsets, and what's at stake for you, without judgment. Assess the situation, explore your choices, and consider your trade-offs. Reach out to bosses, mentors, sponsors, colleagues, friends, family, and even strangers who can help you. Make your decisions. Declare your intentions. Set some goals and plan your next small steps. Visualize them. You've got this.

There is only one thing left to do.

Whether you tell it to someone, write it down, or just live it, create your story.

Make it an exciting one.

Index

Superhero *(cont'd)*
  reflection, recovery by, 203
  resistance faced by, 190–191, 194–196, 202, 203
  risk taking by, 194–195
  self-assessment by, 200
  self-care by, 200
  self-doubt faced by, 202
  sponsors helping, 202
  trials overcome by, 188–189
  unknowns accepted by, 202
Sustainability, 4, 217
Sutton, Bob, 119

T
Taiwanese background, 9, 174
Talking, xiii
Tan, Chade-Meng, 17
Tara, 107, 115–116, 119
Tatiana, 87, 95–96
Team leadership, 159
  in automotive industry, 90–91, 92–94
  bringing on board in, 85–86, 87, 92–94, 97–98, 99
  empathy in, 93–94, 96, 99, 100
  engaging people in, 99–100, 102
  forming team in, 101
  identifying key people in, 99
  interest in others for, 101
  investment for, 100–101
  listening for, 92–93, 98–99, 102–103
  mobilizing support in, 90–91
  by noticing, 94, 95–96
  standing out and, 156, 157
  trust inspired for, 100
Tech company, 12, 43, 174, 235–236
TED Talk, 184
Television
  mistakes in, 56–57
  pressure in, 23–24, 37
  risk taking in, 176–178
Texas, 214
Thich Nhat Hanh, 14
Tipping Point (Gladwell), 97
Tracy, 127, 134–136, 140
Trade-offs, 20

Trinidad, 1, 47, 236, 237
Turkey, 147, 155

U
United Auto Workers (UAW), 92
University dean, 206
Unreasonable Institute, 4

V
Venture capital, 54, 178
Verbal abuse, 106, 107–109, 119
Victor, 3, 9–11, 17
Vision, 20–21
Voice, 146–147, 164
Volatile, uncertain, complex, and ambiguous (VUCA), xii

W
Will, 67, 69–70
William, 225–226, 239
Work, losing interest in, 225
  boss help for, 242, 243
  clear decision after, 240
  at consulting job, 234–235
  by creative type, 232–233
  grit for enduring, 238
  identifying cause of, 239–240
  intentionality for, 241–243
  leaving after, 227, 229–230, 235–236, 237–238
  making best of, 226, 228–230
  mentor help for, 229, 240, 242
  network activated for, 241
  perseverance for enduring, 238
  personal responsibility for, 240–241
  self-care for, 241
  serendipity solving, 232, 233–234, 243
  skill learning for, 243
  sponsor help with, 242
  waiting out, 226, 230–232
Work experiences
  draining, 18, 236
  energizing, 18, 19

Y
Yahoo!, 179

About the Author

After more than 30 years at McKinsey & Company, Joanna Barsh is now a director emerita who continues to serve clients worldwide. She has deep experience leading growth strategy, organization effectiveness, and leadership development projects.

An in-demand speaker, Joanna has given more than 450 keynotes and workshops on leadership in the past decade. She has worked with over 100 companies and organizations, including governments, in more than 20 countries, including Brazil, China, Indonesia, Malaysia, Saudi Arabia, and throughout the Western world. Her goal is to inspire others to step up and lead, and she offers the concepts, tools, and practices to master the capabilities needed to lead well.

A strong advocate for women's advancement, Barsh cochairs the Leadership Working Group of the International Council on Women's Business Leadership. She served on New York City's Commission on Women's Issues from 2002 to 2013, and she led groundbreaking research for the *Wall Street Journal*'s Task Force for Women in the Economy and for the U.S. Chamber of Commerce. She is the author of the bestselling books *How Remarkable Women Lead* and *Centered Leadership*.

Barsh has a BA in English literature from the University of Pennsylvania, an MA in English literature from the University of Chicago, and an MBA from Harvard Business School, where she was a Baker Scholar.

She and her husband divide their time between New York City, their cattle farm upstate, and Tucson. Her two grown-up daughters are the inspiration for this book.